WARTIME DISSENT IN AMERICA

D0760095

WARTIME DISSENT IN AMERICA

A HISTORY AND ANTHOLOGY

Robert Mann

WARTIME DISSENT IN AMERICA
Copyright © Robert Mann, 2010.

All rights reserved.

First published in 2010 by PALGRAVE MACMILLAN® in the United States—a division of St. Martin's Press LLC, 175 Fifth Avenue, New York, NY 10010.

Where this book is distributed in the UK, Europe, and the rest of the world, this is by Palgrave Macmillan, a division of Macmillan Publishers Limited, registered in England, company number 785998, of Houndmills, Basingstoke, Hampshire RG21 6XS.

Palgrave Macmillan is the global academic imprint of the above companies and has companies and representatives throughout the world.

Palgrave® and Macmillan® are registered trademarks in the United States, the United Kingdom, Europe and other countries.

ISBN: 978-0-230-10484-6 (hardcover)
ISBN: 978-0-230-10483-9 (paperback)

Library of Congress Cataloging-in-Publication Data

Mann, Robert, 1958-
   Wartime dissent in America : a history and anthology / by Robert Mann.
      p. cm.
   Includes bibliographical references.
   ISBN 978-0-230-10484-6 (alk. paper) — ISBN 978-0-230-10483-9 (alk. paper)
   1. Peace movements—United States—History. 2. Pacifism—United States—History.
   3. War—Prevention—History. I. Title.
   JZ5584.U6M36 2010
   303.6'6—dc22   2009052221

A catalogue record of the book is available from the British Library.

Design by Scribe Inc.

First edition: August 2010

10 9 8 7 6 5 4 3 2 1

Printed in the United States of America.

To the memory of Roger Guissinger, who taught me so much

CONTENTS

ACKNOWLEDGMENTS

I will never be able to thank properly the friends, colleagues, and scholars who helped make this book possible. I stand on the shoulders of many imminent historians and journalists whose research and insights have enlightened and inspired me. I am also grateful to all those who encouraged my work, especially those who read portions of the manuscript and offered very useful criticism, including Lawrence Velvel, John Maxwell Hamilton, Amy Reynolds, Richard Nelson, and Louis Day. I appreciate the anonymous scholars who read the book in manuscript form and offered very honest and useful criticism and suggestions. I only wish it were possible to acknowledge them by name. My good friend and resourceful research assistant, Katie Knobloch, aided me immensely in numerous ways, including her incisive critiques of several chapters and her dogged research. I am also grateful to my literary agent, Nathan Bransford, and to my careful and cheerful editor at Palgrave Macmillan, Chris Chappell, as well as his colleague Erin Ivy, and Sarah Breeding at Scribe Inc. My colleagues and students at the Manship School of Mass Communication at Louisiana State University were unfailing with friendship and constant encouragement. Finally, as always and beyond measure, I am blessed with the unconditional love and support of my family, particularly Cindy, my wife, my best friend, and in so many ways my inspiration.

INTRODUCTION

STANDING BEFORE AN ATHENIAN JURY IN 399 B.C., CHARGED with heresy and corruption of his city-state's youth, Socrates laid out a most unusual argument: his acquittal would not simply spare an innocent life. If "you put me to death," the seventy-year-old philosopher warned, "you will harm yourselves more than me." He was actually pleading for their lives, he explained, "to save you from misusing the gift of God by condemning me."

Athens, he argued, needed someone to challenge the pious and self-righteous. "When I think that any person is not wise," Socrates said, "I try to help the cause of God by proving that he is not." The Socratic rhetorical style, it seemed, was not well received, even when practiced by its creator.

Nonetheless, Socrates' point was valid and timeless, "If you put me to death, you will not easily find anyone to take my place," he said, perhaps expressing the secret desire of his accusers. Socrates compared Athens to "a large thoroughbred horse which, because of its great size, is inclined to be lazy and needs the stimulation of some stinging fly." Socrates was that metaphorical fly. "All day long I never cease to settle here, there, and everywhere, rousing, persuading, reproving every one of you." As a fly that stung the horse, Socrates' antagonism had awakened Athens. "In your annoyance you will . . . finish me off with a single slap; and then you will go on sleeping till the end of your days, unless God in his care for you sends someone to take my place."

After the jury had pronounced its death sentence, Socrates reconsidered, predicting that his death would spawn more flies to harass the Athenians. "You have brought about my death in the belief that through it you will be delivered from submitting your conduct to criticism; but I say that the result will be just the opposite. You will have more critics, whom up till now I have restrained without your knowing it; and being younger they will be harsher to you and will cause you more annoyance." Timeless in his critique of society's suppression of dissent, Socrates concluded, "The best and easiest way is not to stop the mouths of others, but to make yourselves as good men as you can."[1]

However, his accusers, still insecure in their newly resurrected Athenian democratic state, sentenced Socrates to drink the hemlock. Thus Socrates—contemptuous of free expression for the masses—became the first martyr to free speech in recorded history.

In the 2,345-plus years since, governments and societies have, like horses' tails, swatted at the flies of dissent. An annoyance, at best, and a perceived threat to national security, at worst, dissent often provokes some of the worst behavior of governments and their citizens. It was dissent—"You have heard it said . . . but I say . . ."—that fed the lust for killing Jesus. Dissent cost Gandhi and Martin Luther King Jr. their lives and deprived Galileo, Martin Luther, Nelson Mandela, and Aleksandr Solzhenit-syn of their freedom. Whatever the immediate cost to them and their families, it is remarkable that history has judged kindly so many prominent dissenters. Add to the aforementioned list William Wilberforce, Thomas Paine, William Lloyd Garrison, Susan B. Anthony, Desmond Tutu, Daniel Ellsberg, and Bao Dong.

"All change in history, all advance, comes from the nonconformists," British his-torian A. J. P. Taylor declared in his 1957 chronicle of British dissent, *The Trouble Makers*, "If there had been no troublemakers, no Dissenters, we should still be living in caves." Taylor further asserted, "Posterity does not merely adopt their view of past events—though without acknowledgement; it takes their line in the present. If you want to peer into the future . . . if you want to know what the foreign policy of this country [Britain] will be in twenty or thirty years' time, find out what the Dissenting minority are saying now. The policy being applied will be their policy—maybe at the wrong time and in the way wrong, certainly to a chorus of Dissenting disapproval. Today's realism will appear tomorrow as shortsighted blundering. Today's idealism is the realism of the future."[2]

A review of American wartime dissent suggests that Taylor was correct. The Fed-eralist opponents of the War of 1812 may have contributed to the destruction of their party in national politics, but their opposition—partly born of fear of British military superiority on the seas and in Canada—was reasonable. The deficiencies in U.S. military power—especially the deplorable lack of professionalism in its officer ranks—illuminated by the dissenters in 1812 spawned the drive to invigorate the U.S. Military Academy at West Point, which proved advantageous during the war against Mexico. Opposition to the Mexican War, much of it from northern Whigs opposed to spreading slavery, culminated in slavery's abolition in 1865. Opponents of World War I found their disdain of war and foreign entanglements accepted as national pol-icy throughout the 1920s and 1930s. Some of the cold war opponents who argued for stronger ties with the Soviet Union experienced *glasnost*. Those who marched against the Vietnam War in the 1960s soon saw their warnings about the limitations of U.S. military power (and their abhorrence of an arrogant foreign policy) the ascendant (or at least a respectable) philosophy in Washington for a generation. Those Americans who opposed the war in Iraq in 2003 found themselves, sooner than most dissenters, firmly in the majority by 2005.

"Heretical opinions," John Stuart Mill wrote in his 1859 essay, *On Liberty*, "are generally some of these suppressed and neglected truths, bursting the bonds which kept them down." Mill allowed that dissent often wrongly claims to possess the whole truth, but more forcefully he argued that if one side of an argument "has a better claim than the other, not merely to be tolerated, but to be encouraged and coun-tenanced, it is the one which happens at the particular time and place to be in a minority." Regardless of the correctness of one's position, Mill wrote, "there is always hope when people are forced to listen to both sides."[3]

During times of peace and prosperity, dissent is not so difficult to tolerate (even if it is easier to ignore). A society can be magnanimous with its malcontents when times are good and peace prevails. That is not, however, the variety of dissent this book addresses. Far more daunting is the question of what do about dissent during war, when the nation's leaders and its citizenry perceive a mortal threat to the state. Thus the questions arise: During war, does domestic dissent aid and comfort our enemies? Does it demoralize our troops and confound the citizenry? If so, is that the price of a democracy? Must democracy be preserved at any price, including the diminution of certain civil liberties?

During most wars there are those (usually government officials) who insist that unanimity of thought and purpose is highly beneficial, or even necessary, for victory and therefore dissent must be curtailed for the nation's survival. To those who hold those beliefs, this book should give you pause. It demonstrates not only the breadth and depth of dissent during a dozen wars since 1776, but demonstrates that American democracy has never been threatened by dissent, even the most radical variety. In fact, it was alien and sedition acts prompted by the 1798 quasi-war with France and World War I in 1917 (as well as the "red scare" in 1919 and during the early days of the cold war) that brought us the most repressive periods in American history. Benjamin Franklin was correct, "They that can give up essential liberty to obtain a little temporary safety deserve neither safety nor liberty." By exploring dissent in twelve wars, this book demonstrates that dissent and vigorous debate in wartime is more than a benign act to be tolerated. It strengthens a nation and helps it to prevail.

In 1948, as he studied the Roosevelt administration's management of World War II, the president of the Institute of Public Administration, Luther Gulick, concluded, "the delay caused by debate in wartime America was considerably less than the delay caused by poorly considered and unrefined and inadequate programs in Germany." In other words, dissent and debate over the course of the war strengthened the U.S. war effort. Writing in his book *Administrative Reflections from World War II*, Gulick also concluded that dictatorships were far less efficient in wartime because they suppressed dissent. "In a democracy," he wrote, "not only is the structure of administration designed to flow both ways, with extensive delegation of authority and universal participation in planning and decisions at every level of the organizational structure, but in addition the public and the press have no hesitation in observing and criticising [*sic*] the first evidence of failure once a program has been put into operation."[4]

Unanimity of thought or purpose would seem to be a powerful weapon for a president as he leads the nation in war. However, closer inspection reveals that true unanimity of thought (often coerced or manipulated) mostly strengthens a president's hand domestically. It might help him dominate Congress (for a while), but common sense and experience suggest that it does not necessary translate into a more efficient execution of the war effort. In fact, as most any management consultant or successful chief executive officer (CEO) will attest, when dissent is missing or suppressed, the organization invariably suffers. As Mill wrote, "when there are persons to be found who form an exception to the apparent unanimity of the world on *any* [emphasis added] subject, even if the world is in the right, it is always probably that dissentients have something worth hearing to say for themselves, and that truth would lose something by their silence."[5]

More than a half century ago, then-Senator John F. Kennedy, in his award-winning history of senatorial dissent, *Profiles in Courage*, propounded a deeper and more nuanced concept of democracy—far more than just popular government and majority rule. "The true democracy, living and growing and inspiring, puts its faith in the people—faith that the people will not simply elect men who will represent their views ably and faithfully, but also elect men who will exercise their conscientious judgment—faith that the people will not condemn those whose devotion to principle leads them to unpopular courses, but will reward courage, respect honor and ultimately recognize right."[6]

Over time, our society has decided, in principle at least, that we want such people in Congress and throughout our society. We affirm the value of diverse opinion and vigorous debate in our political affairs. For the most part—although the various sides in American political discourse do what they can to overpower and gain advantage over their adversaries—politics in America is marked by its relative tolerance (if not celebration) of vigorous dissent and its variety of viewpoints. At least, that is what we learned in grade school, and it is the ideal that Americans usually embrace while congratulating themselves for the good fortune to live in the most free and diverse society on earth.

But are we really free? Does our society really encourage diversity of opinion? Do we truly tolerate or encourage dissent? Have our news media really ever served as the marketplace for competing ideas, even radical ones? Or is dissent acceptable in the media in only the narrowest of ranges?

Our society, it seems, is much like the individual. Criticism stings, and therefore we avoid it and work to silence it. "In the abstract we celebrate freedom of opinion as part of our patriotic liturgy," the late Senator J. William Fulbright wrote in his classic condemnation of the Vietnam War, *The Arrogance of Power*. "It is only when some Americans exercise it that other Americans are shocked." The usual reaction to dissent in America called to Fulbright's mind Samuel Butler's observation, "People in general are equally horrified at hearing the Christian religion doubted, and at seeing it practiced."[7]

The debate over slavery provides a good example of the American distaste for dissent. From 1835 to 1844, the U.S. House of Representatives enforced a series of "gag" rules that prohibited even the discussion of abolition in the House—actions that outraged the chief dissident of the era, former President John Quincy Adams. "Your enjoyment of the right of petition to the Congress of the United States, and that of every freeman in this Union," Adams, then a House member from Massachusetts, indignantly told his constituents in 1842, "rests upon the arbitrary fiat of a slave-holding speaker."[8] Adams and his abolitionist allies finally abolished the gag rule, but the suppression of antislavery speech was only beginning. Throughout the South, states prohibited the publication or distribution of newspapers and periodicals that advocated or discussed abolition. Many southerners believed that since slavery was enshrined in the Constitution, neither Congress nor any other body should be allowed to debate it.

This is not to suggest that Americans have been hesitant to voice their dissent, even in times of war, even when threatened by official persecution or prison. Americans loyal to the crown opposed the Revolutionary War at great personal cost. Dissenters during the quasi-war with France were jailed for violating the Sedition Act. New England was a hotbed of dissent during the War of 1812. The Mexican-American

War provoked serious debate and opposition in New England and the South. Despite the intense and bloody passions in the Union and the Confederacy, there was a remarkable amount of debate over the war and its aims. During and after the Spanish-American War—a brief and popular conflict—dissent over U.S. imperialistic aims, and the country's repression of the Philippine insurgency, was widespread and robust. America's entry into the World War in 1917 revealed the ugly and irrational fear of free speech and spawned a new round of laws, reminiscent of the Alien and Sedition Acts of 1798. Even then, however, dissent was lively and widespread.

Then, as the nation entered World War I, something new appeared—official, state-sponsored propaganda, information control, and the sometimes-repressive iron fist of the federal government to enforce, if not unanimity of thought, virtual unanimity of action. At President Woodrow Wilson's behest, Congress criminalized war dissent and funded the ubiquitous Committee on Public Information, the government's omnipresent propaganda machine. Suddenly dissent was treason and thousands of loyal Americans were persecuted for anything less than full-throated support for the war. Federal officials prosecuted and imprisoned hundreds of Americans and shuttered dozens of newspapers for speaking out against the war—or even expressing muted doubts. Following the war, prosecutions continued at the state level. Many states—out of a growing fear that the Bolshevik revolutionary spirit in Russia would take root in the United States—enacted anarchy statutes criminalizing the mere advocacy of the overthrow of the American capitalist system.

What makes this long tradition of wartime dissent so remarkable is that for the first 193 years of the American republic, the Supreme Court did not consider freedom of speech a universal right. It was not until 1931, with the Court's ruling in *Stromberg v. California*, that the nation began to formally put away the long-held assumption that the founders had merely prohibited Congress, not the states, from passing laws restricting freedom of expression.[9]

Despite the Court's growing appreciation of free speech, American citizens and their leaders did not fully embrace the expansive application of this newfound right following the 1931 ruling. During World War II, President Franklin D. Roosevelt harangued the Justice Department to prosecute the "seditionists" who criticized the war effort, and a substantial portion of the public and many in the press fully supported the effort. As world war gave way to cold war, the nation grew even more fearful of free expression, especially anything that smacked of sympathy for the communist beliefs of our erstwhile allies, the Russians. The decade of the 1950s featured a renewed focus on the repressive provisions of the Alien Registration Act of 1940, loyalty oaths, communist witch-hunts led by Senator Joseph McCarthy and his allies, and blacklisting of anyone suspected of sentiments out of line with anticommunist orthodoxy.

Even after the McCarthy era, America remained embroiled in the cold war and what one scholar called "a sense of continuing crisis."[10] The Vietnam War and the mass protests it sparked in the late 1960s and early 1970s disturbed many Americans (perhaps a "silent majority") who accepted the philosophy embraced by presidents Lyndon Johnson and Richard Nixon: radical protest was treasonous.

However, because it lasted so long and eventually engendered such widespread opposition among the public, the Vietnam War may have helped to legitimize dissent in a way that Supreme Court rulings and protests over previous wars did not. By 1971, only about one-fourth of Americans surveyed still believed that the war was worth fighting.[11] Over time, the war's prime supporters—Lyndon Johnson, Richard Nixon, Robert McNamara, and William Westmoreland—were discredited as misguided, at best, and as manipulative deceivers, at worst. It was the war's opponents, particularly the protest movement leaders, who became folk heroes and exemplars of courageous dissent.

Americans who reflect on the cold war era (especially the 1950s) likely congratulate themselves for how far we have come and how much tolerance for dissent has evolved. But have we? Are we far more inclined to tolerate or encourage robust debate over the questions of war and peace than in the 1950s? The evidence suggests our progress is not very impressive. The news media, which should be encouraging a diversity of voices, especially during war, have failed to play a meaningful role as a mediator and facilitator of vigorous debate and dissent.

As W. Lance Bennett, Regina G. Lawrence, and Steven Livingston demonstrate in their remarkable book *When the Press Fails: Political Power and the News Media from Iraq to Katrina*, the quality of public debate in the United States declined once federal regulations no longer required broadcasters to treat news as a public service. Furthermore, "the rise of huge media conglomerates [has] relegated news to the same bottom-line demands as entertainment content—meaning fewer resources for investigative journalism, more infotainment and soft features, and a play-it-safe mentality favoring authorized content over more challenging fare." Adding to this dysfunction, the three scholars wrote, is a "spiral of public disconnection with and antagonism toward both politicians and the press." That means "sustained commitments to independent reporting that challenges individuals and institutions in power seem risky in the absence of demands from citizens and media owners, or government standards to support them."[12] The press, once a watchdog and a source of vital information for dissenters, is now too often an undiscriminating conduit for government propaganda and spin.

While the U.S. government no longer overtly imprisons individuals for dissent during war, it does skillfully manipulate and coerce the news media and thereby manage public opinion (especially during times of war) so that the voices of dissent are silenced or relegated to the margins. Citing a large body of research, Lance Bennett has concluded that "grass roots groups, social movements, and protestors with causes that are not on the government agenda are not only less likely to get their messages reported, but they are far more likely to be portrayed as disruptive, lawless elements than more established political groups." In his 1997 study of journalistic practices, William A. Dorman observed what many others have documented—it is only when "elites defect from a policy consensus . . . that the American press will open up debate on foreign policy or security issues."[13]

Indeed, it is the media's well-documented overreliance on official sources of information about foreign and defense policy that gives these officials a decided, if not overwhelming, advantage in foreign policy "debates." "Journalists who report the news inside the terms of Washington debate," media scholar Jonathan Mermin wrote, "are independent of government in a formal, legal sense but have in effect turned over to official actors [government officials] the power to set the news agenda and the spectrum of debate in the news."[14] The result is that unless the dissent is "official"—a prominent member of Congress, a former president, or a former cabinet secretary— the arguments against war are largely ignored and the government masters of image and spin skillfully dominate the debate.

For example, in the summer of 2002, as then-President George W. Bush threatened war against Iraq, the national network news programs amply reported the elite, official statements of dissent, much of it by Republicans. However, once these Republican voices fell silent or fell in line behind Bush, dissent almost disappeared from the news. One study of television news coverage found that during the week before and after Secretary of State Colin Powell's February 2003 speech to the United Nations, in which he made the case for war against Iraq, the major television networks quoted 393 sources on camera. Of those, only 17 percent were critical of Bush administration policy (most of those were foreign, non-American sources). Of the American sources, only 6 percent opposed war. "Although substantive dissent appeared [in the news]," media scholar Robert M. Entman noted, "much of it originated with low-credibility and low-power foreign sources."[15]

Does this mean that aggressive, official government repression of dissent has been supplanted by a spin-driven news media that marginalize opposing voices? Entman, Mermin, and other media scholars believe so. If American elites do not express their dissent in the arena of foreign policy, Entman wrote, "challenges to the White House's frame will probably not affect policy very much."[16]

Beyond questions about the media, those who are looking for signs of government repression might ask, Has the government simply perfected effective but no-less-nefarious means to punish dissent? As prominent law professor David Cole observed, "the Cold War did most of its damage by targeting people not for their speech, but for their associations." Cole adds, "We have not, it is true, made it a crime to be a member of a terrorist group, but we have made guilt by association the linchpin of the war's strategy, penalizing people under criminal and immigration law for providing 'material support' to politically selected 'terrorist' groups, without regard to whether an individual's support was intended to further or in fact furthered any terrorist activity."[17]

There is another potentially nefarious tool for suppressing dissent—the expanding power Congress has accorded government investigators seeking to conduct domestic antiterrorism surveillance. Ostensibly undertaken to uncover terrorist activity within U.S. borders, another consequence could be the chilling or elimination of communication—written or spoken—that is critical of U.S. policy, especially by Muslim and Arab Americans or other foreign nationals. Before passage of the U.S. Patriot Act, the Foreign Intelligence Surveillance Act (FISA) gave the FBI access to a narrow range of records. The Patriot Act expanded FISA to include business and education documents, library and bookstore records, and Internet histories. In addition, as the controversy over the Bush administration's warrantless wiretapping policy demonstrated, government officials are often not constrained by federal law in their wide-ranging investigations and are largely protected from congressional or judicial oversight.

In the years following September 11, civil libertarians protested the Bush administration's claim that it could arrest and imprison any American citizen—indefinitely and without legal counsel or a trial—after declaring him or her an "enemy combatant." As First Amendment lawyer and activist Nancy Chang wrote, "The costs of political association have risen sharply since September 11, especially when civil disobedience and other forms of peaceful but confrontational protest activities are involved." The kind of protest that once might have "ended in a charge of disorderly conduct under a local ordinance," Chang noted, "can now lead to federal prosecution and conviction for terrorism."[18]

Beyond official government suppression of dissent is the very real fear of retribution by employers against workers who publicly air their dissent, the fear of violating the unwritten rules of political correctness on college campuses or in large organizations, and the pervasive pressure for conformity throughout our society. The result is what one scholar has called "self-silencing."[19] John Stuart Mill observed that "society can and does execute its own mandates," something he called "the tyranny of the majority," which "leaves fewer means of escape, penetrating much more deeply into the details of life, and enslaving the soul itself."[20]

After more than seventy-five years of favorable Supreme Court rulings (and a far more educated and enlightened society), radical dissent is only marginally more welcome in 2010 than in 1798 or 1917. The methods for suppressing dissent have merely evolved and become less overt, but more sophisticated and pervasive. Has aggressive, extensive government surveillance of Americans chilled or eliminated the kind of dissent that some regard as radical? In other words, instead of punishing dissent, have our society and its government perfected the art of *preventing* dissent by various forms of overt and covert coercion?

I have written this book to stimulate readers to deeper reflection and debate on the value of dissent and the necessity of guarding and strengthening free speech rights, especially during wartime. This book's objectives are threefold: First, to celebrate the long and commendable tradition by a wide array of Americans to bravely oppose war at great personal and political risk. Second, to demonstrate that dissent, even during war and national crisis, has never threatened our democracy, but has strengthened it by raising issues worthy of debate. And, finally, to demonstrate that war dissenters are not simply radicals and malcontents who operate on the margins of American society, but are usually perceptive, patriotic Americans who believe, in the words of Senator Fulbright, that "in a democracy dissent is an act of faith. Like medicine, the test of its value is not its taste but its effect, not how it makes people feel at the moment but how it makes them feel and moves them to act in the long run."[21]

Indeed, Americans have opposed wars for a wide variety of reasons. Their dissent has not sprung from any one or two sources of ideological thought, but from more than a dozen distinct ideologies and concerns. Among the reasons for dissent are the following (in parenthesis are wars where some examples of this dissent may be found):

1. Fundamental objections to war for moral or religious reasons (the Mexican, Spanish-American, and Vietnam wars);
2. Opposition to the military strategy being pursued (the cold, Korean, and Vietnam wars and the global war on terrorism);

3. Opposition to military tactics (the Spanish-American and Vietnam wars and the global war on terrorism);

4. Constitutional or procedural objections over the legality of war, that is, protests over wars not properly sanctioned by Congress (Korean and Vietnam wars and the global war on terrorism);

5. Objections over war aims or its perceived outcome (the Revolutionary War, the War of 1812, and the Mexican and Spanish-American wars);

6. Opposition to war because of financial costs (the War of 1812 and the Mexican and Vietnam wars);

7. Isolationism or general opposition to American involvement in any ongoing foreign conflict (World War I, World War II, and Vietnam War);

8. Dissent born of fatigue after a long or unsuccessful war (Korean and Vietnam wars and the global war on terrorism);

9. A belief that war is premature (Gulf War and global war on terrorism);

10. Opposition to war after objectives have changed (Spanish-American and Vietnam wars and the global war on terrorism);

11. Dissent over the absence of a *casus belli* or a belief that the war does not meet the criteria for a "just war" (Mexican and Vietnam wars and the global war on terrorism);

12. Opposition by insiders, such as military leaders and Pentagon or White House officials (Korean and Vietnam wars); and

13. Opposition born of socialism or another ideology that holds that war exploits working people for the benefit of war profiteers (World War I).

The diversity of American wartime dissent is one of its great strengths. Indeed, as this book will demonstrate, the breadth of philosophies guiding antiwar activists makes it impossible for intellectually honest observers to dismiss their words as those of traitors or doe-eyed pacifists. Indeed, it has always been too easy to dismiss dissenters as unpatriotic, partisan, or naive. However, their criticisms are rarely attacks on the country and its leaders, but often helpful guidance on a path toward greater unity of purpose (even if that unity sometimes takes years to develop).

In 1950 Senator Arthur Vandenberg of Michigan endured the scorn of his more partisan Republican colleagues and constituents who wanted sharper distinctions between the Republican and Democratic foreign policy positions. An influential proponent of a bipartisan foreign policy, Vandenberg nonetheless believed that dissent and vigorous debate were essential to unity. "Every foreign policy must be *totally* debated," he wrote to a constituent, "and the 'loyal opposition' is under special obligation to see that it occurs."[22]

Shortly after the United States entered World War II, Republican Senator Robert Taft of Ohio, a former isolationist, made it clear that he would not shrink from criticizing the president's military policies, even during war. Taft believed that "criticism in time of war is essential to the maintenance of any kind of democratic government" and it was wrong to believe that dissent gave aid and comfort to the enemy. "If that comfort makes the enemy feel better for a few moments, they are welcome to it . . . because the maintenance of the right of criticism in the long run will . . . prevent mistakes which might otherwise occur."[23]

The sad fact is that we often find dissent during war a very bad and distasteful medicine—and we have found creative ways to avoid it. Persecution of dissent has given way to the media's marginalization of dissent and government—and corporate-sanctioned prevention. What often passes for dissent on television and in the newspapers are trivial objections, not full-throated disputes over foreign or domestic policy. Compromise, conciliation, and bipartisanship (while worthy objectives) are often treated by the media as antidotes to the poison of vigorous, spirited debate and confrontation. While biased toward coverage of conflict, many in the media also ironically seem to regard dissent and acrimonious debate as threats to democracy.

That is certainly not how our Founding Fathers saw it. As George Washington told his officers in 1783, "For if Men are to be precluded from offering their Sentiments on a matter, which may involve the most serious and alarming consequences, that can invite the consideration of Mankind, reason is of no use to us; the freedom of Speech may be taken away, and, dumb and silent we may be led, like sheep, to the Slaughter."[24]

CHAPTER 1

THE AMERICAN REVOLUTION

"REBELS TO THE LAW OF THE KINGDOM"

THE BOSTON NIGHT WAS BITTERLY COLD, BUT THE REBEL mob that marched on Captain John Malcolm's home was red hot. Wielding clubs, the "Sons of Liberty" summoned Malcolm outside on the evening of Sunday, January 23, 1774. A veteran of the French and Indian War, Malcolm was a royal customs official and a well-known loyalist. Irascible and "inordinately quarrelsome," he was among the most disliked men in a city teeming with hostility to the British government and those who supported it.

The Sons of Liberty converged on Malcolm's home less than six weeks after their now-famous Tea Party, a defiant act that would spark repressive retaliation in the colonies, especially in Boston, the budding rebellion's epicenter. Decrying Britain's increasing taxation and import duties, Boston's citizens, but especially the Sons, were venomous in their hatred for men like Malcolm. Dragging Malcolm from his house, the mob tossed him onto a sled and spirited him along King Street to the Customs House. Stripping him "to the buff and breeches," they pasted his body with tar and feathers, flogged him, and paraded him through the streets of Boston until they reached the Liberty Tree. There, they demanded that he resign his royal office or curse the most prominent object of Massachusetts rebel anger, Thomas Hutchinson, the colony's royal governor. When he refused, the crowd herded him toward the gallows on Boston Neck. Along the way, they forced him to drink quarts of strong tea, each to the health of various royal figures.

Reaching the gallows, the crowd placed the noose around Malcolm's neck and flogged him until he relented and cursed the governor. Sparing his life, they paraded him around town, forcing him to mouth various humiliating oaths. Finally, around midnight, the mob dumped his battered body at his house. Five weeks later, Malcolm sailed for England, proud to be, as he claimed, the first person in America tarred and feathered for loyalty to the British crown.[1]

As this and other episodes would prove, the war for American independence, which many regard as a heroic struggle for basic freedoms ("life, liberty, and the pursuit of happiness"), was not quite that high-minded. A widespread, passionate devotion to free speech as a basic American value would not fully emerge until the early twentieth century. In the case of the American Revolution, our Founding Fathers virtually destroyed freedom of speech. In this war, ostensibly fought for liberty, dissent was largely unwelcome and illegal.

Indeed, while Malcolm may have been among the first dissidents persecuted as a contrarian in the war with Great Britain, he would not be the last. Seven months later—on August 29, 1774—in Hebron, Connecticut, the Reverend Samuel Peters attended a town meeting and opposed a motion to brand the Boston Port Act "unconstitutional, oppressive, and tyrannical." This heresy outraged Hebron's citizens, including the local Sons of Liberty. Peters demanded a public reading of the Boston Port Act and the Magna Carta before any vote, so as "to inform us what is constitutional and what is not." The Sons countered by proposing to contribute to Boston's poor, which Peters also opposed.

Five days later, rumors reached the town that Boston was engulfed in fighting and that the British general, Thomas Gage, was killing old men and babies. Peters tried to calm his aroused parishioners. Even if the reports of violence were true, Peters warned that taking up arms against the British "is high treason." Peters's parishioners were persuaded, but not the Sons of Liberty. A large contingent set off for Boston that day, carrying guns and "cursing General Gage, King George III, [and Prime Minister] Lord North." They quickly found that news of violence in Boston had been false. Yet Peters's dissent left the Sons angry and vengeful. When several hundred of them converged on his house, a "violent affray" ensued. Finally, the pastor emerged to face his accusers and acknowledged that his views were "contrary to the general opinion." The angry crowd hustled him to the village green and forced him swear that King George had "forfeited his Kingdom" and that North, Gage, and the Anglican bishops were "tyrants." Peters soon left for Boston to seek protection from British authorities.[2]

Less than two years later, when public opinion shifted dramatically toward independence, this kind of persecution would be widespread. Lucky for Peters, he escaped Hebron before being tarred and feathered. However, tarring was not the only punishment the Sons of Liberty meted out. Sometimes, after receiving the tar and feathers, victims like John Malcolm were jogged roughly through town straddling "a sharp rail." In 1776, a local Connecticut committee hauled in a farmer, Seth Seely, for the offense of signing a declaration supporting the King's law. The committee ordered the rail for Seely, which also included time in the stock "and besmeared with Eggs."[3] In 1775, the dissent of several loyalists was so vociferous that it attracted the attention of the Continental Congress, which ordered their arrest.[4]

In early 1776, after the public became more aroused against British rule, Congress cracked down further, urging assemblies and committees of safety "by the most speedy and effectual measures" to silence those who opposed the rebellion. By the summer, after Thomas Paine's pamphlet *Common Sense* began turning the public toward independence, Congress became even harsher in its treatment of the loyalists, or Tories. On June 24, Congress recommended that legislatures enact criminal penalties for those who offered aid or comfort to the King or other so-called enemies of the new nation. In September, at a convention in Pennsylvania to write a constitution for the new state, delegates considered a provision to outlaw seditious utterances, defined as any attempt to "obstruct or oppose . . . the measures carrying on by the United States of America for the defense and support of freedom and independence of the said states." The irony of fighting for liberty while suppressing free speech was too much for most delegates, who dropped the provision.[5]

While some legislatures refrained from punishing disloyal persuasion and verbal resistance to the war as treason, several—including Pennsylvania, Maryland, New Jersey, North Carolina, South Carolina, Connecticut, New Hampshire, and New York—criminalized dissent. Moreover, after the Declaration of Independence, some citizens went further and required residents to publicly support the revolution.[6] With the notable exception of Virginia, open loyalty to England was usually punished officially, sometimes by mob violence and almost always by confiscation of personal property.[7]

"Speech and press were not free anywhere during the Revolution," historian Leonard W. Levy noted in his exhaustive 1960 study of free speech, *Legacy of Suppression*. "A long war for independence is scarcely a propitious time for the birth and nurturing of freedom of expression or any civil liberties."[8] The proceedings of the first Continental Congress in 1774 attest to this. In a letter to "the inhabitants of Quebec," the Congress expressed its views about a free press: "The importance of this consists, besides the advancement of truth, science, morality, and arts in general, in its diffusion of liberal sentiments on the administration of Government, its ready communication of thoughts between subjects, and its consequential promotion of union among them, whereby oppressive officers are shamed or intimidated, into more honourable and just modes of conducting affairs."[9]

Although expansive on first blush—robust public discussion in the media had usually been limited to matters of government and religion—Congress had defined acceptable expression as "liberal sentiments" about the various topics. In practice, that would come to mean that "illiberal" sentiments, such as loyalty to the crown, were outside the bounds of accepted speech. For example, the Newport, Rhode Island, Committee of Inspection—among other things, it censored the colony's printers—relied on the congressional letter to reject distribution of the *New-York Gazetteer*, published by James Rivington, a prominent Tory whose belligerent attacks on the rebel cause made his the most widely circulated pro-British paper. The Newport committee accepted the congressional definition of freedom of the press as the "diffusion of liberal sentiments." It rejected Rivington's paper, however, because it and other Tory publications contained "wrong sentiments respecting the measures now carrying on for the recovery and establishment of our rights."[10] By the spring of 1775, more than twenty communities in New York, New Jersey, Connecticut, Rhode Island, and Virginia had banned the paper's distribution. That June, after Rivington's appointment as the King's printer in New York, the local Sons of Liberty destroyed his press and made off with his type.[11]

In South Carolina, in 1778, the legislature decreed, "No person whatever shall speak anything in their religious assembly irreverently or seditiously of the government of this state."[12] Connecticut outlawed speech defaming Congress or the state's General Assembly. Violators could be fined, imprisoned, or disenfranchised. The law was aggressively enforced.[13] Many Quakers in Pennsylvania who refused to support the war or "who talked too freely about the mistakes of Congress, or the virtues of the British government" were harassed, intimidated, imprisoned, or exiled.[14]

Despite the harsh treatment of the loyalists after 1776, open support for the crown was not such a radical notion in the years leading up the war.[15] Even after the war commenced in April 1775, sentiment for independence was confined mostly to Massachusetts. "It is well known," Thomas Jefferson later recalled, "that in July of 1775, a separation from Great-Britain and the establishment of Republican government had never entered into any person's mind."[16] Jefferson may have overstated the case, but his essential point is correct: the vast public as late as December 1775 did not see the struggle with Great Britain as a war for independence. What sparked the dramatic shift in public opinion was the publication, in January 1776, of Thomas Paine's forty-six-page pamphlet, *Common Sense*. The pamphlet's publication coincided with news that King George III had informed Parliament the previous October that he would increase naval and land forces to quell the growing insurrection. Calling the American rebels an "unhappy and deluded multitude," the King graciously signaled his eagerness to "receive the misled with tenderness and mercy" after the war's successful conclusion.[17]

Those words prompted outrage in the American colonies. The simultaneous publication of Paine's pamphlet provided a powerful, if unintended, answer to the King, as well as a vigorous attack on the past. Paine persuasively argued that individual and collective rights emanated not from government. Rather, government was "a necessary evil" created by society for "restraining our vices." In simple, direct language aimed at the common man, Paine discredited the British governmental system and its monarch—"an inveterate enemy to liberty"—and sold the then-radical notion of an irrevocable break with Britain.[18]

Paine's audience was a public—and a Continental Congress—tolerant of the war against Britain, but far from certain about its aim. In Congress, debates raged over escalation of the conflict or reconciliation with Britain. Even many of those who favored the war doubted the colonies could prevail. Independence from Britain was hardly mentioned, as many insisted the war's purpose was not to break from Britain, but rather to invoke the "rights of Englishmen" in pursuit of a peaceful accommodation.[19] *Common Sense* was a turning point in the American Revolution. In its first three months, the pamphlet sold 120,000 copies. By year's end, five hundred thousand would be in circulation, essentially one copy for every household in America.[20] In a matter of months in the spring of 1776, *Common Sense* gave profound new meaning and purpose to a war that would, henceforth, be fought for independence.[21]

Although public opinion moved decisively toward independence, colonial views were far from unanimous. While pro-independence forces controlled most state and local governments, loyalists and neutralists abounded; historians differ on their numbers, perhaps between 13 percent and 30 percent of the population (white and black) at the beginning of the war.[22] While their numbers in the general population might have been significant, the loyalists had little political clout and therefore were easy targets. In 1776, after Congress urged the states to prevent citizens from being "deceived and drawn into erroneous opinion," the states generally complied. Legislatures enacted loyalty oaths and imposed criminal penalties for criticizing war and even the Continental currency. In several states, such speech was treasonous.[23]

By July 4, 1776, the war was no longer a struggle to restore the status quo. *Common Sense* and the Declaration of Independence had fundamentally altered the political landscape, transforming the war into a crusade for independence, not simply from Britain, but from the monarchial past and, in many tragic cases, providing the rationale for the widespread repression of free speech.

JAMES CHALMERS (1727–1806)

Thomas Paine's persuasive arguments for war in Common Sense *shocked prominent loyalists, but none drafted an immediate reply. Finally, on March 16, 1776, more than three months after Paine's pamphlet appeared, Robert Bell—the publisher of the first edition of* Common Sense—*began selling a pamphlet entitled* Plain Truth; *addressed to the inhabitants of America, authored by "Candidus." Unknown to readers, Candidus was a wealthy planter from Maryland's Eastern Shore, James Chalmers.*

Born in Scotland in 1727, Chalmers came to America in 1760. Already prosperous because of business dealings in the West Indies, Chalmers became one of the colony's most respected citizens. Rejecting command of a regiment in the rebel militia, Chalmers enlisted in the British cause in 1776 as a lieutenant colonel of the First Battalion of Maryland Loyalists. Plain Truth—*ironically the working title of Paine's pamphlet—earned a large audience throughout the colonies. Unfortunately for Chalmers, it made for difficult reading. Chalmers's dense pamphlet not only failed to stem the tide of public support for war, it nearly cost him his life. Following the American victories at Trenton and Princeton, a mob attacked Chalmers in the Maryland town of Chestertown.*[24]

PLAIN TRUTH
Pamphlet, 1776

His [Thomas Paine's] first indecent attack is against the English constitution; which with all its imperfections, is, and ever will be the pride and envy of mankind. To this panegyric involuntarily our author subscribes, by granting individuals to be safer in England, than in any other part of Europe. He indeed insidiously attributes this preeminent excellency, to the constitution of the people, rather than to our excellent [British] constitution. To such contemptible subterfuge is our Author reduced. I would ask him, why did not the constitution of the people afford them superior safety, in the reign of Richard the Third, Henry the Eighth, and other tyrannic princes? Many pages might indeed be filled with encomiums bestowed on our excellent constitution, by illustrious authors of different nations. . . .

Can a reasonable being for a moment believe that Great Britain, whose political existence depends on our constitutional obedience, who but yesterday made such prodigious efforts to save us from France, will not exert herself as powerfully to preserve us from our frantic schemes of independency. Can we a moment doubt, that the Sovereign of Great Britain and his ministers, whose glory as well as personal safety depends on our obedience, will not exert every nerve of the British power, to save themselves and us from ruin. . . .

Until the present unhappy period, Great Britain has afforded to all mankind, the most perfect proof of her wise, lenient, and magnanimous government of the Colonies . . . "But (says the Author) the most powerful argument is, that nothing but independence, (that is a Continental form of government) can keep the peace of the Continent, and preserve it inviolate from civil wars. I dread the event of a reconciliation now with Britain as it is more than probable, that it will be followed by revolt somewhere; the consequences of which may be far more fatal than all the malice of Britain. Thousands are already ruined by British barbarity, thousands more will probably share the same fate. These men have other feelings, than those who have nothing suffered: All they now possess is liberty, what they before enjoyed is sacrificed to its service, and having nothing more to lose, they disdain all submission."

Here we cannot mistake our author's meaning, that if one or more of the middle or southern Colonies reconcile with Great Britain, they will have war to sustain with New England; "the consequences of which may be more detrimental, than all the malice of Britain." This terrible denunciation, fortunately for such Colonies, is as futile as its author. Should Great Britain re-establish her authority in the said Colonies by negociation [*sic*], surely it is not temerity to add, that the weight of Britain, in the scale of those provinces, would preponderate against the power of New England. If Britain should reduce the Colonies by arms, (which may Heaven avert!) the New England provinces will have as little inclination, as ability, to disturb the peace of their neighbours. I do indeed most sincerely compassionate those unhappy men, who are ruined by our unfortunate distractions. I do fervantly [*sic*] pray, that Britain, and the Colonies may most effectually consider their peculiar infelicity. Such attention will do infinite honour to the parent state; who cannot view them as enemies, but as men unhappily irritated by the impolitic measures of Great Britain. . . .

Innumerable are the advantages of our connection with Britain; and a just dependence on her, is a sure way to avoid the horrors and calamities of war. Wars in Europe, will probably than heretofore become less frequent; religious rancour, which formerly animated princes to arms, is succeeded by a spirit of philosophy extremely friendly to peace. The princes of Europe are or ought to be convinced by sad experience, that the objects of conquest, are vastly inadequate to the immense charge of their armaments. Prudential motives, therefore, in the future, will often dictate negociation [*sic*], instead of war. . . .

This Continent fifty years hence, infallibly will be richer, and much better peopled than at present; consequently abler to effect a revolution. But alas! e'er that period, our author will forever be forgotten; impelled therefore by his villainous ambition, he would rashly precipitate his country into every species of horror, misery, and desolation, rather than forego his fancied protectorship. "But if you have, (says our author) and still can shake hands with the murderers, then are ye unworthy the name of husband, father, friend, or lover, and whatever may be your rank or title in life, you have the heart of a coward, and the spirit of a sycophant, &c. To talk of friendship with those in whom our reason forbids us to have faith, and our affections wounded through a thousand pores, instructs us to detest is madness and folly."

Ye that are not drunk with fanaticism answer me? Are these words dictated by peace, or base foul revenge, the constant attendant on cowards and sycophants? Does our author so perfectly versed in scripture, mean to conduct us to peace or desolation? or is he fit to legislate for men or devils? Nations after desolating each other, (happily for mankind) forgive, forget, and reconcile; like individuals who quarrel, reconcile, and become friends. Following the laudable example of the CONGRESS; we lately have most readily shaken hands with our inveterate enemies the Canadians, who have scalped nearly as many of our people as the British troops have done: Why therefore may we not forgive and reconcile—By no means, it blasts our author's ambitious purposes. . . .

Nations, like individuals, in the hour of passion attend to no mediation. But when heartily drubbed, and tired of war, are very readily reconciled, without the intervention of mediators; by whom, belligerents were never reconciled, until their interests or passions dictated the pacification. If we may use our author's elegant language, mediation is "farsical." I grant however, that the idea of our forcing England by arms to treat with us is brilliant. "It is unreasonable continues (our author) to suppose that France and Spain will give us any kind of assistance, if we mean only to make use of that assistance for the purpose of repairing the breach, and strengthening the connection between Britain and America; because those powers would be sufferers by the consequences." . . .

Volumes were insufficient to describe the horror, misery and desolation, awaiting the people at large in the syren form of American independence. In short, I affirm that it would be most excellent policy in those who wish for TRUE LIBERTY to submit by an advantageous reconciliation to the authority of Great Britain; "to accomplish in the long run, what they cannot do by hypocrisy, fraud and force in the short one."[25]

CHARLES INGLIS (1734–1816)

Although his father was an Anglican priest in his native Ireland, Charles Inglis had no formal education. The elder Inglis died when Charles was young, forcing his mother to instruct him at home. Arriving in America in 1755, Inglis found work teaching in the Church of England school at Lancaster, Pennsylvania, after which the church ordained him in 1758. He became a curate at Trinity Church in New York in 1765.

As relations between America and England grew more hostile, Inglis concluded that England gave its colonial subjects too much freedom. "America is too unwieldy for the feeble, dilatory administration of democracy," he asserted. In 1776, after publication of Thomas Paine's Common Sense, Inglis published his own response, True Interest of America Impartially Stated. *He later composed other loyalist pamphlets and letters to the press under the pseudonym "Papinian." After rebels seized and burned copies of the first pamphlet, Inglis doggedly published two more editions in Philadelphia.*

Inglis's dissent enraged New York rebels. When a group of armed men entered his church one Sunday morning, demanding that he cease offering prayers for the King, he refused and proceeded to pray for George III.[26] Inglis fled England in 1783 when the British evacuated New York. He returned to North America in 1787 to live out his years as the church's first bishop of Nova Scotia.[27]

THE TRUE INTEREST OF AMERICA IMPARTIALLY STATED
Pamphlet, 1776

I think it no difficult matter to point out many advantages which will certainly attend our reconciliation and connection with Great-Britain, on a firm, constitutional plan. I shall select a few of these; and that their importance may be more clearly discerned, I shall afterwards point out some of the evils which inevitably must attend our separating from Britain, and declaring for independency. On each article I shall study brevity.

1. By a reconciliation with Britain, a period would be put to the present calamitous war, by which so many lives have been lost, and so many more must be lost, if it continues. This alone is an advantage devoutly to be wished for. This author [Thomas Paine] says—*"The blood of the slain, the weeping voice of nature cries, Tis time to part."* I think they cry just the reverse. The blood of the slain, the weeping voice of nature cries—*It is time to be reconciled*; it is time to lay aside those animosities which have pushed on Britons to shed the blood of Britons; it is high time that those who are connected by the endearing ties of religion, kindred and country, should resume their former friendship, and be united in the bond of mutual atfection [*sic*], as their interests are inseparably united.

2. By a Reconciliation with Great-Britain, Peace—that fairest offspring and gift of Heaven—will be restored. In one respect Peace is like health; we do not sufficiently know its value but by its absence. What uneasiness and anxiety, what evils, has this short interruption of peace with the parent-state, brought on the whole British empire! . . .

3. Agriculture, commerce, and industry would resume their wonted vigor. At present, they languish and droop, both here and in Britain; and must continue to do so, while this unhappy contest remains unsettled.

4. By a connection with Great-Britain, our trade would still have the protection of the greatest naval power in the world. England has the advantage, in this respect, of every other state, whether of ancient or modern times. . . .

5. The protection of our trade, while connected with Britain, will not cost a fiftieth part of what it must cost, were we ourselves to raise a naval force sufficient for this purpose.

6. Whilst connected with Great-Britain, we have a bounty on almost every article of exportation; and we may be better supplied with goods by her, than we could elsewhere. . . .

7. When a Reconciliation is effected, and things return into the old channel, a few years of peace will restore everything to its pristine state. Emigrants will flow in as usual from the different parts of Europe. Population will advance with the same rapid progress as formerly, and our lands will rise in value. . . .

Let us now, if you please, take a view of the other side of the question. Suppose we were to revolt from Great-Britain, declare ourselves Independent, and set up a Republic of our own-what would be the consequence?—I stand aghast at the prospect—my blood runs chill when I think of the calamities, the complicated evils that must ensue, and may be clearly foreseen—it is impossible for any man to foresee them all. . . .

1. All our property throughout the continent would be unhinged; the greatest confusion, and most violent convulsions would take place. . . . The common bond that tied us together, and by which our property was secured, would be snapt [*sic*] asunder. . . .

2. What a horrid situation would thousands be reduced to who have taken the oath of allegiance to the King: yet contrary to their oath, as well as inclination, must be compelled to renounce that allegiance, or abandon all their property in

America! How many thousands more would be reduced to a similar situation; who, although they took not that oath, yet would think it inconsistent with their duty and a good conscience to renounce their Sovereign; I dare say these will appear trifling difficulties to our author; but whatever he may think, there are thousands and thousands who would sooner lose all they had in the world, nay life itself, than thus wound their conscience. A Declaration of Independency would infallibly disunite and divide the colonists.

3. By a Declaration for Independency, every avenue to an accommodation with Great-Britain would be closed; the sword only could then decide the quarrel; and the sword would not be sheathed till one had conquered the other. . . .

The importance of these colonies to Britain need not be enlarged on, it is a thing so universally known. The greater their importance is to her, so much the more obstinate will her struggle be not to lose them. The independency of America would, in the end, deprive her of the West-Indies, shake her empire to the foundation, and reduce her to a state of the most mortifying insignificance. Great-Britain therefore must, for her own preservation, risk every thing, and exert her whole strength, to prevent such an event from taking place. This being the case—

4. Devastation and ruin must mark the progress of this war along the sea coast of America. Hitherto, Britain has not exerted her power. Her number of troops and ships of war here at present, is very little more than she judged expedient in time of peace—the former does not amount to 12,000 men—nor the latter to 40 ships, including frigates. Both she, and the colonies, hoped for and expected an accommodation; neither of them has lost sight of that desirable object. . . . But as soon as we declare for independency, every prospect of this kind must vanish. Ruthless war, with all its aggravated horrors, will ravage our once happy land-our seacoasts and ports will be ruined, and our ships taken. Torrents of blood will be split, and thousands reduced to beggary and wretchedness. . . .

The Americans are properly Britons. They have the manners, habits, and ideas of Britons; and have been accustomed to a similar form of government. But Britons never could bear the extremes, either of monarchy or republicanism. Some of their Kings have aimed at despotism; but always failed. Repeated efforts have been made towards democracy, and they equally failed. . . . Limited monarchy is the form of government which is most favourable to liberty—which is best adapted to the genius and temper of Britons; although here and there among us a crack-brained zealot for democracy or absolute monarchy, may be sometimes found.

Besides the unsuitableness of the republican form to the genius of the people, America is too extensive for it. That form may do well enough for a single city, or small territory; but would be utterly improper for such a continent as this. America is too unwieldy for the feeble, dilatory administration of democracy.[28]

JAMES RIVINGTON (1724–1802) AND
WILLIAM SMITH (1728–1793)

Born in London to a publishing family, James Rivington made a small fortune in England publishing Tobias Smollett's History of England—*and then squandered it. Destitute, he headed for America in 1760 at age 33. He set up printing shops in Philadelphia, Boston, and finally in New York, where he began publishing America's first daily newspaper in March 1773. Known as the* New-York Gazetteer *and the* Connecticut, New Jersey, Hudson's River, and Quebec Weekly Advertiser, *the publication was a huge success, quickly achieving a circulation of 3,600 throughout the colonies and a reputation as the best newspaper in the country.*

    When war came, Rivington reported both sides, but eventually began publishing editorials sympathetic to the British, angering the Sons of Liberty. In early 1775, when a New Jersey mob hanged him in effigy, Rivington scoffed at the indignity and ran a sketch of the hanging in his paper. Not long thereafter, a group of more than seventy Sons visited his shop and destroyed several printing plates.

    By May, his editorials proved so offensive that the Sons had him arrested. Friends in the Continental Congress arranged for his release in hopes that, given a second chance, Rivington would tone down his editorials. He refused, and in November the Sons were back—this time destroying the shop and carting off his type, vowing to melt down the metal for bullets. Undaunted, Rivington set sail for Britain in January 1776 and returned two years later with new type and another press. He also now had the title of King's Printer in America and publisher of the Royal Gazette.[29]

    Throughout the war, Rivington published his avidly pro-British publication in British-occupied New York. After his death in 1802, evidence emerged suggesting that Rivington was a spy for the Continental Army, at least during the war's later years. Whatever his loyalties, Rivington's paper was a Tory publication until the war's end. Although American authorities allowed him to continue publishing in New York after the war, his readership plummeted and the once-fiery Tory organ went bust in 1783.[30]

    The following is an excerpt from a 1780 pamphlet Rivington republished in 1781 for William Smith (1728–1793), chief justice of the colonial government of New York. Formerly a critic of British taxation policies (John Adams praised his role in the Stamp Act crisis of 1765), Smith remained neutral in the war, believing both sides were at fault. He finally expressed loyalty to the Crown in 1778, support the British rewarded in 1780 by appointing him chief justice.[31]

THE CANDID RETROSPECT, OR THE A
MERICAN WAR EXAMINED BY WHIG PRINCIPLES
Pamphlet, 1780

Who then are the real enemies of America, if not *they* who have perverted the *virtuous aims* of the *main body* of the people for the defence of their rights and priviledges [*sic*], into a war for dominion? . . .

    It being manifest that nothing will satisfy the directors of the American Councils (by whom several of the Colonies suffer themselves to be ruled) but measures incompatible with the safety of the many millions of the same natural stock with themselves in Europe, Asia and Africa, and in the contented dispersions in the Islands, as well as on the continent of America, Great-Britain will be justifiable in exerting the powers she enjoys for her preservation, to render the rebelled Plantations as *impotent* as they appear to be *unfriendly*, to the welfare of that vast community, with whom they may be, as they once were, happily united; and from whom they are now sullenly severed, upon principles of partiality, reprobated by great multitudes of their own country-men, who have suffered insults, imprisonments, fines, sequestrations, and many of them *death itself* . . .

That the sufferings of the loyalists in all parts of the continent, from the hands of fellow subjects, who while violating the rights of private judgment, are nevertheless appealing in their fasts, prayers and thanksgivings, to the God of love and mercy, for their innocence, will eternally demonstrate the hypocrisy, avarice and profligacy of some, and the fanaticism of the rest of their oppressors; as the forbearance of Great-Britain, in not having yet executed a single rebel in her power, and in restraining from the devastations and complicated calamities, she might have brought upon the avowed ally of her inveterate enemy, is of her lenity and generosity: And that it will become her in future, to have a tender regard, not only to her friends in America, but to discriminate the ignorant, the timid, the helpless, the uninformed and the seduced, by proportionable indulgences; and to remember at the final termination of the war in a re-union, the fidelity and affection she found here, and to strike hands with the Colonies, in a free and generous establishment of their privileges, bought by the blood of the *American*, as well as the *European* loyalist.

Lastly, That Great-Britain independent of her own interest in the controversy, is, all circumstances considered, bound by justice and honour to prevent the ruin of her American friends, at every risk short of certain destruction to herself: And that it will be her duty, if compelled by adversity to conclude a disadvantageous peace, and to part with one or more of her Colonies to France, Spain or any other foreign nation, to stipulate in clear and strong terms, in behalf of the loyalists who may be found there, for every advantage of disposing of their estates, and free liberty to remove to such of the Colonies or Dominions, as may not be unfortunately surrendered at the end of the war, to a popish or arbitrary power.[32]

CHAPTER 2

THE WAR OF 1812

"WEED OUR COUNTRY OF TRAITORS"

AMERICAN GRIEVANCES AGAINST THE BRITISH REACHED A FEVER PITCH in the spring and early summer of 1812. On June 1, President James Madison—prodded and cajoled by a group of bellicose Republican House members—asked Congress to declare war on Britain in response to what he called "a series of acts hostile to the United States as an independent and neutral nation."

As Madison indignantly noted, British cruisers had for years been seizing American ships and pressing hapless passengers into naval service. "Thousands of American citizens, under the safeguard of public law and of their national flag," Madison said, "have been torn from their country and from everything dear to them." All efforts at diplomacy had failed, Madison said.

Adding to the American outrage, the British—beginning in 1807 with the so-called Orders in Council—imposed a naval blockade of the European coast, shutting down U.S. trade with European nations by seizing American-flagged ships that did not first visit and pay duties at British ports. In effect, the United States was an innocent but very injured bystander in the long-running conflict between Britain and France, both hoping to cripple the other by eliminating foreign commerce. In that sense, the British were not alone in their hostility to American shipping. While almost 400 American ships were seized by the British between 1807 and 1812, the French seized more than 550.[1] "Our commerce has been plundered in every sea," Madison told the Congress, "the great staples of our country have been cut off from their legitimate markets, and a destructive blow aimed at our agricultural and maritime interests. . . . We behold, in fine, on the side of Great Britain, a state of war against the United States, and on the side of the United States a state of peace toward Great Britain."[2]

Madison's call for war was the culmination of months of work by a group of new, young Republican members of Congress—about a dozen fierce, self-styled patriots eager to defend the nation's sovereignty and its national honor against Britain's belligerence. They were, in the words of one historian, "ardent patriots too young to remember the horrors of the last British war and thus willing to run the risks of another to vindicate the nation's rights."[3] Among these zealous men—they were known as the "War Hawks"—were two of Congress's most respected leaders, Henry Clay of Kentucky and John C. Calhoun of South Carolina. Short of his thirty-fifth birthday and a freshman congressman, Clay was so widely admired that his colleagues made him speaker upon his arrival in Washington. From that position, he afforded his fellow War Hawks a prominent and influential voice in the debate over war.

In November 1811, the War Hawks engineered passage of military preparedness legislation to increase the army's size to ten thousand men, put all naval vessels into active commission, increase the militias' numbers to ten thousand, strengthen coastal fortifications, and arm merchant vessels. Doubtful, however, of the nation's ability to compete with Britain on the seas, Congress rejected proposals for a drastic expansion of naval forces—an unfortunate decision, as the coming war would be fought almost entirely on the seas and the Great Lakes.[4]

Congress also rejected the notion of fighting the French and the British. Among those supporting a dual war over American rights on the high seas was Calhoun. "The Devil himself could not tell [whether] England or France is the most wicked," said a Republican House ally of Calhoun, Nathaniel Macon of North Carolina. Cooler and more sentimental heads prevailed. In addition to the folly of fighting wars against two powerful nations, France—despite its aggression against U.S. shipping—retained the affection of many Americans who fondly remembered that country's support of the American Revolution and who supported the French Revolution. After considering the prospect of war with both countries, the Senate rejected the idea—although just barely—in an 18 to 14 vote.[5]

Another enticing possibility appealed to the War Hawks and their followers—seizing Canada from the British as a bargaining tool to persuade Britain to end its aggression against the United States. As an added benefit, one historian noted, it would also "diminish the threat of British-inspired Indian wars on the northern frontier."[6] To the deluded Republicans it seemed a simple matter. Canada, they presumed, was poorly defended and a military invasion would be a near-effortless enterprise. "The acquisition of Canada this year will be a mere matter of marching," Thomas Jefferson asserted.[7]

One war supporter, Hezekiah Niles, publisher of an influential Baltimore newspaper, the *Weekly Register*, summarized the political pressures that no doubt weighed on the minds of some antiwar congressmen. Noting that the "whole number of the opponents of the present administration is far short of the number of the tories we had in the revolutionary war," Niles believed that most members of Congress would side with Madison. Niles framed the question for House and Senate members as "*For America or for England?*" He believed that "a very small and contemptible portion, indeed, will fail to rally round the standard of government" and he was confident that the war would "*weed our country of traitors.*"[8]

Among the war's fierce opponents was Congressman John Randolph, a feisty Republican from Virginia, who spoke for many southerners when he told the House Foreign Relations Committee in late 1811 that the brewing conflict was not a matter of self-defense, but a "war of conquest, a war for the acquisition of territory and subjects."[9] Randolph's dissent, and his efforts to obstruct the House's march to war, had little effect. Once Madison formally requested war, the House, under Clay's leadership, moved quickly to overpower outnumbered Federalists (still largely pro-British) and some Republicans who wanted to open the debate to public scrutiny. Instead, House members debated the measure in closed session and, on June 4, voted 79 to 49 for war with Great Britain. It was clearly not the overwhelming vote of confidence that Clay and Madison desired. All of the pro-war votes were from Republicans, while 40 Federalists and 22 Republicans were opposed (a quarter of the Republicans in the House abstained). The proponents mostly represented the South and the West (Kentucky, Tennessee, and Ohio)—and they were younger than the opponents, mostly younger than forty. The votes against war came almost entirely from New England and New York—among those opposed were eight of ten New England senators and eleven of fourteen New York representatives. Despite the strong New England dissent, six congressmen from Massachusetts and most of the Vermont and New Hampshire delegations supported the war—helping provide the declaration its margin of victory in the House.[10] The Senate, meanwhile, approached the matter with more deliberation. After debating the issue for several weeks—following many attempts by opponents to defeat the resolution—senators voted 19 to 13 for war on June 17.[11]

Despite the war declaration's passage, the nation was clearly not united in wanting war with Britain—nor was it entirely sure of the war's purpose. "Many nations have gone to war in pure gayety of heart," wrote Henry Adams in his history of the Madison presidency, "but perhaps the United States were the first to force themselves into a war they dreaded, in the hope that the war itself might create the spirit they lacked."[12] The war, observed the *Connecticut Courant*, "was commenced in folly, it is proposed to be carried on with madness, and (unless speedily terminated) will end in ruin."[13]

The nation was woefully unequipped for combat with one of the world's most potent military powers. Legislation increasing the size of the U.S. army had failed. That meant the only force remotely prepared to fight by April 1812 was the navy. Funds to finance the war were scarce. After years of resolving to reduce the nation's Revolutionary War debt, the Republicans were loath to borrow the funds for the conflict. Congress, complained one New York Federalist, had nothing to show for its effort but "paper preparations."[14]

In July came the first Federalist broadside against the war, in the form of an eleven-thousand-word document signed by thirty-four House members. The statement rebutting Madison's arguments was widely read throughout the country. The nation, the congressmen asserted, was happily "removed from the bloody theatre of Europe" and had "nothing to fear" from invasion; "from acquisition nothing to hope." Affirming the document, the Federalist-dominated Massachusetts House condemned the war as "impolitic, unnecessary, and ruinous."[15] Massachusetts Governor Caleb Strong agreed and called for a fast to atone for the war "against the nation from which we are descended." Strong had plenty of company. He and other New England governors, with the exception of New Hampshire's chief executive, refused to honor presidential requisitions for state militia.[16]

Dissent was slow to spread to the other states, where the conflict was still popular. In July 1813, a mob in Baltimore destroyed the printing facilities of the *Federal Republican*, a newspaper edited by fierce war critic Alexander L. Hanson. The ensuing violence resulted in several deaths and seriously injured one of Hanson's defenders, Henry Lee III, the Revolutionary War general and former governor of Virginia, who never fully recovered from his wounds.[17]

Throughout 1813, the struggle went badly for the United States as British forces continually thwarted American efforts to establish a strong foothold in Canada. In September, U.S. naval forces commanded by Commodore Oliver Hazard Perry defeated a British squadron in the Battle of Lake Erie, securing American control of the strategic lake. The next month, the United States won another modest victory. This time, U.S. and Kentucky militiamen commanded by William Henry Harrison defeated British troops and their Indian allies in the Battle of the Thames near Chatham, Ontario, in Upper Canada. Afterwards, U.S. troops cleared British forces out of Detroit and western Ontario. Most important, the defeat broke the back of the British-Indian alliance in the northwest.[18]

Despite this modest American success, it was evident to President Madison that a peaceful resolution was far more likely than a military victory. The need for a negotiated settlement became even more evident in the spring of 1814 when Napoleon abdicated, ending Britain's war with France. This meant that Britain now had the time and resources to devote full attention to its war in America. As Madison moved toward negotiations with the British, the war was at best a stalemate, and with the British navy blocking American ships from leaving port, the conflict now threatened to strangle the young nation's economy.

In March 1814, Congress overwhelmingly repealed the unpopular trade embargoes enacted in 1806 to 1808 that had hurt U.S. shipping interests (especially in New England) far more than the intended target. Britain plundered coastal communities, including burning Washington, DC, and an unsuccessful attack on Baltimore. (The attack on the southern states of Virginia and Maryland—especially the British attack on Washington, DC—was partly out of revenge for the Americans' reckless burning in April 1813 of York, the capital of Upper Canada.)[19]

The British attacks on the South were also motivated by that region's war fervor and the corresponding opposition to war in New England. While they initially left New York and New England alone, by May 1814 the British extended their blockade to include the entire American coast, hoping to exacerbate dissent in New York, Boston, and other New England shipping communities. By June 1814, British troops blockaded several New England ports, staged violent raids on coastal towns and captured much of eastern Maine in a military operation that many assumed would eventually extend to Boston. As the British hoped, the fact that they had attacked New England communities with impunity, with virtually no defense from U.S. troops, only fueled the region's antagonism toward Washington.[20] Worse, the U.S. treasury was almost broke and the government desperately needed loans from New England banks—something many of the region's recalcitrant bankers opposed in order to force Madison to abandon plans to invade Canada.[21] In fact, Henry Adams later speculated, New England probably "lent to the British government during the war more money than she lent to her own."[22]

In response to the dire situation, Governor Strong of Massachusetts summoned the state's General Court (or Legislature) into special session in early October to condemn, not the British, but President Madison. The outcome was a resolution proposing a convention of New England state representatives to address what one member called "the destructive policy by which a state of unparalleled national felicity has been converted into one of humiliation, of danger, and distress."[23] The resulting convention in Hartford, Connecticut, brought together representatives of Massachusetts, Connecticut, and Rhode Island, mostly moderates who hesitated to go as far as some of their angry colleagues who favored secession. Indeed, the Hartford Convention rhetoric was far less incendiary than some feared. Meeting privately from December 15, 1814, to January 5, 1815, the delegates produced rampant speculation that they were hatching a treasonous plot or a plan of secession. What they produced were proposals for seven constitutional amendments that dealt not so much with the conduct of the war, but addressed perceived Republican abuses and New England's declining influence in national affairs.[24]

It was, however, the speculation about what the convention *might* have done that characterized it. Its members and its product were indelibly stained with the tint of treason and disloyalty, despite its moderate tone and relatively modest objectives. What altered the perception about the convention and, in turn, the Federalists, was the news of General Andrew Jackson's stunning and decisive defeat of the British at New Orleans and the peace treaty negotiated at Ghent. The British decision to restore the prewar status quo took the Federalists by surprise, exposed them to public ridicule and scorn, and virtually destroyed the party's political standing. Before the battle of New Orleans, the U.S. position had appeared hopeless. Now, after Jackson's heroic victory, the Federalists were hopeless.[25]

The national celebration of the New Orleans battle, which was fought after the war-ending Treaty of Ghent, dealt the Federalists a fatal blow. The public now viewed the party as defeatist and unpatriotic. Their members' pragmatic and sometimes-principled dissent against the nation's most unpopular war (prior to Vietnam) earned them the scorn of a euphoric nation that mythologized the U.S. "victory"—promptly forgetting how the United States almost lost the war. The nation's ire was directed at the "disloyalty" of the commercial interests in New England who controlled the party. Hobbled by his party's opposition to the now-popular war, the Federalist presidential candidate in 1816, Rufus King, lost badly to James Monroe. Four years later, the almost-nonexistent party had no presidential candidate at all. By 1824, the Federalist Party—shipwrecked on the shoals of a nearly disastrous conflict—was dead.[26]

JOHN RANDOLPH (1773–1833)

A renowned orator, John Randolph represented Virginia in Congress from 1799 through 1813. Although a Republican, he was motivated less by his devotion to Jeffersonian ideals then by his hatred of the Federalists. "I know not how gentlemen calling themselves Republicans can advocate such a war," he told the House in December 1811.[27] He was brilliant, well educated, and had the feisty spirit of a warrior as well as the soul of a poet. He was also quite eccentric. He would sometimes enter the House chamber fresh from a fox hunt, strolling down the aisle wearing spurs, followed by his foxhound.[28]

Opposed to war with England, Randolph's considerable rhetorical and parliamentary skills were no match for the War Hawks led by his nemesis, Henry Clay, with whom he engaged in a duel in 1826. Neither man was injured, although Clay's second shot hit Randolph's coat. When he died in 1833, Randolph was buried, by his instructions, facing west toward Kentucky, so that he might keep an eye on Clay.[29]

In 1811, as Congress debated military preparedness legislation, Randolph protested, especially angered by American designs on British-controlled Canada.

OPEN LETTER TO HIS CONSTITUENTS
May 30, 1812

France has for years past offered us terms of undefined commercial arrangement, as the price of a war with England, which hitherto we have not wanted firmness and virtue to reject That price is now to be paid. We are tired of holding out; and, following the example of continental Europe, entangled in the artifices, or awed by the power of the destroyer of mankind, we are prepared to become instrumental to his projects of universal dominion. *Before these pages meet your eye, the last republic of the earth will have enlisted under the banners of the tyrant and become a party to his cause.* The blood of the American freemen must flow to cement his power, to aid in stifling the last struggles of afflicted and persecuted man, to deliver up into his hands the patriots of Spain and Portugal, to establish his empire over the ocean and over the land that gave our fathers birth—to forge our own chains! And yet, my friends, we are told, as we were told in the days of Mr. Adams, *"the finger of heaven points to war."* Yes, the finger of heaven *does* point to war! It points to war, as it points to the mansions of eternal misery and torture—as a flaming beacon warning us of that vortex which we may not approach but with certain destruction. . . .

These are no ordinary times; the state of the world is unexampled; the war of the present day is not like that of our revolution, or any which preceded it, at least in modern times. It is a war against the liberties and the happiness of mankind; it is a war in which the whole human race are the victims, to gratify the pride and lust of power of a single individual. I beseech you, put it to your own bosoms, how far it becomes you as freemen, as Christians, to give your aid and sanction to this impious and bloody war against your brethren of the human family. To such among you, if any such there be, who are insensible to motives not more dignified and manly than they are intrinsically wise, I would make a different appeal I adjure you by the regard you have for your own safety and property, for the liberty and inheritance of your children—by all that you hold dear and sacred—to interpose your constitutional powers to save your country and yourselves from the calamity, the issue of which it is not given to human foresight to divine. . . .

My friends, do you expect to find those who are now loudest in the clamor for war, foremost in the ranks of battle? Or, is the honor of this nation indissolubly connected with the political reputation of a few individuals, who tell you *they* have gone too far to recede, and that you must pay, with *your ruin*, the price of their *consistency*? . . .

The destiny of the American people is in their own hands. The net is spread for their destruction. You are enveloped in the toils of French duplicity, and if—which may Heaven in its mercy forbid—you and your posterity are to become hewers of wood and drawers of water to the modern Pharaoh, it shall not be for the want of my best exertions to rescue you from the cruel and abject bondage. This sin, at least, shall not rest upon my soul.[30]

JOSIAH QUINCY (1772–1864)

Born into one of the wealthiest and most prominent New England families, Quincy trained as a lawyer, but soon spurned the law for his true love—politics. A Federalist, he represented Boston in the U.S. House from 1804 to 1813, when he resigned in disgust over the War of 1812. Although as the House Federalist leader he originally supported President Madison's military preparedness measures, he switched course in early 1812 and actively opposed the war declaration.

After leaving Congress, Quincy won a seat in the Massachusetts Senate, where he continued speaking out against the war. Quincy later served as Boston's mayor and then as president of Harvard College. A dissident to the end, in his retirement Quincy published a series of antislavery pamphlets.[31]

In Federalist Protest, *written by Quincy and signed by 34 Federalist House members, the war's opponents denounced the political leaders who they believed had goaded President Madison and Congress into war for political reasons, including the conquest of Canada—not for the ostensible reason of redressing injuries inflicted by the British.[32]*

FEDERALIST PROTEST
1812

A nation like the United States, happy in its local relations; removed from the bloody theatre of Europe; with a maritime border, opening a vast field for enterprise; with territorial possessions exceeding every real want; its firesides safe; its altars undefiled; from invasion nothing to fear; from acquisition nothing to hope; how shall such a nation look to Heaven for its smiles, while throwing away, as though they were worthless, all the blessings and joys which peace and such a distinguished lot include? With what prayers can it address the Most High, when it prepares to pour forth its youthful rage upon a neighboring people; from whose strength it has nothing to dread, from whose devastation it has nothing to gain?

If our ills were of a nature that war would remedy; if war would compensate any of our losses, or remove any of our complaints, there might be some alleviation of the suffering, in the charm of the prospect. But how will war upon the land protect commerce upon the ocean? What balm has Canada for wounded honor? How are our mariners benefitted by a war, which exposes those who are free, without promising release to those who are impressed?

But it is said that war is demanded by honor. Is national honor a principle, which thirsts after vengeance, and is appeased only by blood, which, trampling on the hopes of man, and spurning the law of God, untaught by what is past and careless of what is to come, precipitates itself into any folly of madness, to gratify a selfish vanity or to satiate some unhallowed rage? If honor demands a war with England, what opiate lulls that honor to sleep over the wrongs done us by France? On land, robberies, seizures, imprisonments, by French authority; at sea, pillage, sinkings, burnings, under French orders. These are notorious. Are they unfelt because they are French? Is any alleviation to be found in the correspondence and humiliation of the present Minister Plenipotentiary of the United States at the French Court? In his communications to our Government as before the public, where is the cause for now selecting France as the friend of our country, and England as the enemy?

If no illusion of personal feeling, and no solicitude for elevation of place, should be permitted to misguide the public councils; if it is indeed honorable for the true statesman to consult the public welfare, to provide in truth for the public defence, and to impose no yoke of bondage; with full knowledge of the wrongs inflicted by the French, ought the Government of this country to aid the French cause, by engaging in war against the enemy of France? To supply the waste of such a war, and to meet the appropriation of millions extraordinary for the war expenditures, must our fellow citizens, throughout the Union, be doomed to sustain the burden of war-taxes, in various forms of direct and indirect imposition? . . .

It would be some relief to our anxiety, if amends were likely to be made for the weakness and wildness of the project, by the prudence of the preparation. But in no aspect of this anomalous affair can we trace the great and distinctive properties of wisdom. There is seen a headlong rushing into difficulties, with little calculation about the means, and little concern about the consequences. With a navy comparatively nominal, we are about to enter into the lists against the greatest marine on the globe. With a commerce unprotected and spread over every ocean, we propose to make profit by privateering, and for this endanger the wealth of which we are honest proprietors. An invasion is threatened of the colonies of a Power which, without putting a new ship into commission, or taking another soldier into pay, can spread alarm or desolation along the extensive range of our seaboard. The resources of our country, in their natural state, great beyond our wants or our hopes, are impaired by the effect of artificial restraints. Before adequate fortifications are prepared for domestic defence; before men, or money, are provided for a war of attack, why hasten into the midst of that awful contest which is laying waste Europe? It cannot be concealed, that to engage in the present war against England is to place ourselves on the side of France, and exposes us to the vassalage of States serving under the banners of the French Emperor.

The undersigned cannot refrain from asking, what are the United States to gain by this war? Will the gratification of some privateersmen compensate the nation for that sweep of our legitimate commerce by the extended marine of our enemy, which this desperate act invites? Will Canada compensate the Middle States for New York; or the Western States for New Orleans? Let us not be deceived. A war of invasion may invite a retort of invasion. When we visit the peaceable, and as to us innocent, colonies of Great Britain with the horrors of war, can we be assured that our own coast will not be visited with like horrors? At a crisis of the world such as the present, and under impressions such as these, the undersigned could not consider the war, in which the United States have in secret been precipitated, as necessary, or required by any moral duty, or any political expediency.[33]

JOHN LOWELL (1769–1840)

John Lowell was a Boston lawyer and Federalist who served in the Massachusetts legislature from 1798 to 1800. By 1803, overwork destroyed his health. After returning from a three-year recuperation in Europe, Lowell began publishing spirited pamphlets and letters to the editor. His strident opposition to the trade embargo, President Madison, and the War of 1812 earned him the nickname, "the Boston Rebel." Lowell opposed the Hartford Convention because delegates would not urge their states to withhold resources from the war effort. While not widely distributed throughout the states, his pamphlets were influential in New England. In 1812, he wrote two widely read discourses on the war—Mr. Madison's War and Perpetual War.[34]

MR. MADISON'S WAR
Pamphlet, 1812

It may be said, and it is often said, it is now too late to discuss the merits of the declaration of war. The Rubicon is passed. It is your duty to submit and aid as much as possible in the prosecution of the war. It is not patriotic to vindicate the conduct of a nation whom your government has declared your enemy. Let us before we part, my fellow citizens, consider this subject. Every war is supposed to have some *definite object*. That object ought to be a legitimate and honest one, otherwise the war is unjust. It ought also to be a practicable and attainable one, otherwise the war is inexpedient. It ought not to expose us to greater evils and dangers than those which we would wish to remedy, otherwise it is rash and destructive. In order then to know for *what* we are to fight, and *how long* we ought to fight, and what we are to *insist upon* as an ultimatum from our enemy, it is necessary to discuss before the people, (who have as yet heard *only one side of the question* from the inflamed speeches of members of Congress) the whole merits of this war.

If we are bound *forever* to *approve* this war, because a majority of six senators only, (no wiser nor better than ourselves) saw fit to declare it in complaisance to the president, why we may as well give up the right of suffrage at once to this oligarchy, and let them save us the trouble of future elections. But if we have a right to change our rulers and to put in better men, men who love peace, rather than a hopeless war; it is necessary that we should also have the right and power to shew, that the present men have abused their trust by plunging us into an unjust war which might and ought to have been avoided. What limit will our friends of freedom set to right of discussing the merits or propriety of continuing the war?

Suppose after ten or twenty years of war, our posterity shall find the country impoverished, our commerce destroyed, our young men sacrificed in fruitless expeditions, the nation ground to powder by taxes and paper money—and suppose our enemy still triumphant on the ocean, and that all the prophecies about her downfall, shall prove illusory, would not some future patriot in 1832, be authorized to address the people, and assure them that the war was ruinous, that the points for which we were contending were not worth the contests, and that Britain it was evident could not be compelled to yield them, and that for these reasons, they ought to turn out those who were for continuing the war, and put in those who would restore peace?

Would not such a man be a true patriot?

Well then, where will you draw the line as to the *time* when the war may be opposed? Shall it be fixed at six months, a year, ten years, or twenty?

I should say, that from the moment war is declared, those who conscientiously opposed its declaration have a right, and to preserve consistency, are *bound*, to endeavor to bring about a peace by shewing the folly, the wickedness and the evils of the war.

Nay, I go farther—the sooner you do this, and the more strenuously, and vigorously, and undauntedly you urge it, the more true patriotism you discover. For by these means you may put an end to the war before its evils are fully realized, and while the country still possesses some commerce worth saving; but there will be little or no merit in opposing the war some twenty years hence, when an oppressed, and impoverished, and desperate people rise as they will eventually do, and look around in despair for the authors of their calamities who will then seek refuge in caves and mountains, and call upon the rocks and hills to cover them.[35]

CHAPTER 3

THE MEXICAN WAR

"THIS MISERABLE WAR"

PRESIDENT JAMES K. POLK WANTED WAR WITH MEXICO. HAVING campaigned in 1844 for aggressive westward expansion—including bringing into the Union Oregon and the disputed Texas territory south of the Nueches River—Polk knew that war was the most direct route to fulfilling his promises. By May 1846, he would get his war.[1] A Democrat, Polk led a party dedicated to Manifest Destiny, believing the United States' "destiny" was to expand its territory throughout North America. "That which constitutes the strength of the Union, the wealth and independence of its people," a Polk ally explained, "is the boundless expanse of territory laid open to their possession." As the *Post* of Boston asserted, "This 'miserable war' will do more for the spread of commercial and political freedom, the prosperity of the United States, than any other event since the Declaration of Independence."[2]

From the beginning, the issue was Texas; actually, a small part of Texas. After the Texas Revolution of 1836, the Mexican government denied the independence of its former possession, straining U.S.-Mexico relations. By March 1845, Mexico severed diplomatic relations with the United States. In response, Polk further antagonized Mexico by siding with Texas officials who claimed that the Texas-Mexico border was not the long-recognized Nueches River, but the Rio Grande, 150 miles to the southwest. Polk then sent General Zachary Taylor and his 1,500-man army to Corpus Christi, on the border of the disputed territory. In August, Polk reinforced Taylor's army when Mexican forces began massing along the Rio Grande.

Under guise of a diplomatic mission, Polk sent diplomat and former Louisiana Congressman John Slidell to Mexico City to discuss payment of damage claims by American citizens, the disputed boundary, and the purchase of California and New Mexico. Slidell's mission was doomed and Polk likely knew it. Slidell was "envoy extraordinary and minister plenipotentiary," a title guaranteed to offend Mexican officials who agreed to receive only a "commissioner." Rejected by the Mexican government in March 1846, the American diplomat left Mexico City in a huff.[3]

That Polk knew Slidell's mission would fail is evidenced by his order to Taylor in October 1845—before Slidell's departure for Mexico—to advance his army from Corpus Christi to the Rio Grande. By late March 1846—about the time Slidell arrived in Mexico City—Taylor's army established fortifications across the river from the Mexican village of Matamoros. In April, when a Mexican cavalry force crossed the Rio Grande, it clashed with a small unit of Taylor's army. In the skirmish, Mexican forces killed eleven Americans and took forty-seven prisoners.[4]

"Hostilities may now be considered as commenced," Taylor helpfully reported to Polk after the incident. Proclaimed one Washington newspaper on April 26, "American blood has been shed on American soil."[5] In his message to Congress on May 11, 1846, Polk disingenuously said the United States evinced "the strong desire to establish peace with Mexico on liberal and honorable terms." Despite his attempts at diplomacy, Polk said, the Mexican army "invaded our territory and shed the blood of our fellow-citizens on our own soil." After recounting the details of Slidell's aborted mission and the skirmish at Matamoros, Polk declared that a state of war existed between the two nations.[6]

Polk's message was crafty and deceitful. It marked the first time an American president had requested a war declaration by stating that the war had begun. Accompanying Polk's message was legislation authorizing acceptance of militia and volunteers. Over vigorous opposition by some House and Senate members, denied time to read the documents that accompanied Polk's message, both houses quickly endorsed the war—174 to 14 in the House and 40 to 2 in the Senate. All the no votes were Whigs. In the *Boston Whig*, an abolitionist paper, Charles Francis Adams (son of former president and then-House member John Quincy Adams), labeled the war declaration's preamble "one of the grossest national lies that was ever deliberately told." In the *New York Tribune*, Horace Greely derided Polk as "the Father of Lies" for portraying the United States as the victim of Mexican aggression.[7]

Not completely against expansionism, Whigs were generally opposed to acquiring these new lands quickly and by force.[8] "The true glory of our Republic," one Whig leader maintained, "consists not so much in the wide extent of our domain, as in . . . that devotion to the cause of *equal and exact justice*." Some Whigs believed that the rush to expand the nation's territory revealed Americans as "greedy for the acquisition of territory."[9] Northern Whig opposition was further stoked by the belief that Polk's expansionism was a backdoor attempt to extend slavery to the new states and territories.[10]

Many southern slave-owning Whigs were no less opposed to the war than their northern allies. None other than Democratic Senator John C. Calhoun of South Carolina—a fierce defender of slavery and former War Hawk of 1812—vehemently opposed the conflict, insisting Polk had "forced" Congress into war by asserting the conflict had already begun. Presciently, Calhoun observed, "It sets an example, which will enable all future Presidents to bring about a state of things, in which Congress shall be forced, without deliberation, or reflection, to declare war, however opposed to its convictions of justice or expediency."[11]

Like most Whigs, however, Calhoun believed he had little choice but to support the war. Recalling how the Federalist Party destroyed itself over its hostility the War of 1812, most Whigs opposed Polk's war policies, but supported the troops (still a familiar wartime refrain and cudgel).[12] This philosophy was explained well by Representative Alexander Stephens of Georgia, who said "now the fires of war are raging on our frontier, all good citizens should render their willing aid, as I most cheerfully do."[13] The Whig dissent did not trouble Polk as he pressed for an offensive to take New Mexico and California while Taylor's army secured the disputed Texas region. U.S. troops easily seized Santa Fe and then, after scattered Mexican opposition, California.[14] In the aftermath, support for the war spiked. "Our people are like a young man of 18," Calhoun wrote, "full of health and vigour and disposed for adventure of any discription [sic], but without wisdom or experience to guide him."[15]

In his State of the Union message in December 1846, Polk assailed critics who characterized the war "as one of [U.S.] aggression." Employing rhetoric that future presidents would use to smear critics of other wars, Polk charged that "a more effectual means could not have been devised to encourage the enemy and protract the war than to advocate and adhere to their cause, and thus give them aid and comfort."[16] Polk essentially labeled his critics traitors.

By early 1847, Polk and General Winfield Scott, general in chief of the U.S. Army, agreed on a bold strategy to end the war. After Scott's army successfully assaulted the Mexican Gulf coast city of Vera Cruz, he and Polk prepared to capture Mexico City. By September 1847, Scott's army overcame stiff Mexican resistance and took the Mexican capital. By February of the following year, both sides agreed that the United States could keep the territories that had been Polk's original objectives—land that would eventually become California, New Mexico, Arizona, Nevada, Colorado, and Utah. In all, Polk captured half of Mexico's land (adding 1.2 million square miles of new land to the United States). In addition, the Rio Grande was the accepted boundary between the new state of Texas and Mexico, another of Polk's original objectives. For this, the United States paid Mexico $15 million.[17]

The war had been an expensive adventure, costing the United States more than $100 million and thirteen thousand American soldiers' lives (the vast majority died from disease).[18] At its conclusion, Americans still generally supported the war's aims but were ready for the end, partly evidenced by Whig victories in the election of 1846 in which Democrats lost both houses. When the Treaty of Guadalupe Hidalgo arrived in Washington, Polk was unenthusiastic about its terms, but had little choice but to sign it. Antiwar Whigs controlled the House and, with it, continued funding for the military to hold captured territory. Facing growing dissent, including from newspapers that attacked the war's rising costs, Polk submitted the treaty to the Senate, which quickly ratified it. The House, meanwhile, displayed its displeasure with Polk in early January 1848, when it narrowly approved an amendment of censure that deplored "a war unnecessarily and unconstitutionally begun by the President of the United States."[19]

By 1848, the country was deeply divided over slavery, a wound to the national psyche that debate over the war only aggravated—and exposed. Opposition to the war "left behind sectional strains that began the process of breaking the old bonds of the union," historian Frederick Merk argued, "especially the national political parties, and replacing them with sectionalized parties."[20] More than anything, it was the Wilmot Proviso that transformed the Mexican War into the prelude to the civil war. The proviso—legislation proposed by Congressman David Wilmot of Pennsylvania in 1846 during debate over funding the war—would have outlawed slavery from any U.S. territory acquired from Mexico during the war. Although it never became law, it sparked a long, bitter national debate over slavery that ended in civil war. What began as a grand crusade to expand the limits of the Union to its farthest reaches also sparked the bitter and violent debate that would eventually tear apart the same Union. As one Massachusetts Whig worried in 1847, "Are not matters coming to such an issue as will inevitably alienate one portion from another. I try to avert my eye from such a prospect—but is it not looming up in the mist—dark and portentous?"[21]

CHARLES SUMNER (1811–1874)

The renowned abolitionist U.S. senator from Massachusetts, Charles Sumner served from 1851 until his death in 1874. Before he found his abolitionist passion, he opposed the looming war with Mexico. Invited to give Boston's esteemed Independence Day oration in 1845, Sumner chose as his theme, "What is the true grandeur of nations?"

To the crowd at Boston's Tremont Temple, including about one hundred army and naval officers from local forts, Sumner presented his thesis, asking, "Can there be in our age any peace that is not honorable, any war that is not dishonorable?" Sumner's speech, in which he imagined the eventual creation of the United Nations, offended the military guests and shocked many in the audience, who expected a conventional patriotic address. "The young man has cut his throat," a former Boston mayor exclaimed. However, the speech marked Sumner as a powerful speaker and an intrepid political leader with a bright future. The oration made him an instant celebrity in New England and marked the beginning of a remarkable political career in which he would distinguish himself as one of the leading Republican critics of the South in the years before the Civil War.

In 1856 he delivered a speech in the Senate in which he passionately opposed the introduction of slavery into Kansas and pointedly attacked three of the plan's Democratic proponents—Stephen A. Douglas, Andrew Pickens Butler, and James Murray Mason. Two days later, Butler's nephew, Representative Preston Brooks of South Carolina, stalked onto the Senate floor and beat Sumner into unconsciousness with a cane. Sumner's injuries were so severe that he could not resume his Senate duties for four years. The attack, meanwhile, fueled the fires of northern hostility toward the South.

After the war, Sumner was a leader of the Radical Republicans, and at the time of his death in 1874, was among the leading proponents of Reconstruction-era civil rights legislation, which Congress enacted the following year.[22]

THE TRUE GRANDEUR OF NATIONS
Speech at Boston's Tremont Temple, July 4, 1845

It is not in the power of man, by any subtle alchemy, to transmute wrong into right. Because War is according to practice of the world, it cannot follow that it is right. For ages the world worshipped false gods; but these gods were not less false, because all bowed before them. At this moment the larger portion of mankind are Heathen; but Heathenism is not true. It was once the *practice* of nations to slaughter prisoners of war; but even the Spirit of War recoils now from this bloody sacrifice. . . .

There is still another influence which stimulates War, and interferes with the natural attractions of Peace; I refer to a selfish and exaggerated *love of country*, leading to its physical aggrandizement, and political exaltation, at the expense of other countries, and in disregard of the principles of True Greatness. Our minds, nursed by the litera-ture of antiquity, have imbibed the narrow sentiment of heathen patriotism. Exclu-sive love for the land of birth, was a part of the religion of Greece and Rome. It is an indication of the lowness of their moral nature, that this sentiment was so material as well as exclusive in its character. . . .

It has been a part of the policy of rulers, to encourage this exclusive patriotism; and the people of modern times have all been quickened by the feeling of antiquity. I do not know that any one nation is in a condition to reproach another with this patriotic selfishness. All are selfish. Men are taught to live, not for mankind, but only for a small portion of mankind. The pride, vanity, ambition, brutality even, which we rebuke in individuals, are accounted virtues when displayed in the name of country. . . .

But War crushes, with bloody heel, all beneficence, all happiness, all justice, all that is God-like in man. It suspends every commandment of the Decalogue. It sets at naught every principle of the Gospel. It silences all law, human as well as divine, except only that blasphemous code of its own, the *Laws of War*. If, in its dismal annals, there is any cheerful passage, be assured that it is not inspired by a mar-tial Fury. Let it not be forgotten—let it ever be borne in mind, as you ponder this theme—that the virtues, which shed their charm over its horrors, are all borrowed of Peace; they are emanations of the Spirit of Love, which is so strong in the heart of man, that it survives the rudest assaults. The flowers of gentleness, of kindliness, of fidelity, of humanity, which flourish, in unregarded luxuriance, in the rich meadows of Peace, receive unwonted admiration when we discern them in War, like violets, shedding their perfume on the perilous edges of the precipice, beyond the smiling borders of civilization. God be praised for all the examples of magnanimous virtue, which he has vouchsafed to mankind! . . .

If I have succeeded in imposing, on your minds, the truths, which I have endeav-ored to uphold today, you will be ready, as faithful citizens, alike of our own Republic and of the universal Christian Commonwealth, to join in efforts to abolish the Arbit-rament of War, to suppress International *Lynch Law*, and to induce the Disarming of the Nations as measures indispensable to the establishment of Permanent Peace—that grand, comprehensive blessing, at once the child and parent of all those *guardian virtues*, without which there can be no National Honor, no National Glory, no True Grandeur of Nations![23]

JOHN C. CALHOUN (1772–1850)

One of the most controversial political leaders of his era, John C. Calhoun was also the most prominent advocate of slavery, an institution he praised as "a posi-tive good." Elected to the U.S. House from South Carolina in 1810, he was among the War Hawks demanding war against Britain in 1812. Enormously talented and charismatic, he was, one admirer said, "a cast iron man who looks as if he had never been born and could never be extinguished."

From 1817 to 1825, he was secretary of war under President James Monroe and then vice president under John Quincy Adams and Andrew Jackson. He resigned his office in a dispute with Jackson in 1832 and entered the Senate, where he battled the abolitionists until he left to become President John Tyler's secretary of state in 1843. In that position, Calhoun tried unsuccessfully to persuade the Senate to annex Texas. He returned to the Senate in 1845 and, while privately opposed to the war against Mexico, he voted yes partly to support troops that Polk claimed were already engaged in war. Among his reasons for opposing Polk's policy, outlined in his 1848 Senate speech, were concerns about abuse of presidential power and his opposition to "placing these colored races [Mexicans and Indians] on an equality with the white race."[24]

CONQUEST OF MEXICO
Speech to the House of Representatives, January 4, 1848

. . . I know further, sir, that we have never dreamt of incorporating into our Union any but the Caucasian race—the free white race. To incorporate Mexico, would be the very first instance of the kind of incorporating an Indian race; for more than half of the Mexicans are Indians, and the other is composed chiefly of mixed tribes. I protest against such a union as that! Ours, sir, is the Government of a white race. The greatest misfortunes of Spanish America are to be traced to the fatal error of placing these colored races on an equality with the white race. That error destroyed the social arrangement which formed the basis of society. The Portuguese and ourselves have escaped—the Portuguese at least to some extent—and we are the only people on this continent which have made revolutions without being followed by anarchy. And yet it is professed and talked about to erect these Mexicans into a Territorial Government, and place them on an equality with the people of the United States. I protest utterly against such a project.

Sir, it is a remarkable fact, that in the whole history of man, as far as my knowledge extends, there is no instance whatever of any civilized colored races being found equal to the establishment of free popular government, although by far the largest portion of the human family is composed of these races. And even in the savage state we scarcely find them anywhere with such government, except it be our noble savages—for noble I will call them. They, for the most part, had free institutions, but they are easily sustained among a savage people. Are we to overlook this fact? Are we to associate with ourselves as equals, companions, and fellow-citizens, the Indians and mixed race of Mexico? Sir, I should consider such a thing as fatal to our institutions.

The next two reasons which I assigned, were, that it would be in conflict with the genius and character of our institutions, and subversive of our free government. I take these two together, as intimately connected; and now of the first—to hold Mexico in subjection. . . .

Sir, he who knows the American Constitution well—he who has duly studied its character—he who has looked at history, and knows what has been the effect of conquests of free States invariably, will require no proof at my hands to show that it would be entirely hostile to the institutions of the country to hold Mexico as a province. There is not an example on record of any free State even having attempted the conquest of any territory approaching the extent of Mexico without disastrous consequences. The nations conquered have in time conquered the conquerors by destroying their liberty. That will be our case, sir. The conquest of Mexico would add so vast an amount to the patronage of this Government, that it would absorb the whole power of the States in the Union. This Union would become imperial, and the States mere subordinate corporations. But the evil will not end there. The process will go on. The same process by which the power would be transferred from the States to the Union, will transfer the whole from this department of the Government (I speak of the Legislature) to the Executive. All the added power and added patronage which conquest will create, will pass to the Executive. In the end, you put in the hands of the Executive the power of conquering you.[25]

ABRAHAM LINCOLN (1809–1865)

Running for Congress in 1845, Abraham Lincoln never discussed the looming war with Mexico. However, he later claimed that he opposed "enlarging our field." Once in Congress in 1847, the conflict was essentially over. Lincoln delivered his January 12, 1848, speech to the U.S. House just weeks before the Senate ratified the peace treaty.

Lincoln also offered resolutions demanding proof that Mexican attacks on American soil provoked the war. He insisted on evidence to "establish whether the particular spot of soil on which the blood of our citizens was so shed, was, or was not, our own soil." Lincoln also supported a Whig resolution condemning the war as "unnecessarily and unconstitutionally begun." Back in Illinois, Lincoln encountered significant criticism of his position, even from some Whig allies. Although he did not seek reelection because of his pledge to serve one term, it is likely that opposing a popular war would have hurt his reelection effort.[26]

THE WAR WITH MEXICO
Speech to the U.S. House of Representatives, January 12, 1848

The President, in his first war message of May 1846, declares that the soil was ours on which hostilities were commenced by Mexico; and he repeats that declaration, almost in the same language, in each successive annual message, thus showing that he esteems that point, a highly essential one. In the importance of that point, I entirely agree with the President. To my judgment, it is the very point, upon which he should be justified, or condemned. In his message of December, 1846, it seems to have occurred to him, as is certainly true, that title—ownership—to soil, or anything else, is not a simple fact; but is a conclusion following one or more simple facts; and that it was incumbent upon him, to present the facts, from which he concluded, the soil was ours, on which the first blood of the war was shed. . . .

Now I propose to try to show, that the whole of this,—issue and evidence—is, from beginning to end, the sheerest deception. The issue, as he presents it, is in these words "But there are those who, conceding all this to be true, assume the ground that the true western boundary of Texas is the Nueches, instead of the Rio Grande; and that, therefore, in marching our army to the east bank of the latter river, we passed the Texan line, and invaded the territory of Mexico." Now this issue is made up of two affirmatives and no negative. The main deception of it is, that it assumes as true, that one river or the other is necessarily the boundary; and cheats the superficial thinker entirely out of the idea, that possibly the boundary is somewhere between the two, and not actually at either. A further deception is that it will let in evidence, which a true issue would exclude. A true issue, made by the President, would be about as follows "I say the soil *was ours*, on which the first blood was shed; there are those who say it was not." . . .

His first item is, that the Rio Grande was the Western boundary of Louisiana, as we purchased it of France in 1803; and seeming to expect this to be disputed, he argues over the amount of nearly a page, to prove it true; at the end of which he lets us know, that by the treaty of 1819, we sold to Spain the whole country from the Rio Grande eastward to the Sabine. Now, admitting for the present, that the Rio Grande, was the boundary of Louisiana, what, under heaven, had that to do with the *present* boundary between us and Mexico? How, Mr. Chairman, the line, that once divided your land from mine, can *still* be the boundary between us, after I have *sold* my land to you, is, to me, beyond all comprehension. And how any man, with an honest purpose only, of proving the truth, could ever have *thought* of introducing such a fact to prove such an issue, is equally incomprehensible. The outrage upon common *right*, of seizing as our own what we have once sold, merely because it *was* ours *before* we sold it, is only equaled by the outrage on common *sense* of any attempt to justify it.

The President's next piece of evidence is, that "the Republic of Texas always *claimed* this river (Rio Grande) as her western boundary." That is not true, in fact. Texas has claimed it, but she has not *always* claimed it. There is, at least, one distinguished exception. Her state constitution—the Republic's most solemn, and well considered act; that which may, without impropriety, be called her last will and testament, revoking all others—makes no such claim. But suppose she had always claimed it. Has not Mexico always claimed the contrary? So that there is but *claim* against *claim*, leaving nothing proved, until we get back of the claims, and find which has the better *foundation*. . . .

Now sir, for the purpose of obtaining the very best evidence, as to whether Texas had actually carried her revolution, to the place where the hostilities of the present war commenced, let the President answer the interrogatories, I proposed, as before mentioned, or some other similar ones. Let him answer, fully, fairly, and candidly . . . And if, so answering, he can show that the soil was ours, where the first blood of the war was shed—that it was not within an inhabited country, or, if within such, that the inhabitants had submitted themselves to the civil authority of Texas, or of the United States . . . then I am with him for his justification. In that case I, shall be most happy to reverse the vote I gave the other day.[27]

CHAPTER 4

THE CIVIL WAR

"THIS WAR IS MURDER, & NOTHING ELSE"

DISSENT IN THE CONFEDERACY

"SECESSION IS RESISTING THE POWERS THAT BE, AND THEREFORE it is a violation of God's command." The words that Rev. John H. Aughey bravely spoke to his congregation at the Poplar Creek Presbyterian Church in Choctaw, Mississippi, jeopardized his life. The sermon, delivered in the winter of 1860 following Abraham Lincoln's election as president, aimed to persuade the pastor's east-central Mississippi parishioners to resist the passionate rush toward secession and war sparked by the election results. Aughey asked, "Why should we secede, and thus destroy the best, the freest, and the most prosperous government on the face of the earth, the government which our patriot fathers fought and bled to secure?" Soon thereafter, Mississippi citizens voted on secession. When Aughey voted, he requested a Union ticket. Telling him that none had been printed, the election official also advised a vote for secession. Aughey refused and, "amidst the frowns, murmurs, and threats of the judges and bystanders," claimed that he cast the only antisuccession vote in his precinct.

When Mississippi's secessionist convention convened in January 1861, the outcome was preordained by raging emotions, but also by the intimidation and coercion encountered by Aughey and other pro-Union citizens. Mississippi was the second state to leave the Union, after South Carolina, and was soon followed by Florida, Georgia, Alabama, Texas, and Louisiana. "It was dangerous to utter a word in favor of the Union," Aughey wrote, adding that "self-constituted vigilance committees sprang up all over the country, and a reign of terror began." In short order, "one of these august tribunals" summoned the renegade parson to appear and answer the charge that he was an abolitionist and a Unionist. Appearing before the committee several days later, Aughey professed to antisecession and antislavery sentiments. The committee would not convict him, fearful, Aughey said, that other locals might "think this to be an unwarranted and illegal proceeding." Later that night, several men appeared at Aughey's door with apparent plans to finish what the vigilante committee had started.

Aughey fled Choctaw for Tishomingo County, where "I found that the great heart of the county still beat true to the music of the Union."[1]

The notion of a South united in its defense of slavery and the Confederacy was widespread then and now. However, it is fiction. Although about six hundred thousand out of two million eligible southern white men enlisted in the cause, considerable opposition to the war flourished in almost every Confederate state.[2] In Virginia, Arkansas, and Missouri, voters sent a majority of Unionists to their secessionist conventions. Voters in North Carolina and Tennessee initially decided against holding a convention. Secretary of State William Seward recognized that this sentiment represented the conditional nature of secessionist sentiment in these states. "Every thought that we think," he told President Abraham Lincoln in January, "ought to be conciliatory, forbearing and patient, and so open the way for the rising of a Union Party in the seceding states which will bring them back into the Union." Lincoln had his doubts, but accepted Seward's advice.[3]

When the war began, the antisecessionist No-Nothing Party controlled the governments of several major cities, including Richmond, Atlanta, Raleigh, Mobile, New Orleans, Galveston, and Austin. In almost every southern state, conventions to consider secession had among their members men of strong pro-Union sentiment. When Union forces attacked Fort Sumter on April 12, 1861, Virginia, North Carolina, Arkansas, and Tennessee were caught up in the emotion of the war and finally joined the Confederacy.[4]

One former state senator from Tennessee claimed that he "held out firmly against the Disunion movement . . . until the war . . . commenced, and . . . all his dear friends and kindred, including his own sons, had enlisted in the disunion cause." In Mississippi, Union sympathizers were outnumbered but undeterred. Known throughout the South as "scalawags," they were usually ostracized or attacked for their dissent and in some cases forced to enlist and fight for the Confederacy. In Vicksburg, Mississippi, the Confederate commander in 1861 notified potential scalawags that they would be "imprisoned, Shot or Sent Out of the Country."[5]

The western part of Virginia was almost entirely either pro-Union or neutral. Such was the level of dissent that citizens in northwestern Virginia separated from Virginia in 1863 to form the new pro-Union state of West Virginia. Eastern Tennessee was ardently pro-Union. A majority of the citizens in that region opposed secession in 1861 "and many of them never pretended to support the Confederacy at any time during its existence," historian Georgia Lee Tatum wrote in her remarkable 1934 book, *Disloyalty in the Confederacy.*[6]

One prominent opponent of secession was feisty Whig publisher Reverend William G. Brownlow, a Methodist preacher who excoriated the Tennessee aristocrats supporting the war. During debate over secession, Brownlow ran for governor, warning that secessionist leaders would "go down to their graves without any halo of glory surrounding their brows, while on their heads would be gathered this hissing curses of all generations, terrible as the fork-tongued snakes of Medusa."[7] Brownlow's campaign failed, as did his Unionist cause. The public in Tennessee and several other recalcitrant states shifted in favor of secession in early 1861 when Lincoln called for states to provide their quota of troops.[8] Tennessee's governor, for example, vowed that his state would "not furnish a single man for the purpose of coercion, but fifty thousand if necessary for the defense of our rights and those of our southern brothers."[9]

Dissent was widespread in northwest Arkansas, northern Mississippi, northern Alabama, North Carolina, and Texas. While a majority in Georgia supported secession, one-third of the delegates to the state's secession convention opposed leaving the Union.[10] Georgia Governor Joseph Brown actively opposed the Confederacy's conscription act throughout the war, arguing that it violated his state's sovereignty. By early 1862, more than half of the state's volunteers from northeast counties reportedly deserted their posts and returned home to tend to families and farms. When Congress raised the draft age to forty-five, Brown angrily fought the law and furloughed all of the state's militia forces.[11] Disaffection with the Confederacy was so high in some parts of Georgia that citizens continued to fly the Union flag after the state seceded. In Pickens County, one official complained to Governor Brown, "a United States flag was raised upon a pole, soon after secession, and kept afloat in bold open defiance of Confederate authorities for several weeks." When asked to dispatch Confederate soldiers to remove the flag, Brown demurred, not wanting to antagonize the area's dissidents.[12]

One official in Huntsville, Alabama, reported in October 1862 that many citizens in that region were in open rebellion to the Confederacy, some buying and selling cotton for the Union and others serving as spies and informants. A few Confederate officers in the area, the official speculated, were loyal to the Union. To avoid conscription, some citizens "were developing chronic diseases that their neighbors never suspected them of," but that doctors eagerly diagnosed. "In fact, when the conscription act went into effect," Georgia Lee Tatum wrote, "health began to break down in all sections of the state." Some even severed fingers or toes to avoid military service. In late 1862, in Randolph County, Alabama, defiance of the conscription act was so widespread that an armed mob stormed the county jail and released the deserters.[13]

At least three well-organized secret peace societies— opposed to the war and the Confederacy—operated throughout a large swath of the South, including parts of Arkansas, Alabama, Georgia, Mississippi, North Carolina, and possibly Florida and South Carolina. Members generally urged Confederate soldiers to desert and advocated enlistment in and support of the Union army. As evidenced by the experiences of the members of the Peace and Constitutional Society of Arkansas—about 1,700 strong—this form of dissent sometimes provoked stern repression. In October 1861, Confederate officials arrested twenty-seven peace society members in Van Buren County, Arkansas, sending them to Little Rock for trial. The following month, officials arrested one hundred more. In December, local officials charged 111 additional suspects in two counties, but instead of sending them to Little Rock for trial, persuaded authorities to allow them to enlist in the Confederate army.[14]

Hostility to the Confederacy was pronounced in northern Arkansas, from which a stream of Unionist dissenters flocked into Springfield, Missouri, to enlist in the Union army. When Federal troops occupied northwest Arkansas in early 1863, "disloyal" citizens from around the region descended on them, asking for protection. Many enlisted in the Union army. One Federal official estimated that as many as five thousand men from northwest Arkansas might be willing to fight against the Confederacy. In November 1862, in response to the growing "disloyalty" in Arkansas, the legislature approved the death penalty for those providing aid and comfort to the enemy. Officials apparently never had the opportunity to enforce the new law, as the Union presence in Arkansas steadily increased throughout 1863. By the fall, Federal troops controlled Little Rock.[15]

The reason for this widespread Southern dissent? In most cases, opposition to secession was concentrated in regions where slave labor was not the dominant economic force. In these mostly upcountry areas, the anger of poor whites was often directed more at the rich, landed slave owners whose thumping for armed confrontation with the U.S. government over slave rights had little to do with them—other than the potential to further depress their region's economy and cause them to be drafted into a "rich man's cause."

The southern upcountry ambivalence about slavery might have been more prevalent had it not been for widespread censorship of antislavery publications. Since 1835, when several northern antislavery societies begin flooding southern leaders with antislavery literature, southern states regularly blocked distribution of newspapers, books, and pamphlets advocating abolitionism. U.S. Postmaster General Amos Kendall and President Andrew Jackson supported censoring what the president called "incendiary publications intended to instigate the slaves to insurrection." There was little indignation or protest in the North about the freedom of the mails and its importance to free speech. The antislavery societies eventually abandoned the effort and, as a result, most southerners were blissfully ignorant about the vigorous debate over slavery that raged in the North. One paper that did protest censorship of the mails was the New York *Evening Post*. Perhaps presaging the consequences of a much broader and more rigorously enforced censorship of the mails that would come more than eighty years later during World War I, the paper asserted, "If the government once begins to discriminate as to what is orthodox and what heterodox in opinion, what is safe and what unsafe in tendency, farewell to our freedom."[16]

DISSENT IN THE UNION

On April 27, 1861, only two weeks after the war began with the Confederate attack on Fort Sumter, Union volunteers from Massachusetts marched through Baltimore (a bastion of pro-Confederacy sentiment) en route to Washington. A pro-Confederate mob attacked the soldiers, killing several in violence that eventually became a widespread riot. When the Baltimore mayor moved to prevent more Union troops from passing through his city—by destroying railroad bridges north of the city—President Lincoln feared for Washington's security. Hoping to quash a growing prosecessionist rebellion, Lincoln suspended *habeas corpus*, which allowed Federal and military officers to arrest—without warrant—those suspected of subversive activity.

Among those arrested was a wealthy landowner, John Merryman, suspected of a role in the destruction of bridges and telegraph lines outside Baltimore. When Merryman petitioned the Federal court for a writ of *habeas corpus*, the presiding judge, Chief Justice Roger B. Taney, complied. Local military officials, however, defied

Taney and kept Merryman imprisoned. In late May, when Taney—acting as a circuit court judge—ruled that Lincoln's order violated the Constitution, Lincoln persisted. Lincoln maintained that the power to suspend the writ was an emergency power the president could exercise in times of rebellion. Waiting for Congress to assemble and consider the matter was impractical, he argued. "Are all the laws, *but one* [habeas corpus], to go unexecuted," Lincoln asked, "and the government itself go to pieces, lest that one be violated?"[17]

Several weeks later, Lincoln suspended habeas corpus in Florida. In all, he would do so eight times, most dramatically in September 1862, when he suspended the writ throughout the nation.[18] While Taney objected, Congress was far more compliant, ratifying his actions retroactively and authorizing future suspensions. Despite the apparent severity of the order, Lincoln was not obsessed with suppressing dissent. He was primarily concerned with draft evasion, sabotage, treason, and trading with the enemy.[19]

Occasionally, however, military authorities arrested someone for disloyal speech. "Lincoln generally learned of these arrests, if at all, only after the fact, and he was almost always displeased," legal scholar Geoffrey R. Stone concluded. In fact, Stone wrote, Lincoln had grown weary of politically motivated arrests by 1863 and indicated that they should stop "unless the *necessity*" for the arrests was "*manifest* and *urgent*." While expressing his displeasure over such arrests, Lincoln did little to prohibit them, choosing, in Stone's words, "to defer to the judgment of his commanders."[20]

Perhaps the most prominent example of Lincoln's deference to his military officers in this realm is the notorious case of Clement Vallandigham, an Ohio congressman and leader of the Peace Democrats, also known as Copperheads. From almost the first days of the conflict, some members of the Democratic Party, particularly in southern regions of western states like Illinois, Ohio, and Indiana, opposed the war. Secession, these Peace Democrats believed, was constitutional.

Many northern Democratic opponents of the war had southern roots or were German or Irish immigrants, especially Catholics, and had little affinity for the Union. Perhaps far more significant, most opponents were strict constitutional constructionists. These Democrats supported the Union and, whatever their feelings about slavery, believed the dispute between North and South should be peacefully negotiated. The "same portion of our people," one New Yorker observed, were those who "do not esteem cutting the throats of one's countrymen as proof of patriotism or rely upon bombardments of a city as the best way of cultivating union and fraternal love with its inhabitants."[21]

Another factor in the Copperheads' lack of passion for the war was their racist views.[22] One prominent Philadelphian, Charles Ingersoll, publicly declared, "I look upon Negro property as being sacred as any other property, and I sympathize with the South in their desire to preserve it." Ingersoll's brother Edward agreed. "It is not African slavery that is the root of all evil, it is this mad philosophy of Abolitionism."[23]

To the Copperheads, Lincoln's approach was appalling and unconstitutional. They deplored his proclaiming war unilaterally, his suspension of habeas corpus, and his call for seventy-five thousand troops—all without prior congressional approval. "We are hourly in danger at such times as these, of slipping thoughtlessly out of our constitution moorings, and then all is lost," the Columbia, Ohio, *Crisis* said in an editorial. Further enraging the Copperheads was Lincoln's Emancipation Proclamation, preliminarily issued in September 1862, which freed slaves in Confederate territory under Union military control. Two days later came Lincoln's executive order suspending habeas corpus across the North. "It will unite the whole South, and protract the war indefinitely," one Connecticut critic wrote. "I did not think Lincoln could be such an obstinate old fool."[24]

By early 1863, the peace faction of the Democratic Party may well have represented a majority, according to historian James M. McPherson. In New York, for example, a large gathering of Democrats approved a resolution declaring that the war "against the South is illegal, being unconstitutional, and should not be sustained." The state's governor, Horatio Seymour, supported the Union, but strongly denounced emancipation as "bloody, barbarous, revolutionary." So intense was dissent in the Midwest—fed by Union defeats on the battlefield and the economic disruptions caused by the war—that some Democrats in Ohio, Indiana, and Illinois talked of a "Northwest Confederacy." Such a confederation would have conceivably broken from abolitionist New England and formed a southern alliance.[25]

No one personified the dissent of Peace Democrats more than Vallandigham. Although the peace faction had gained ground in Ohio, Indiana, and Pennsylvania in the fall 1862 congressional elections, Vallandigham—gerrymandered into a prowar district by the Republican-controlled state legislature—lost to a Republican war hero backed by Lincoln.[26] A charismatic leader who preached limited government, Vallandigham became the lightening rod for Republican vitriol against the Copperheads. Even after his defeat, he returned to Congress to oppose the draft and to deliver a farewell speech in which he insisted that Republicans were fighting, not for the Union, but against slavery. "The people of the West demand peace, and they begin to more than suspect that New England is in the way," Vallandigham warned. "If you of the East, who have found this war against the South, and for the negro, gratifying to your hate or profitable to your purse, will continue it . . . [be prepared for] *external divorce between the West and the East.*"[27]

Like many Peace Democrats, Vallandigham was outraged in March 1863 by congressional passage of conscription legislation. Facing declining enlistments that posed a threat to the war, Congress authorized a draft. The process was rife with fraud and abuse and led to violence throughout the North, but particularly in New York City, where ethnic tensions would later combine with general discontent to spark a massive, bloody riot in July. In May, Vallandigham—campaigning for governor—delivered a speech in Mount Vernon, Ohio, at the state Democratic Party convention. He was well aware that his words were in blatant violation of General Order No. 38, an edict by Major General Ambrose Burnside, the new commander of the Department of the Ohio. With Ohio and Illinois on the verge of erupting in outright rebellion, the general had impetuously outlawed the "habit of declaring sympathy for the enemy," punishable by arrest and prosecution in military court.[28]

With Burnsides's agent taking notes, Vallandigham condemned the general's order as "a bane usurpation of arbitrary power." For two hours, Vallandigham ranted, calling the war "wicked, cruel, and unnecessary" and a struggle "for the freedom of the black and the enslavement of the whites." Attacking the president as "King Lincoln,"

Vallandigham urged his audience to use the ballot box to "hurl" Lincoln "from his throne." Many in the crowd cheered.[29]

Burnside promptly had the former congressman arrested. After a two-day trial, a military tribunal convicted him, finding that his speech "could but induce in his hearers a distrust of their own Government and sympathy for those in arms against it, and a disposition to resist the laws of the land." Instead of a death sentence, however, the tribunal imprisoned Vallandigham for the war's duration. Vallandigham's appeal failed, but Ohio Democrats treated him as a hero, and nominated him for governor. Despite the condemnation of Democrats, and even some Republicans, Burnside was undaunted. "Why should such speeches from our own public men be allowed?" he asked "My duty requires me to stop license and intemperate discussion, which tends to weaken the authority of the government and army." Lincoln, who mainly wanted to punish draft dodgers and terrorists, was embarrassed. The president upheld his general, but ordered Vallandigham banished to the Confederacy.[30]

Answering critics who attacked Lincoln for condoning suppression of political speech, the president agreed that mere criticism of the administration and its war policies was not grounds for prosecution. "If there were no other reason for the arrest," Lincoln wrote in a public letter, "then I concede that the arrest was wrong." Lincoln, however, argued that Burnsides had arrested Vallandigham for "laboring, with some effect, to prevent the raising of troops, to encourage desertions from the army; and to leave the Rebellion without an adequate military force to suppress it." To emphasize his point, Lincoln posed the following rhetorical question, "Must I shoot a simple-minded soldier boy who deserts, while I must not touch a hair of a wily agitator who induces him to desert? . . . I think that in such a case to silence the agitator, and save the boy is not only constitutional, but withal a great mercy."

To the question of how the Constitution should apply to free speech in wartime, Lincoln observed that the Constitution "is not, in its application, in all respects the same, in cases of rebellion or invasion involving the public safety, as it is in time of profound peace and public security." For example, Lincoln noted, the Constitution allowed the suspension of habeas corpus. "I can no more be persuaded that the Government can constitutionally take no strong measures in time of rebellion, because it can be shown that the same could not be lawfully taken in time of peace, than I can be persuaded that a particular drug is not good medicine for a sick man, because it can be shown not to be good for a well one." Historians argue that Vallandigham never advocated civil disobedience. Vallandigham correctly protested that he had merely uttered "words of criticism of the public policy of the Administration, addressed to an open and public political meeting of my fellow-citizens of Ohio lawfully and peaceably assembled."[31]

Following his exile to the Confederacy, Vallandigham escaped to Bermuda and then to Canada. In his absence, his campaign for governor failed. In 1864 he returned to the United States in violation of his exile (Lincoln tolerated his return) and later helped draft the Democratic Party's platform planks that condemned Lincoln's "suppression of freedom of speech and the press" and demanded an immediate end to the war.[32]

Meanwhile, the war's carnage in the spring and summer of 1864 continued to shock the public in the North. In Virginia, at the Wilderness near Chancellorsville, the Union sustained seventeen thousand casualties on May 5. Ten days later, at Drewry's Bluff, near Richmond, more than four thousand Union soldiers died. Two days later, at Spotsylvania, another battle with Confederate forces resulted in 6,800 casualties. On June 1, at Cold Harbor, Confederate forces killed or wounded about seven thousand Union troops in less than an hour. "There is death at the heart of this glory & greatness," wrote a New York Copperhead. "This war is murder, & nothing else, and every man who gives a dollar or moves his finger to aid is an aider & abettor of murder." The slaughter undermined public support for the war and for Lincoln.[33]

By the fall of 1864, however, the tide of war began to turn and, with it, Lincoln's sagging political fortunes. Soldiers, allowed to vote for the first time, cast ballots in overwhelming numbers for Lincoln over his Democratic opponent, George McClellan, the former Union general. Perhaps as many as four out of five soldiers voted for Lincoln over McClellan, whose party had advocated "a cessation of hostilities." Although McClellan supported the war, he was in the unfortunate position of running on a peace platform written by Vallandigham and other Copperheads. Lincoln's allies preferred to call the nominating convention "the Chicago Surrender." Finally, McClellan denounced his own party's platform, but it was too late. On September 4, just two days after the convention, Lincoln received news that sealed his reelection—a telegram from General William T. Sherman, "Atlanta is ours, and fairly won." Shortly thereafter came the additional good news that Union forces had captured Mobile, the last Gulf port held by Confederate forces.[34] By the spring of 1865, the Civil War would be over. In the November elections, Lincoln and his Republican allies crushed the Democrats. The defeat, abetted by their vigorous dissent during the war, would cost the Democrats dearly. It would be another twenty years until a Democrat, Grover Cleveland, would occupy the White House.[35]

JAMES GOVAN TALIAFERRO (1798–1876)

A Whig and Scalawag, James Taliaferro practiced law, operated a cotton gin, and edited a newspaper in Harrisonburg, Louisiana. An early and vocal opponent of secession, Taliaferro used the pages of his newspaper, the Harrisonburg Independent, *to argue against a course that he maintained "would inevitably lead to war and bloodshed." To Taliaferro, the Confederacy was a "wretched oligarchy." In 1856 he wrote, "Secession can only exist as a revolutionary right. It can never exist as a peaceful remedy." As the Catahoula Parish delegate to Louisiana's secession convention in January 1861, Taliaferro was the only participant to speak out against the secession ordinance. During the roll call, delegates allowed Taliaferro to explain his vote, but refused to publish his remarks in the convention's official journal. His speech later appeared in the* New Orleans Daily Crescent *and in Taliaferro's newspaper. Taliaferro returned to his hometown to discover that vigilantes had destroyed his cotton gin. After the war, as an associate justice of the Louisiana Supreme Court and president of the state's constitutional convention, Taliaferro helped secure Louisiana's readmission to the Union.[36]*

TALIAFERRO'S PROTEST

Speech to the Louisiana Secession Convention, January 1861

I oppose the act of secession because, in my deliberate judgment, the wrongs alleged as the cause of the movement might be redressed under the Constitution by an energetic execution of the laws of the United States, and that, standing on the guarantees of the Constitution, in the Union, Southern rights might be triumphantly maintained under the protection and safeguards which the Constitution affords.

Because, in secession, I see no remedy for the actual and present evils complained of, and because the *prospected* evils depicted so gloomily may never come, and if they should, the inalienable right to resist tyranny and oppression might then be exercised as well and successfully as now.

Because I see no certainty that the seceding States will ever be confederated again; none that the border States will secede at all; and if they should, I see no reliable ground for believing that they would incorporate themselves with the Gulf or cotton States in a new government. I see no surety, either, that Texas will unite with them.

Because the Gulf or cotton States alone, were they to unite in a separate confederacy, would be without the elements of power, indispensable in the formation of a government to take a respectable rank among the nations of the earth.

Because I believe that peaceable secession is a right unknown to the Constitution of the United States; that it is a most dangerous and mischievous principle in the structure of any government; and when carried into the formation of the contemplated Confederacy of the Gulf States will render it powerless for good, and complete its incapacity to afford the people permanent security for their lives, liberty and property.

Because it is my solid and deliberate conviction that the distraction of the Southern States by separate secession will defeat the purpose it is intended to accomplish and that its certain results will be to impair instead of strengthening the security of Southern institutions.

Because the proper status of Louisiana is with the border States, with which nature has connected her with the majestic river which flows through her limits; and because an alliance with a weak government in the Gulf States east of her is unnatural and antagonistic to her obvious interests and destiny.

Because, by separate secession, the state relinquishes all its rights within the Government, it surrenders its equal rights to the common territories—to the vast public domain of the United States, and to the property of every king blessing to the Nation. And for this reason I oppose secession as being emphatically submission.

Because secession may bring anarchy and war, as it will assuredly bring ruinous exactions upon property, in the form of direct taxation, a withering blight on the prosperity of the State, and a fatal prostration of all its great interests.

Because, the act of dissolving the ties which connect Louisiana with the Federal Union is a revolutionary act, that this Convention is, of itself, without authority from the people of the State, and refusing to submit its action to them for their sanction in the grave and vital act of changing their government, this Convention violates the great and fundamental principles of American government, that the will of the people is supreme.[37]

RICHARD KEITH CALL (1792–1862)

A veteran of Florida's Creek and Seminole wars, Richard Call was an aide and protégé of General Andrew Jackson and later a brigadier general in Florida's militia. In the 1820s, after the Creek War, Call helped establish Florida's territorial government.

Serving in the state legislative council, and then as Florida's delegate to Congress, he eventually became territorial governor, serving until 1845. Over the years, he was a Democrat, Whig, Know-Nothing, and finally, a Constitutional Unionist. Call opposed secession in the weeks following Lincoln's election and published a pamphlet, An Address to the People of Florida from General R. K. Call, *in which he labeled disunion "high treason against our constitutional government." The following is from Call's second pamphlet of dissent published and widely distributed in 1861, the text of a letter sent to the chairman of the Pennsylvania delegation to the 1860 Constitutional Union Convention in Baltimore.*

UNION.-SLAVERY.-SECESSION

Open Letter to John S. Littell, of Germantown, Penn., February 12, 1861

A great nation has been dismembered. The bonds of the American Union, the work of Washington, of Franklin, of Madison, and other great sages and statesmen of a glorious age, have been rent and snapped like cobwebs; and the greatest fabric of human government, without complaint of wrong or injustice, has been destroyed in a few months—madly and rashly destroyed, without reflection, and without loss of life or stain of blood.

Star after star from the once glorious, but now drooping, banner has fallen, others are waning in their light, and the whole heavens are covered with the gloomy portent of universal distinction. When shall this ruin end? Where is the rock which will stand and throw back the mad destructive waves of revolution, and arrest the fearful, fatal, desolating progress of secession! Through the mist of the tempest, I think I see that rock rising in moral power and sublimity along the whole southern line of North Carolina, Tennessee, and Arkansas, supported by Missouri, Kentucky, Virginia, Maryland, and Delaware, and above the mad, riotous, and exulting shout of successful secession and triumphant revolution. From that rock I hear a voice, like the voice of God, saying to the raging sea, "Thus far shalt thou go and no further, and here shall thy proud waves be stayed." Here I trust, is the rock of safety, standing in the centre of the American Union. The extremities may become cold, and lose their sensibilities, their love for our gallant flag, their pride for our prestige and national glory, won on so many battle-fields, and consummated by so many civic achievements; they may retire to the idolatrous worship of their local and sectional divinities, but the American heart will love and worship the God of our fathers; it will continue to beat in the American bosom, in the centre of the American Union; its warm blood will continue to circulate on both sides of the line of slavery, binding together, in national bonds, the kindred affections of one race in different communities.

Here, I trust in God and in the wisdom and virtue of my countrymen, that there is and that there ever will be an American Union, bearing as the emblem of its power and glory, the broad stripes and bright stars, the banner of freedom at home, and the sign and hope of liberty to the world. Here, at least, I hope, a glorious Union of sovereign States may stand forever, to vindicate the success of the representative Republican system, to vindicate the success of the great experiment of popular government, to rebuke despotic power, to disrobe tyranny of its pomp and pride, to rebuke anarchy and riot in the sanctuary of secession; to sustain the cause of law and government, the holy cause of civil and religious liberty; to bless the living, honor the dead, justify the blood of our glorious Revolution. . . .

Disunion, under certain contingencies, may be justified; it may become an imperative necessity, but it should be the last resort; like the rite of extreme unction, it should be reserved for the last, and administered only in the dying hour of the only remaining hope within the Union. Disunion must be fatal!—fatal to the peace, safety, and happiness of both divisions of the country—fatal to the progress of liberty and civilization—fatal to the pride and glory of the American name. . . .

Every State has a right to exclude slavery, or abolish slavery, within the limits of its own jurisdiction. But no State has a right to disregard its nationality; no State has a right to secede from the moral and legal national obligations to sustain the institution of African slavery where it is, or where it may be lawfully established. I have opposed secession persistently, vehemently. I have thrown myself in the breach to oppose it. In resisting it I have stood almost alone, while others gave way to its angry surges which dashed around. I dared to oppose it, because I thought secession, whether in the majority or the minority, whether supported by one man, or by millions of men, wrong, eminently wrong, and that the approval of multitudes can never make it right. If it has a principle in the philosophy of human government, it is a principle of destruction. The secession of a Southern State from the Union is not more disloyal to the government, not more revolutionary, than the treachery, insubordination and hostile resistance, of a Northern State to the obligations of the Constitution. They are both violations of the public law—both defiant of the public authority—with this difference in favor of the Southern State, that she is not the aggressor, that she has not stricken the first blow. . . .

The offending Northern States act with no passionate precipitation. She deliberately meditates and coolly consummates a violation of the Constitution. While she withdraws her allegiance to the government, by denying the authority of its judicial, and legislative, power in special cases, while she withholds her allegiance to some of the bonds of the Constitution, she sings anthems of praise and glory to the Union she has violated, and claims all the blessings and advantages of the government to which she renders only a partial fealty, a selfish allegiance. It is thus that the two extremities are madly rending the vitals of our once great and glorious country. It is thus the American Union, once the pride of every American heart, once the admiration and wonder of the whole civilized world, has been disrupted and destroyed. It is thus the public peace has been broken, and we stand on the verge of calamitous, desolating, ruinous, civil war. . . . The "Ides of March" is at hand; then, for the first time, a sectional [Republican] party will take possession of our government. The fate of the nation may be decided by the policy that party may inaugurate. The application of any coercive measure to drive back a seceded State, will be fatal to the last remaining hope of the Union.

Although I deny the right of secession, I acknowledge the right of revolution and hold to the principles enunciated in our Declaration of Independence. And if it be the will of the majority of the people of the seceded States to form an independent government, they have the right, and it can be only a question of power. No coercive measures can reunite them with the North. It is forbidden by the genius of our free institutions, and any attempt at coercion must unite every Southern State and every Southern man in the most determined and energetic resistance. I was opposed to the seizure of the fortifications, and other property, of the government in the South, but they can never be restored to the government until every constitutional right of the South shall have been fully acknowledged by the North. If it should be the determination of Mr. Lincoln and the party which has brought him into power, to confine slavery to its present limits, the day of battle need not be deferred, and, when it comes, I trust in God that every Southern man will be ready and willing to die rather than yield to a proposition so unjust, so abhorrent, and so dishonorable.

I rejoice at the noble and patriotic stand taken by the conservative Southern States, in resisting the impulse of secession, not because I am disposed to submit to wrong and injustice, not because I am willing to preserve the Union longer than it continues to be the Union of the Constitution, but because I hope they will do, what I had hoped the whole South would have done. Because I hope they will with one voice demand of the North a full and perfect recognition of every constitutional right and privilege of the South, and if this just demand should not be complied with, then with my long-cherished devotion to the Union of our fathers, I shall be reconciled to see it end forever! The North and South can never live in peace together except on terms of perfect social and political equality, therefore a separation, with war, and all its attendant calamities, will be far better than a discontented unity, with the confinement of slavery to its present limits. This I shall regard not only as the greatest indignity and insult to the South, but the greatest calamity which could he inflicted, and rather than bear this insult, and endure this calamity, I prefer that the last Southern man should fall, on the last battle-field of the terrible war, in which we may soon be engaged.[38]

CLEMENT VALLANDIGHAM (1820–1871)

As the most prominent Peace Democrat during the Civil War, Clement Vallandigham became a symbol of treason and disloyalty for many northern supporters of the war. The son of a Presbyterian minister, Vallandigham's obstinate nature was evident early in life. He left college before graduation after a bitter dispute with the school's president over a matter of constitutional law. He later became a lawyer, but found politics and journalism more interesting. He served several terms in the Ohio House, including a term as speaker, and became part owner and editor of the Dayton Empire. *Elected to Congress in a disputed election in 1856, he made his mark early with strong denunciations of the Republican Party's antislavery positions. During the secession crisis of 1860 and 1861, he pushed for compromise with the South. After his defeat in 1862, Vallandigham continued speaking out, returning to Washington one last time to deliver a strong speech in favor of peace with the South. The following year, in Ohio, a defiant speech to a Democratic Party convention resulted in Vallandigham's arrest and conviction for treason. Embarrassed, Lincoln simply banished his adversary to the Confederacy. By 1864, Vallandigham was back in Ohio in time to help write portions of the Democratic Party's antiwar platform. In the following speech, Vallandigham presages the early twentieth and twenty-first century debates over violations of civil liberties during wartime, including the rights of prisoners and charges that the government illegally violated the sanctity of private communication.[39]*

EXECUTIVE USURPATION
Speech to the U.S. House, July 10, 1861

Sir, the Constitution not only confines to Congress the right to declare war, but expressly provides that "Congress (not the President) shall have power to raise and support armies;" and to "provide and maintain a navy." In pursuance of this authority, Congress, years ago, had fixed the number of officers, and of the regiments, of the different kinds of service; and also, the number of ships, officers, marines, and seamen which should compose the navy. Not only that, but Congress has repeatedly, within the last five years, refused to increase the regular army. More than that still: in February and March last, the House, upon several test votes, repeatedly and expressly refused to authorize the President to accept the service of volunteers for the very purpose of protecting the public property, enforcing the laws, and collecting the revenue. And, yet, the President, of his own mere will and authority, and without the shadow of right, has proceeded to increase, and has increased, the standing army by twenty-five thousand men; the navy by eighteen thousand; and has called for, and accepted the services of, forty regiments of volunteers for three years, numbering forty-two thousand men, and making thus a grand army, or military force, raised by executive proclamation alone, without the sanction of Congress, without warrant of law, and in direct violation of the Constitution, and of his oath of office, of eighty-five thousand soldiers enlisted for three and five years, and already in the field. And, yet, the President now asks us to support the army which he has thus raised, to ratify his usurpations by a law ex post facto, and thus to make ourselves parties to our own degradation, and to his infractions of the Constitution. Meanwhile, however, he has taken good care not only to enlist the men, organize the regiments, and muster them into service, but to provide, in advance, for a horde of forlorn, worn-out, and broken-down politicians of his own party, by appointing, either by himself, or through the Governors of the States, major-generals, brigadier-generals, colonels, lieutenant-colonels, majors, captains, lieutenants, adjutants, quarter-masters, and surgeons, without any limit as to numbers, and without so much as once saying to Congress, "By your leave, gentlemen."

Beginning with this wide breach of the Constitution, this enormous usurpation of the most dangerous of all powers—the power of the sword—other infractions and assumptions were easy; and after public liberty, private right soon fell. The privacy of the telegraph was invaded in the search after treason and traitors; although it turns out, significantly enough, that the only victim, so far, is one of the appointees and especial pets of the Administration. The telegraphic dispatches, preserved under every pledge of secrecy for the protection and safety of the telegraph companies, were seized and carried away without search-warrant, without probable cause, without oath, and without description of the places to be searched, or of the things to be seized, and in plain violation of the right of the people to be secure in their houses, persons, papers, and effects, against unreasonable searches and seizures. One step more, sir, will bring upon us search and seizure of the public mails; . . .

Sir, the rights of property having been thus wantonly violated, it needed but a little stretch of usurpation to invade the sanctity of the person; and a victim was not long wanting. A private citizen of Maryland, not subject to the rules and articles of war—not in a case arising in the land or naval forces, nor in the militia, when in actual service—is seized in his own house, in the dead hour of the night, not by any civil officer, nor upon any civil process, but by a band of armed soldiers, under the verbal orders of a military chief, and is ruthlessly torn from his wife and his children, and hurried off to a fortress of the United States—and that fortress, as if in mockery, the very one over whose ramparts had floated that star-spangled banner immortalized in song by the patriot prisoner, who, "by dawn's early light," saw its folds gleaming amid the wreck of battle, and invoked the blessings of heaven upon it, and prayed that it might long wave "o'er the land of the free, and the home of the brave."

And, sir, when the highest judicial officer of the land, the Chief Justice of the Supreme Court, upon whose shoulders, "when the judicial ermine fell, it touched nothing not as spotless as itself," the aged, the venerable, the gentle, and pure-minded [Chief Justice Roger] Taney, who, but a little while before, had administered to the President the oath to support the Constitution, and to execute the laws, issued, as by law it was his sworn duty to issue, the high prerogative writ of habeas corpus—that great writ of right, that main bulwark of personal liberty, commanding the body of the accused to be brought before him, that justice and right might be done by due course of law, and without denial or delay, the gates of the fortress, its cannon turned towards, and in plain sight of the city, where the court sat, and frowning from its ramparts, were closed against the officer of the law, and the answer returned that the officer in command has, by the authority of the President, suspended the writ of habeas corpus. And thus it is, sir, that the accused has ever since been held a prisoner without due process of law; without bail; without presentment by a grand jury; without speedy, or public trial by a petit jury, of his own State or district, or any trial at all; without information of the nature and cause of the accusation; without being confronted with the witnesses against him; without compulsory process to obtain witnesses in his favor; and without the assistance of counsel for his defense. And this is our boasted American liberty? . . .

As to the pretense, sir, that the President has the Constitutional right to suspend the writ of habeas corpus, I will not waste time in arguing it. The case is as plain as words can make it. It is a legislative power; it is found only in the legislative article; it belongs to Congress only to do it. . . .

Sir, some years hence—I would fain hope some months hence, if I dare—the present generation will demand to know the cause of all this; and, some ages hereafter, the grand and impartial tribunal of history will make solemn and diligent inquest of the authors of this terrible revolution.[40]

BENJAMIN CURTIS (1809–1874)

President Millard Fillmore appointed Benjamin Curtis, a native of Watertown, Massachusetts, to the Supreme Court in 1851. One of the two dissenters from the Court's notorious proslavery Dred Scott *decision in 1857, Curtis resigned that year in a dispute with the decision's author, Chief Justice Roger Taney, over the release of his dissent to the press before its formal release by the Court. During the Civil War, as a lawyer in private practice, Curtis supported the North but strongly objected to the Emancipation Proclamation, as well as President Abraham Lincoln's suspension of habeas corpus, arguing that those actions exceeded Lincoln's constitutional authority. After Lincoln's death, Curtis defended President Andrew Johnson during his Senate impeachment trial.*

In this pamphlet published in Boston in 1862, Curtis asserted that Lincoln was prosecuting the war by unconstitutional means, an argument that would be made in subsequent wars about presidents accused of abusing their wartime powers.[41]

EXECUTIVE POWER
1862

The war in which we are now engaged is a just and necessary war. It must be prosecuted with the whole force of this government till the military power of the South is broken, and they submit themselves to their duty to obey, and our right to have obeyed, the Constitution of the United States as "the supreme law of the land." But with what sense of right can we subdue them by arms to obey the Constitution as the supreme law of *their* part of the land, if we have ceased to obey it, or failed to preserve it, as the supreme law of *our* part of the land. . . .

I do not propose to discuss the question whether the first of these proclamations [the Emancipation Proclamation] of the President, if definitively adopted, can have any practical effect on the unhappy race of persons to whom it refers; nor what its practical consequences would be, upon them and upon the white population of the United States, if it should take effect; nor through what scenes of bloodshed, and worse than bloodshed, it may be, we should advance to those final conditions; nor even the lawfulness, in any Christian or civilized sense, of the use of such means to attain *any* end.

If the entire social condition of nine millions of people has, in the providence of God, been allowed to depend upon the executive decree of one man, it will be the most stupendous fact which the history of the race has exhibited. But, for myself, I do not yet perceive that this vast responsibility is placed upon the President of the United States. I do not yet see that it depends upon his executive decree, whether a servile war shall be invoked to help twenty millions of the white race to assert the rightful authority of the Constitution and laws of their country, over those who refuse to obey them. *But I do see that this proclamation asserts the power of the Executive to make such a decree. . . .*

The proclamation of emancipation, if taken to mean what in terms it asserts, is an executive decree, that on the first day of January next, all persons held as slaves, within such States or parts of States as shall then be designated, shall cease to be lawfully held to service, and may by their own efforts, and with the aid of the military power of the United States, vindicate their lawful right to their personal freedom.

The persons who are the subjects of this proclamation are held to service by the laws of the respective States in which they may reside, enacted by State authority, as clear and unquestionable, under our system of government, as any law passed by any State on any subject.

This proclamation, then, by an executive decree, proposes to repeal and annul valid State laws which regulate the domestic relations of their people. Such is the mode of operation of the decree.

The next observable characteristic is, that this executive decree holds out this proposed repeal of State laws as a threatened *penalty* for the continuance of a governing majority of the people of each State, or part of a State, in rebellion against the United States. So that the President hereby assumes to himself the power to denounce it as a punishment against the entire people of a State, that the valid laws of that State which regulate the domestic condition of its inhabitants, shall become null and void, at a certain future date, by reason of the criminal conduct of a governing majority of its people. . . .

When the Constitution says that the President shall be the commander-in-chief of the army and navy of the United States, and of the militia of the several States when called into the actual service of the United States, does it mean that he shall possess military power and command *over all citizens of the United States;* that, by military edicts, he may control all citizens, as if enlisted in the army or navy, or in the militia called into the actual service of the United States? Does it mean that he may make himself a legislator, and enact penal laws governing the citizens of the United States, and erect tribunals, and create offices to enforce his penal edicts upon citizens? Does it mean that he may, by a prospective executive decree, repeal and annul the laws of the several States, which respect subjects reserved by the Constitution for the exclusive action of the States and the people? The President is the commander-in-chief of the army and navy, not only by force of the Constitution, but under and subject to the Constitution, and to every restriction therein contained, and to every law enacted by its authority, as completely and clearly as the private in his ranks.

He is general-in-chief; but can a general-in-chief *disobey any law of his own country?* When he can, he superadds to his *rights* as commander the *powers* of a usurper; and that is military despotism. In the noise of arms have we become deaf to the warning voices of our fathers, to take care that the military shall always he, or whoever is acting for him, may choose. They hold the citizen to trial before a military commission appointed by the President, or his representative, for such acts or omissions as be subservient to the civil power? Instead of listening to these voices, some persons now seem to think that it is enough to silence objection, to say, true enough, there is no civil right to do this or that, but it is a military act. They seem to have forgotten that every military act is to be tested by the Constitution and laws of the country under whose authority it is done. And that under the Constitution and laws of the United States, no more than under the government of Great Britain, or under any free or any settled government, the mere authority to command an army, is not an authority to disobey the laws of the country.[42]

CHAPTER 5

THE SPANISH-AMERICAN WAR AND THE PHILIPPINE WAR

"THE BLIND PASSIONS OF THIS COUNTRY"

AMERICA'S WAR AGAINST SPAIN BEGAN IN EARNEST IN THE U.S. Senate on March 17, 1898. On that day, Senator Redfield Proctor, a respected Republican businessman from Vermont, spoke in the Senate about his recent trip to war-torn Cuba. "It is desolation and distress, misery and starvation," Proctor told colleagues, who listened as the usually unemotional senator passionately described the suffering and deprivation he had witnessed. As senators knew, the Madrid government, to isolate the people from the influence of Cuban insurgents fighting against Spanish rule, ordered the wholesale relocation of villages and towns, herding the Cuban people into compounds, or *reconcentrados*. It was reports about the deplorable conditions in these camps that prompted Proctor's mission. His tale shocked the Senate and much of the nation—and moved Congress decisively toward war.

In the horrid conditions of these "towns," Proctor said, death and disease was widespread. "It is not within the narrow limits of my vocabulary to portray it," he said. Of the 1.6 million Cubans in the camps, Proctor reported that nearly two hundred thousand had died in recent months from starvation and disease. The solution? Until the Cuban people can return to their villages and rebuild, Proctor said, "the American people must, in the meantime, care for them."[1]

Proctor's riveting speech was not simply a report on the conditions of war-ravaged Cuba; it was a call to arms sounded by one of President William McKinley's most important Senate allies.[2] Among those still not converted was the irascible Republican House speaker, Thomas "Czar" Reed of Maine. Noting Proctor's reputation as "the marble king" of Vermont, Reed wryly observed, "A war will make a large profit for gravestones." Reed, however, undoubtedly knew he was swimming against the current of public opinion.[3]

Fueling the anti-Spanish sentiment were newspapers in New York, Washington, New Orleans, and Florida, all with reporters in Cuba. These papers featured a stream of sensational stories of Spanish atrocities. Artists, including Frederic Remington, supplied newspapers with dramatic, emotional depictions of the Cubans' suffering and depravation.[4] Most aggressive were two New York papers—the *World*, published by Joseph Pulitzer, and the *Journal*, published by William Randolph Hearst. Typical of the *World*'s early reporting was this dispatch from 1896, "The skulls of all were split to pieces down to the eyes. Some of these were gouged out. All the bodies had been stabbed by sword bayonets and hacked by sabres [*sic*] until I could not count the cuts; they were indistinguishable. The bodies had almost lost semblance of human form."[5]

A headline on a June 25, 1896, story in the *World* screamed, "The Worst Has Not Been Told; Even Little Children Are Slain by the Spanish; Bodies Sometimes Shamefully Mutilated."[6] The *Journal* was no less sensational. With Remington supplying the disturbing pen sketches, correspondent Richard Harding Davis arrived in Cuba in January 1897 to "report" on Spanish atrocities.[7]

Hearst made no secret of his desire for war. When the United States finally declared war, the publisher boasted, "DO YOU LIKE THE JOURNAL'S WAR?"[8] While newspaper reports likely generated some public support for war, the sinking of the USS *Maine* in Havana Harbor in February 1898 inflamed passions, especially after a naval inquiry concluded that an external explosion, mostly likely a submarine mine, had killed 266 men.[9]

Other prowar newspapers joined in. "Spain stands as an imbecile among the powers of Europe," the Chicago *Inter-Ocean* asserted in January 1898. The *Chicago Tribune* agreed: Spain "is a poor, broken down, decrepit, bankrupt nation. The United States, the most powerful nation on the globe, in a conflict with Spain would only have to crook its little finger, the job would be so easy."[10]

War was particularly popular among Republicans who sponsored, in 1896, nonbinding resolutions urging diplomatic recognition of the Cuban insurgents as the nation's legitimate leaders. When Democratic President Grover Cleveland ignored the resolutions, Cuban independence became even more closely associated with the Republican Party.[11] Some prominent Republicans, however, adamantly opposed the war. Speaker Reed made no secret of his antipathy and actively worked to derail efforts to vote on prowar legislation.[12] In the Senate, Republican Senator George Hoar of Massachusetts (his state was among the most reliably antiwar bastions since the War of 1812) sternly warned his colleagues of the consequences of picking a fight with Spain. "If we enter upon this war, we are to subject our ships to many disasters like that of the *Maine* and our soldiers to pestilence and yellow fever . . . to say nothing of the increase of the debt and of the pension list." Another Republican senator, George Wellington of Maryland, declared, "If war comes, the thunder of guns . . . will bring death and disaster to our men, sorrow to our homes, contaminating diseases to our shores."[13]

Hoar and Wellington opposed the conflict, not because of fundamental opposition to war, but rather because their revulsion at the idea of an American empire—and they feared the United States might lose. Some newspapers shared those concerns. The day after the *Maine* exploded, the *New York Commercial Advertiser* warned, "The incident will be worth the cost of it if it teaches us humility and abates our thirst for war. If peace is so perilous to our battleships when there is real powder in their magazines, what would war be?"[14]

At a mass meeting of war opponents in Boston in April 1898, noted lawyer Moor-field Storey attacked the "irresponsible mercenaries" in the New York media and elsewhere who "are madly shrieking for war." Storey rightly doubted the stories of widespread Cuban suffering. "This has been a campaign of lies waged by the Cubans in the United States through the newspapers," he said. Even if the stories were true, "Shall we help it by bombarding Havana or Matanzas and depriving innocent people of their homes and their means of livelihood?"[15] Another prominent opponent of war was Harvard scholar Charles Eliot Norton, later vice president of the New England Anti-Imperialist League. In a speech in Cambridge in June 1898, Norton mourned the nation's decision to "enter into a path of darkness and peril."[16]

Facing a growing war clamor, President McKinley searched for a diplomatic solution. Despite Spanish attempts to avert the confrontation, the *Maine's* sinking overwhelmed the impact of the modest proposed reforms. The Cuban insurgents, meanwhile, said they would accept nothing less than complete independence, some-thing Spanish officials knew they could not grant without dire domestic political consequences. Even after the spectacular news of the *Maine's* explosion, McKinley wanted more time for diplomacy.[17] By April 1898, time ran out. "Mr. President," Vice President Garrett Hobart told him, "I can no longer hold back the Senate. They will act without you if you do not act at once."[18] As the French ambassador to the United States reported to his government in early April, "Whatever happens next, one must respect a president who has resisted, for as long as he has, the blind passions of this country."[19]

On April 11, McKinley asked Congress for military intervention "in the cause of humanity and to put an end to the barbarities, bloodshed, starvation and horrible miseries." McKinley justified intervention because of "the very serious injury to the commerce, trade, and business of our people." While he did not specifically ask for a war declaration, McKinley made it clear that U.S. military action in Cuba was his intention—but only as a means to secure peace. "In the name of humanity, in the name of civilization, in behalf of endangered American interests which give us the right and the duty to speak and to act, the war in Cuba must stop."[20]

The Hearst newspapers, angry that McKinley did not demand a war declaration, decried the president's message, charging that he had "profoundly disappointed the American people; instead of a call to arms," McKinley had "sounded a summons to retreat." Further angering war proponents was McKinley's failure to demand Cuban independence. Despite some opposition, especially in the Senate, Congress authorized military intervention in Cuba—42 to 35 in the Senate and 310 to 6 in the House.[21]

What followed was a "war" lasting one hundred days. By July 17, U.S. naval and ground forces secured the island and forced Spain into peace negotiations. In the United States, the "splendid little war," as Secretary of State John Hay called it, was wildly popular.[22] The war was not only about Cuba; the U.S. Army was aimed at two other Spanish possessions—Puerto Rico and the Philippines. Both were acquired after minimal fighting—the Spanish clearly did not have the heart or military might for a protracted war—and the two sides soon concluded peace negotiations. In March 1899, the Senate approved a treaty with Spain in which the United States acquired Cuba, Puerto Rico, and—in exchange for $20 million—the Philippine archipelago.[23]

While the initial military engagement in the Philippines was successful—U.S. forces under Commodore George Dewey decisively defeated the Spanish at Manila Bay in May 1898—the subsequent occupation of the island chain sparked a lengthy and violent insurrection. For the next four years, American forces would struggle to establish control, while in the United States, a war of words erupted over whether the nation should embrace its new imperialist status.[24]

While the nation spun into expansionist frenzy, McKinley was circumspect, yet also mindful of the political risks of lending any support to the anti-imperialist cause. "The truth is I didn't want the Philippines," he later said, "and when they came to us as a gift from the gods, I did not know what to do about them." Eventually, McKinley said, he concluded that "we could not give them back to Spain—that would be cowardly and dishonorable; . . . that we could not leave them to themselves—they were unfit for self-government . . . [and so] there was nothing left for us to do but to take them all . . . uplift and civilize and Christianize them."[25]

As it became clear that the United States would have to fight the insurgents to secure in the Philippines what it had "purchased" from Spain, opponents of American policy emerged. In Boston, in November 1898, a politically diverse group formed the Anti-Imperialist League. Other state chapters quickly formed. While led by mostly liberal Republicans, the movement also featured prominent Democrats like William Jennings Bryan and other respected individuals, including Samuel Clemens (Mark Twain), former President Grover Cleveland, and Rev. Adolph A. Berle.[26]

The first major struggle was over congressional approval of the peace treaty and appropriation of the $20 million to purchase the Philippines. A vigorous and effective opponent of the treaty was Senator Hoar, who told the Senate on January 9, 1900:

> Our imperialistic friends seem to have forgotten the use of the vocabulary of liberty. They talk about giving good government. "We shall give them such a government as we think they are fitted for." "We shall give them a better government than they had before." Why . . . that one phrase conveys to a free man and a free people the most stinging of insults. In that little phrase, as in a seed, is contained the germ of all despotism and of all tyranny. Government is not a gift. Free government is not to be given by all the blended powers of earth and heaven. It is a birthright. It belongs, as our fathers said and as their children said, as Jefferson said and as President McKinley said, to human nature itself. There can be no good government but self-government.[27]

McKinley's treaty eventually passed, but with only two votes to spare. It was, perhaps, the support of one prominent anti-imperialist that carried the day. Bryan, the 1896 Democratic presidential nominee, urged his Senate allies to support the treaty so that imperialism would be the dominant campaign theme in the approaching 1900 presidential election.[28] One vigorous opponent of the treaty, Andrew Carnegie, was disgusted with Bryan's seemingly expedient tactics, "One word from Mr. Bryan would have saved the country from disaster."[29]

From the beginning, racism was an important factor in the debate over what to do with Cuba, Puerto Rico, and the Philippines. "Are we to have a Mongolian state in this Union?" Representative John F. Fitzgerald of Massachusetts (grandfather of future President John F. Kennedy) asked. Far more than racist views motivated the anti-imperialists; freedom and self-determination were also dominant themes.[30] "With cheek unblushing we go on in the prosecution of this war as though our ideas of civilization were to be accepted by every grade of people from the tropics to the arctics [sic]," George S. Boutwell, the first president of the national Anti-Imperialist League, said at an anti-imperialist mass meeting in Boston in September 1899. "In all the public policy of this war, and especially in the proclamations of the President to the Filipinos, there may be seen, and only half concealed, the arrogant pretension that whatever we have is good and that whatever has been accepted by the inhabitants of the Philippines is bad."[31]

Perhaps the most notorious dissent against the American war against Philippine insurgents was published by Edward Atkinson, a prominent Massachusetts business-man and the founder of the Anti-Imperialist League. In addition to the standard anti-imperialist arguments, Atkinson included in his pamphlet a section, "The Hell of War and its Penalties," describing the various tropical and sexual diseases to which the American troops were exposed. In April 1899, he announced plans to send cop-ies to several hundred American troops in the field. When the government refused him a mailing list, Atkinson mailed copies to the leading military officers stationed in the Philippines. The U.S. Postmaster General seized the pamphlets. Publicity from the incident created a clamor for Atkinson's publication. In all, he distributed about 135,000 copies.[32]

Just as propaganda helped persuade Americans to support the war, it also gener-ated dissent. In May 1899, the Anti-Imperialist League published a collection of letters from American soldiers. While it could not vouch for the veracity of the state-ments, or even the identity of every author, the league offered them as "a valuable source of information as to the real situation." The pamphlet purported to attest to not only the brutality involved in suppressing the insurgency, but also the doubts of the soldiers about the morality and brutality of their mission. Perhaps the most shocking letter was allegedly penned by a soldier identified as A. A. Barnes, Battery G, Third United States Artillery:

> The town of Titatia was surrendered to us a few days ago, and two companies occupy the same. Last night one of our boys was found shot and his stomach cut open. Immedi-ately orders were received from General Wheaton to burn the town and kill every native in sight, which was done to a finish. About one thousand men, women, and children were reported killed. I am probably growing hard-hearted, for I am in my glory when I can sight my gun on some dark-skin and pull the trigger. Let me advise you a little, and should a call for volunteers be made for this place, do not be so patriotic as to come here. Tell all my inquiring friends that I am doing everything I can for Old Glory and for America I love so well.[33]

An outraged New York Times attacked the league as treasonous and said the group should "send rifles, Maxim guns, and stores of ammunition to the Filipinos," because that would "be more openly and frankly treasonable."[34] The letters had an incendiary impact on the anti-imperialists. When Bryan ran for president in 1900 on an anti-imperialist platform, he enjoyed the support of many who previously had scoffed at his shopworn "free silver" position. Upon his nomination to run against McKinley for a second time (McKinley had defeated Bryan in the 1896 election), Bryan argued for self-government, which he said was "the overshadowing political fact" of the previous century.[35] A thrilling orator, Bryan tried to stoke anti-imperialist sentiment. The country, however, was in no mood.[36] On election day, Bryan's support was no better than four years earlier, suggesting that McKinley's role in making the United States a bona fide world power was popular with at least a narrow majority of voters.

As the insurrection dragged on—throughout 1901 and 1902—the anti-imperialist message earned a wider audience. Part of the reason was the growing brutality on both sides. Although McKinley and the U.S. governor of the islands, William Howard Taft, insisted that American troops treat Philippine civilians with dignity, Secretary of War Elihu Root argued that tough tactics were necessary to deal with "barbarous cruelties" by Philippine insurgents.[37]

In fact, both sides engaged in deplorable behavior opposed by McKinley and Philippine insurgent leader Emilio Aguinaldo.[38] The commanding U.S. general, Arthur MacArthur, condoned harsh methods to quell the uprising and pacify the population, including torture and executions. After Vice President Theodore Roosevelt became president upon McKinley's assassination in 1901, the conduct of the war by both sides deteriorated considerably. The worst example occurred on the eastern islands of Samar when U.S. troops responded to a vicious rebel attack with equally vicious methods. "I want no prisoners," General Jacob Smith told his troops. "I wish you to kill and burn, the more you kill and burn the better it will please me." Smith ordered his men to kill anyone of fighting age, which he defined as ten years and older. After the resulting wholesale massacre at Samar, the Army court-martialed and convicted Smith in May 1902, but Roosevelt did almost nothing to discourage the ruthless tactics of other commanders.[39]

In January 1902, the U.S. Senate, prodded by Senator Hoar, investigated the alleged atrocities. Chaired by Massachusetts Senator Henry Cabot Lodge, the hearings were probably a whitewash.[40] In a report submitted to the committee by two of its lawyers—Moorfield Storey and Julian Codman—the extent of the American atrocities were clear. The men, both active in anti-imperialist organizations, concluded "that the destruction of Filipino life during the war has been so frightful that it cannot be explained as the result of ordinary civilized warfare." They cited evidence of torture and "the practice of burning native towns and villages and laying waste the country."[41]

"Who of our people, if the decision rested solely with him, would set fire to his neighbors' houses and slaughter a thousand men to increase his business and demonstrate his strength?" asked Bolton Hall, a prominent New York anti-imperialist in *The Arena* in July 1902.[42] Also in *The Arena*, another anti-imperialist, Ernest Crosby, wrote, "There is something fine in the unsimulated strength of a wild beast, but when a nation steals the soil from under your feet and enslaves you to its own uses, and in the meantime prates of Christianity and civilization and benevolent intentions, it turns the stomach of an honest man."[43]

News of the atrocities finally began to erode public support for the war (just as news of official torture and "prisoner abuse" would turn many Americans against the Iraq War more than a century later). By July 1902, Roosevelt declared the struggle ended, the conclusion achieved by policies that had partially taken the nation to war in the first place—the forceful removal of civilians into concentration camps. The U.S. policy worked and the guerilla warfare soon abated. The war cost 4,200 American lives and killed 20,000 insurgents. Civilians suffered the most—two hundred thousand dead from disease and famine.[44]

The new American empire, acquired from 1898 to 1902, included Cuba, Puerto Rico, and the Philippines. While many celebrated the entry of the United States into the fraternity of empires, others believed the country had gone badly astray. Lamented former President Grover Cleveland in 1904, "It was a mockery of Fate that led us to an unexpected and unforeseen incident in this conflict, and placed in the path of our Government, while professing national righteousness, representing an honest and liberty-loving people, and intent on a benevolent, self-sacrificing errand, the temptation of sordid aggrandizement and the false glitter of world-power."[45] Cleveland's warning was prescient. In little more than a decade, the United States—now a world power—would enter into the folly of a disastrous and costly world war.

CHARLES ELIOT NORTON (1827–1908)

Charles Eliot Norton was an influential writer and professor of history at Harvard where he discouraged his students from enlisting in the U.S. military. A hotbed of anti-imperialist sentiment near the end of the nineteenth century, Boston was the site of Norton's famous speech against the war on June 7, 1898, to the Men's Club of the Prospect Street Congregational Church in Cambridge. The speech and sentiment it stirred sparked formation of the Anti-Imperialist League that November. Along with Charles Francis Adams and Grover Cleveland, Norton was among the league's original honorary vice presidents.[46]

TRUE PATRIOTISM
Address before the Men's Club of the Prospect Street Congregational Church, Cambridge, Massachusetts, June 7, 1898

A generation has grown up that has known nothing of war. The blessings of peace have been poured out upon us. We have congratulated ourselves that we were free from the misery and the burdens that war and standing armies have brought upon the nations of the Old World. "Their fires"—I cite a fine phrase of Sir Philip Sidney in a letter to Queen Elizabeth—"Their fires have given us light to see our own quietness." And now all of a sudden, without cool deliberation, without prudent preparation, the nation is hurried into war, and America, she who more than any other land was pledged to peace and good-will on earth, unsheathes her sword, compels a weak and unwilling nation to a fight, rejecting without due consideration her earnest and repeated offers to meet every legitimate demand of the United States. It is a bitter disappointment to the lover of his country; it is a turning-back from the path of civilization to that of barbarism.

"There never was a good war," said [Benjamin] Franklin. There have indeed been many wars in which a good man must take part, and take part with grave gladness to defend the cause of justice, to die for it if need be, a willing sacrifice, thankful to give life for what is dearer than life, and happy that even by death in war he is serving the cause of peace. But if a war be undertaken for the most righteous end, before the resources of peace have been tried and proved vain to secure it, that war has no defense; it is a national crime. And however right, however unavoidable a war may be, and those of us who are old enough to remember the war for the Union know that war may be right and unavoidable, yet, I repeat the words of Franklin, "There never was a good war." It is evil in itself, it is evil in its never-ending train of consequences. . . .

There are, indeed, many among us who find justification of the present war in the plea that its motive is to give independence to the people of Cuba, long burdened by the oppressive and corrupt rule of Spain, and especially to relieve the suffering of multitudes deprived of their homes and of means of subsistence by the cruel policy of the general who exercised for a time a practical dictatorship over the island. The plea so far as it is genuine deserves the respect due to every humane sentiment. But independence secured for Cuba by forcible overthrow of the Spanish rule means either practical anarchy or the substitution of the authority of the United States for that of Spain. Either alternative might well give us pause. And as for the relief of suffering, surely it is a strange procedure to begin by inflicting worse suffering still. It is fighting the devil with his own arms. . . .

But the war is declared; and on all hands we hear the cry that he is no patriot who fails to shout for it, and to urge the youth of the country to enlist, and to rejoice that they are called to the service of their native land. The sober counsels that were appropriate before the war was entered upon must give way to blind enthusiasm, and the voice of condemnation must be silenced by the thunders of the guns and the hurrahs of the crowd. Stop! A declaration of war does not change the moral law. "The ten commandments will not budge" at a joint resolve of Congress. Was James Russell Lowell[47] aught but a good patriot when during the Mexican war he sent the stinging shafts of his matchless satire at the heart of the monstrous iniquity, or when, years afterward, he declared, that he thought at the time, and that he still thought, the Mexican war was a national crime? Did John Bright[48] ever render greater service to his country than when, during the Crimean war, he denounced the Administration which had plunged England into it, and employed his magnificent power of earnest and incisive speech in the endeavor to repress the evil spirit which it evoked in the heart of the nation? No! the voice of protest, of warning, of appeal is never more needed than when the clamor of fife and drum, echoed by the press and too often by the pulpit, is bidding all men fall in and keep step and obey in silence the tyrannous word of command. Then, more than ever, it is the duty of the good citizen not to be silent, and spite of obloquy, misrepresentation and abuse, to insist on being heard, and with sober counsel to maintain the everlasting validity of the principles of the moral law. . . .

My friends, America has been compelled against the will of all her wisest and best to enter into a path of darkness and peril. Against their will she has been forced to turn back from the way of civilization to the way of barbarism, to renounce for the time her own ideals. With grief, with anxiety must the lover of his country regard the present aspect and the future prospect of the nation's life. With serious purpose, with utter self-devotion he should prepare himself for the untried and difficult service to which it is plain he is to be called in the quick-coming years.[49]

WILLIAM JENNINGS BRYAN (1860–1925)

The Democratic Party's presidential nominee in 1900, William Jennings Bryan was one of the most energetic and thrilling campaigners of his era. A former congressman from Nebraska, Bryan became the nation's most prominent anti-imperialist spokesperson. He and his followers believed that the U.S. occupation of the Philippines violated the principles and values of the Founding Fathers. Bryan, who McKinley had defeated in 1896, demanded the immediate independence of the Philippines. Campaigning for President McKinley, Vice President Theodore Roosevelt argued that the United States had a duty to first civilize the Philippine people before granting them independence. Despite Bryan's effort to make the Philippine occupation an issue, McKinley beat Bryan by a margin even larger than in 1896. Bryan would later serve as Secretary of State under President Woodrow Wilson. In that post, he became a vigorous proponent of peaceful conflict resolution, negotiating arbitration treaties with thirty nations in which they agreed to first seek peaceful resolutions before resorting to war. Bryan resigned in protest in 1915 when Wilson began to abandon neutrality in the wake of the sinking of the British ship Lusitania.

THE PARALYZING INFLUENCE OF IMPERIALISM
Speech to the Democratic National Convention, Kansas City, Missouri, July 1900

If it is right for the United States to hold the Philippine Islands permanently and imitate European empires in the government of colonies, the Republican Party ought to state its position and defend it, but it must expect the subject races to protest against such a policy and to resist to the extent of their ability.

The Filipinos do not need any encouragement from Americans now living. Our whole history has been an encouragement, not only to the Filipinos, but to all who are denied a voice in their own government. If the Republicans are prepared to censure all who have used language calculated to make the Filipinos hate foreign domination, let them condemn the speech of Patrick Henry. When he uttered that passionate appeal, "Give me liberty or give me death," he expressed a sentiment which still echoes in the hearts of men.

Let them censure Jefferson; of all the statesmen of history, none have used words so offensive to those who would hold their fellows in political bondage. Let them censure Washington, who declared that the colonists must choose between liberty and slavery. Or, if the statute of limitations has run against the sins of Henry and Jefferson and Washington, let them censure Lincoln, whose Gettysburg speech will be quoted in defense of popular government when the present advocates of force and conquest are forgotten.

Someone has said that a truth once spoken can never be recalled. It goes on and on, and no one can set a limit to its ever widening influence. But if it were possible to obliterate every word written or spoken in defense of the principles set forth in the Declaration of Independence, a war of conquest would still leave its legacy of perpetual hatred, for it was God Himself who placed in every human heart the love of liberty. He never made a race of people so low in the scale of civilization or intelligence that it would welcome a foreign master.

Those who would have this nation enter upon a career of empire must consider not only the effect of imperialism on the Filipinos but they must also calculate its effects upon our own nation. We cannot repudiate the principle of self-government in the Philippines without weakening that principle here.

Lincoln said that the safety of this nation was not in its fleets, its armies, its forts, but in the spirit which prizes liberty as the heritage of all men, in all lands, everywhere, and he warned his countrymen that they could not destroy this spirit without planting the seeds of despotism at their own doors.

Even now we are beginning to see the paralyzing influence of imperialism. Heretofore this nation has been prompt to express its sympathy with those who were fighting for civil liberty. While our sphere of activity has been limited to the Western Hemisphere, our sympathies have not been bounded by the seas. We have felt it due to ourselves and to the world, as well as to those who were struggling for the right to govern themselves, to proclaim the interest which our people have, from the date of their own independence, felt in every contest between human rights and arbitrary power. . . .

A colonial policy means that we shall send to the Philippine Islands a few traders, a few taskmasters, and a few officeholders, and an army large enough to support the authority of a small fraction of the people while they rule the natives.

If we have an imperial policy we must have a great standing army as its natural and necessary complement. The spirit which will justify the forcible annexation of the Philippine Islands will justify the seizure of other islands and the domination of other people, and with wars of conquest we can expect a certain, if not rapid, growth of our military establishment. . . .

What is our title to the Philippine Islands? Do we hold them by treaty or by conquest? Did we buy them or did we take them? Did we purchase the people? If not, how did we secure title to them? Were they thrown in with the land? Will the Republicans say that inanimate earth has value but that when that earth is molded by the Divine Hand and stamped with the likeness of the Creator it becomes a fixture and passes with the soil? If governments derive their just powers from the consent of the governed, it is impossible to secure title to people, either by force or by purchase. . . .

There is an easy, honest, honorable solution of the Philippine question. It is set forth in the Democratic platform and it is submitted with confidence to the American people. This plan I unreservedly endorse. If elected, I will convene Congress in extraordinary session as soon as inaugurated and recommend an immediate declaration of the nation's purpose: first, to establish a stable form of government in the Philippine Islands, just as we are now establishing a stable form of government in Cuba; second, to give independence to the Cubans; third, to protect the Filipinos from outside interference while they work out their destiny, just as we have protected the republics of Central and South America, and are, by the Monroe Doctrine, pledged to protect Cuba.[50]

CHAPTER 6

WORLD WAR I

"THE POISON OF DISLOYALTY"

CONTROVERSY FOLLOWED DAVID STARR JORDAN, THE SIXTY-SIX-YEAR-OLD PRESIDENT OF Stanford University. Since the spring of 1917, the renowned naturalist, explorer, and peace activist had traveled the East Coast speaking against American involvement in the European war. "Whatever the primal nature of war," Jordan said, "its every act is murder or robbery."[1] In two and a half years of fighting in Europe, nearly five million men had died.[2] Appalled by the notion that American armament makers, "hard pressed for capital," were hoping the United States would enter the conflict, Jordan arrived in Baltimore to deliver a speech on April 1—the day before President Woodrow Wilson would ask Congress to declare war on Germany.

Several days earlier, in New York's Madison Square Garden, a near riot had erupted as Jordan addressed a large antiwar gathering.[3] Two days later, in New Jersey, officials at Princeton University would not allow Jordan to speak on campus. When he did speak, at a nearby church, some undergraduates answered his criticism of Wilson with hisses and whistles.[4]

When Jordan reached Baltimore, a sympathetic crowd of five thousand greeted him at a gathering organized by a local minister. Barely into his speech, however, a thousand-person mob stormed the building, marched down the aisles waving an American flag, stopping Jordan in midsentence. The crowd disbanded after police arrived and began swinging clubs and arresting two wagonloads of protesters.[5] A large man who stood six foot three inches tall, Jordan strolled peacefully to his host's home. As Jordan later learned, while he slept, a large crowd had paraded throughout the city, searching hotels for him while singing, "We'll hang Dave Jordan to a sour apple tree." Jordan spoke in Washington to a peace conference the next day, stopping his prepared remarks to inform his audience that Wilson had just asked Congress to declare war.[6]

Wilson's April 2 speech was the culmination of a vast shift on the war. In early 1914, after only one year in office, Wilson had declared, "Every [social] reform we have won will be lost if we go into this war."[7] In the beginning, at least, Wilson appeared to set aside his British sympathies for strict neutrality. He tried several times to broker peace between Britain and Germany. Nonetheless, as war raged and German hostility toward the United States increased, Wilson gradually launched a military preparedness campaign. In November 1915 he proposed expanding the nation's land and naval forces, not to counter an imminent threat, but to be prepared if the war threatened U.S. security. The evidence of Wilson's ostensible desire to downplay the prospect of U.S. troops in combat: the Democratic Party's slogan during his 1916 reelection campaign was "He Kept Us Out of War."[8]

While the party's slogan stressed peace, Wilson laid the groundwork for war. In particular, his efforts to influence the 1916 Democratic Party platform plank on loyalty foreshadowed the repression that would mark his second term. The language that Wilson approved said, in part: "The indivisibility and incoherent strength of the nation is the supreme issue this day . . . all men of whatever origin or creed who would count themselves Americans [should] join in making clear to all the world, the unity and consequent power of America. This is an issue of patriotism. To taint it with partisanship would be to defile it."[9]

That statement partly reflected Wilson's growing distrust of foreign-born Americans—and his distaste for dissent. "The gravest threats against our national peace and safety have been uttered within our own borders," he told Congress in December 1915. "There are citizens of the United States, I blush to admit, born under other flags but welcomed by our generous naturalization laws to the full freedom and opportunity of America, who have poured the poison of disloyalty into the very arteries of our national life."[10] In another speech, Wilson said, "I am in a hurry to have a line-up, and let the men who are thinking first of other countries stand on one side, and all those that are for America first, last, and all the time, on the other side."[11]

It was particularly German Americans who felt the sting of suspicion and distrust in the years after a German submarine had sunk the British ship *Lusitania* in May 1915, killing 1,198 people, 123 of them Americans. In 1917, German Americans were about eight percent of the nation and the second largest ethnic group.[12] While their significant numbers initially offered German Americans some protection, German maritime aggression quickly devoured the good will and tolerance of many Americans. Hoping to cripple Britain by choking off the importation of vital commodities and munitions—and in response to a British blockade of Germany—the German navy targeted ships bound for England. Besides those who died on the *Lusitania*, American passengers and seamen were perishing in increasing numbers on foreign- and American-flagged ships. When, in the spring of 1917, Germany declared unrestricted naval warfare against shipping near Britain and in the Mediterranean, U.S.-German relations collapsed. When a potential military alliance between the Germans and Mexican officials came to light in March 1917 (in the notorious Zimmerman telegram, the Germans proposed helping Mexico retake parts of Texas and Arizona lost during the Mexican-American War), war with Germany seemed certain.

It is not clear, however, that the majority of Americans yet favored war. Evidence of public ambivalence is that congressional sentiment was far from unanimous. Some members simply feared getting the nation entangled with Europe. Others worried about the impact of conscription and the consequence of casting millions of young men into a war that had already killed millions. Others worried that potential war profits were behind some of the sentiment for war, while others challenged the essential morality of war itself.

"I do not question your patriotism, and I do not permit you to question my patriotism when I say that I am not willing to give a million American boys to avenge the lives of those people who sought to run the [naval] blockade laid down either by the English or the German Government," Republican Representative William Mason of Illinois said to applause from colleagues on April 5. Democratic Representative Edward Keating of Colorado argued that the congressional elections the previous year were a national referendum against war. "Who among you last October and November, when you were asking for the votes of your constituents," he asked, "dared to suggest to them that if elected you would send their boys to Europe?"[13]

Those arguments enraged Democratic Representative James Thomas Heflin of Alabama. "God of our fathers! Where is the patriotism and the courage of these gentlemen who today are trying to tie the hands of this Government so that it cannot defend itself from the dangers that threaten it?" In a refrain whose spirit future political leaders would adopt during times of war, Heflin added, to applause, "You are with the Kaiser and the Imperial German Government or you are standing with the president and the people of the United States."[14]

In the Senate, Republican George Norris of Nebraska echoed the suspicions of those who wondered if the cries for war were motivated by the desire for profits from munitions and other military supplies. "We are going into war upon the command of gold," he said. "I feel that we are about to put the dollar sign on the American flag." Some colleagues responded to those remarks with angry shouts of "Treason! Treason!"[15]

Six senators and fifty House members voted against war.[16] Perhaps Democratic Representative Henry Flood of Virginia best summed up the prowar sentiment: "This war is not of our choosing," he told the House on April 5. "For wrongs committed by the German Government to democracy, to humanity, and to civilization we have ample cause for declaring war; for wrongs done to American citizens and the American flag we have no course but to go to war."[17] Even a renowned pacifist such as David Starr Jordan changed his mind. "Our country is now in war and the only way out is forward," Jordan wrote to the *San Francisco Bulletin* on April 10. "We must now stand together, with the hope that our entrance into Europe may in some way advance the cause of democracy and hasten the coming of lasting peace."[18]

Although once a free-speech advocate, Wilson's attitude was transformed. Demanding support for the war, Wilson warned Congress, "If there should be disloyalty, it will be dealt with with a firm hand of stern repression," he said. "But, if it lifts its head at all, it will lift it only here and there and without countenance except from a lawless and malignant few."[19] In a Flag Day speech in June, Wilson expanded on this theme, suggesting that all dissent was disloyalty. "Woe be to the man or group of men who seeks to stand in our way in this day of high resolution when every principle we hold dearest is to be vindicated and made secure for the salvation of the nation."[20]

Wilson and Congress backed up those words with aggressive action. On the day Congress declared war, Wilson signed an executive order regarding "enemy aliens" that, among other things, prohibited them from publishing any attack on the government, the armed forces, or policies of the United States. The next day, Wilson issued a secret order empowering federal agencies to remove employees suspected of disloyalty. The order later became part of the federal Sedition Act of 1918.[21]

To maintain public support for the war, in April 1917 Wilson created the Committee on Public Information (CPI), headed by the muckraking journalist George Creel. Using propaganda and public relations techniques—in fact, Creel and his staff created and professionalized modern propaganda—the committee found creative ways to influence Americans of every stripe. "It was the fight for the *minds* of men, for the 'conquest of their convictions,' and the battle-line ran through every home in every country," Creel later wrote.[22] The committee-policed voluntary censorship of the media—others, with Creel's support, would attend to the compulsory censorship—produced almost unanimous "patriotic" war coverage.[23] Using two dozen war expositions in cities throughout the country, six thousand press releases, seventy-five million copies of prowar pamphlets, the committee's information and propaganda easily aroused the patriotic passions of journalists and their readers.[24] While America's young men were enlisting—and being drafted—to fight in Europe, the CPI enlisted artists, writers, advertisers, and educators in its campaign to sell the war and vilify the Germans.[25] The CPI recruited another seventy-five thousand Americans as "Four-Minute Men" who gave four-minute prowar speeches to more than 134 million people in motion picture houses and other venues throughout the country. The propaganda effort worked better than Wilson and Creel could have imagined. In a matter of months, a largely pacifistic nation had become, in Creel's words, "one white hot mass instinct with fraternity, devotion, courage and deathless determination."[26] To many, this new prowar sentiment was a dangerous strain of violent and repressive patriotism that infected the body politic and destroyed civil liberties in order to spread and preserve democracy.

Creel's committee provided the persuasion; Congress and Wilson provided the coercion. The most repressive laws the president received from Congress were the Espionage and Trading with the Enemy acts of 1917 and the Sedition Act of 1918. Originally Wilson wanted a press censorship provision in the Espionage Act, imposing a $10,000 fine and ten years in prison for anyone convicted of publishing information deemed useful to the enemy.[27] "To attempt to deny to the press all legitimate criticism either of Congress or the Executive is going very dangerously far," Republican Senator Henry Cabot Lodge of Massachusetts argued.[28] Members of Congress removed that provision and toned down several others, apparently believing they had eliminated all opportunities to suppress speech. They had not.

One provision imposed up to a $10,000 fine and twenty years in prison, or both, for those who, during war "shall wilfully [*sic*] make or convey false reports or false statements with intent to interfere with the operation or success of the military or naval forces of the United States or to promote the success of its enemies."[29] Justice Department officials later employed this provision to prosecute 2,168 individuals, convicting 1,055 for speaking against the war. Those convicted would include ninety-seven leaders of the Industrial Workers of the World labor union, a U.S. Senate candidate in Minnesota, and Eugene V. Debs, the Socialist Party's 1912 presidential candidate.[30]

Another provision gave the U.S. Postmaster General broad authority to suppress free speech and dissent. Anything mailed that violated the act or advocated "treason, insurrection, or forcible resistance to any law of the United States" could be seized by postal officials. Violators could be imprisoned for five years or fined $5,000. This made Postmaster General Albert S. Burleson the nation's censor-in-chief, with near-absolute control over the content of small-circulation newspapers that relied almost exclusively on mail subscriptions.[31] All of this was too much for some in Congress. Said Democratic Senator Oscar Underwood of Alabama, "I do not believe the time has come when it is necessary for the Congress to betray the fundamental principles of the government in order to carry on the war at this time."[32]

Despite the law's potential for repression, the Wilson administration was not satisfied. In October 1917, the White House pressured Congress to enact the Trading with the Enemy Act, which enlarged the postmaster general's censorship powers. The law required all foreign-language newspapers to obtain Post Office Department permission before mailing publications with news about the government, its enemies and their policies, or the progress of the war. By mid-1918, the act achieved its goal: virtually every German-language newspaper had either endorsed U.S. war policy or stopped discussing the issue altogether.[33]

Congress and the Wilson administration further restricted free speech in May 1918 with passage of amendments to the Espionage Act (the collection of amendments were also called the Sedition Act). Responding to Attorney General Thomas Gregory's complaints about the "lack of laws relating to disloyal utterances" and "flagrant disloyalty," Congress created a handful of new offenses punishable by a $10,000 fine, up to twenty years in prison, or both. The First Amendment notwithstanding, Congress made it a crime to "wilfully [sic] utter, print, write, or publish any disloyal, profane, scurrilous, or abusive language about the form of government of the United States, or the Constitution of the United States, or the military or naval forces of the United States, or the flag." Criminal activity also included any "word or act [that] support[ed] or favor[ed] the cause of any country with which the United States is at war."[34]

The bill outraged Wilson's most prominent critic, former President Theodore Roosevelt, who attacked, in the *Kansas City Star* on April 6, "the foolish or traitorous persons who endeavor to make it a crime to tell the truth about the administration when [it] is guilty of incompetence. . . . It is a proposal to make Americans subjects instead of citizens."[35]

Later that year, in October, Congress overrode Wilson's veto to enact the Alien Act, which excluded from immigration into the United States anyone "who is a member of or affiliated with any organization entertaining or teaching disbelief in or opposition to organized government." Those convicted could be deported. The U.S. Justice Department would enforce the law energetically in 1919, deporting hundreds of "disloyal" aliens.[36]

Meanwhile, the Post Office busily censored the mail and closed "disloyal" newspapers and the Justice Department—and its U.S. attorneys with wide discretion about whom to prosecute—aggressively enforced the Espionage Act. John Lord O'Brian, assistant to the attorney general, later observed that the enormous publicity given the law "fanned animosities into flame."[37] Among the government's favorite targets were Socialist Party members and the Industrial Workers of the World (IWW). In fact, the Justice Department successfully prosecuted almost one hundred IWW members, including union leader William D. Haywood, whose conviction earned him a $30,000 fine and a twenty-year prison sentence.[38] Almost half of the government's prosecutions for violations of the Espionage Act occurred in thirteen of the nation's eighty-seven federal judicial districts, and most of those were in the West, where IWW activity was strongest. Various state officials also imprisoned scores of citizens for violating state sedition laws, particularly in the West. In Montana, officials prosecuted more than 130 people in 1918 and 1919.[39]

Another victim of the federal crackdown on free speech was a Lithuanian-born naturalized citizen, Emma Goldman, whose passionate and eloquent anarchist speeches made her an international figure. In March 1917, Goldman published a powerful essay, "The Promoters of the War Mania," in the anarchist monthly, *Mother Earth*, "If the opponents of war, from the Atlantic to the Pacific, would immediately join their voice into a thunderous No!, then the horror that now menaces America might yet be averted."[40] In June 1917, federal officials arrested Goldman for participating in mass anticonscription rallies. A jury convicted her. She remained in prison until officials deported her following the war.[41]

The national leader of the Socialist Party, Eugene V. Debs, met much the same fate in 1918 after a speech in Canton, Ohio. Debs, who had received more than nine hundred thousand votes when he ran for president in 1912, had just left a prison after visiting three socialists jailed for opposing the war. Speaking to supporters, Debs said, "it is extremely dangerous to exercise the constitutional right of free speech in a country fighting to make democracy safe in the world." Debs added, "They tell us that we live in a great free republic; that our institutions are democratic; that we are a free and self-governing people. This is too much, even for a joke."[42] The speech got Debs arrested under the Espionage Act for obstructing the enlistment of soldiers. He was convicted and sentenced to ten years in prison. The U.S. Supreme Court unanimously upheld the conviction, but President Warren Harding pardoned Debs in 1921, the year after Congress repealed the Sedition Act.[43]

Debs and Goldman were just two of the thousands of Americans prosecuted for expressing contrary opinions about the war—or, in some cases, for failing to express their supportive opinions strongly enough. A citizen-inspired investigative force, sanctioned by the Justice Department, deputized 250,000 people in 600 cities and towns to spy on fellow citizens. The American Protective League, created by a Chicago advertising executive, charged a one-dollar membership fee for a badge that said, "Secret Service Division." Thusly armed, league members ran roughshod. They spied, opened mail, wiretapped phones, burglarized private offices, and intimidated and even arrested those suspected of disloyal activities.[44] Attorney General Thomas Gregory bragged, "After the first six months of the War, it would have been difficult for fifty persons to have met for any purpose, in any place, from a Church to a dance hall in any part of the United States, without at least one representative of the Government being present."[45]

Another group of repressive organizations were state councils of defense, also called public safety committees or loyalty bureaus. While these organizations often helped the federal government sell war bonds and raise money and supplies for the troops, they also harassed and intimidated citizens for expressing opposition to (or lack of enthusiasm about) the war. Some organizations *required* that citizens donate money to the war effort.[46] Most of this intimidation of citizens and suppression of dissent was condoned and encouraged by Gregory, a Texas antitrust lawyer with no appreciation for civil liberties. "May God have mercy on them," he said of the war opponents in 1918, "for they need expect none from an outraged and an avenging government."[47]

Discrimination against German Americans was widespread. By 1918 almost half the states restricted or outlawed the speaking of German. German-language books were burned. Montana banned a history textbook for its "pro-German" views, apparently for asserting that "Christianity advanced from the Rhine to the Elbe." A study in the spring of 1918 by the midwestern field representative of the Council of National Defense reported numerous instances of violence and intimidation against German Americans for minor or imagined "offenses." The official reported, "All over this part of the country men are being tarred and feathered and some are being lynched. . . . [A]s a rule, it has the complete backing of public opinion."[48]

For all the patriotic support that Wilson and the CPI created—and the Justice Department and others coerced—the war took its toll on the Democratic Party's political standing and, more important, Wilson's ability to sell the peace treaty to the American people. Progressives were originally attracted to Wilson's liberal, progressive stance on many social issues. Among other things, he had passed antitrust legislation and created the Federal Trade Commission to prohibit unfair business practices, outlawed child labor, and limited railroad workers to an eight-hour day.[49] Wilson's attacks on free-speech undermined his standing with progressives. Wilson, however, appeared to believe that anything—even the destruction of civil liberties—was justified in pursuit of a righteous cause. "There is a great wind of moral force moving through the world, and every man who opposes himself to that wind will go down in disgrace," Wilson told an audience in France in December 1918.[50]

The war ended in November 1918 when the Germans signed the armistice. Wilson spent six months in Paris (he returned to the United States only once), negotiating the Versailles Treaty and creating the League of Nations. The Washington he left behind in December 1918, however, was very different. Republicans gained control of Congress in the 1918 midterm elections. That electoral loss was partly attributed to Wilson's repression of dissent and the way his Justice Department harassed and imprisoned his natural allies—progressives and union members. Faced with a hostile majority in Congress, Wilson further injured the treaty's chances by refusing to compromise with Republicans on its provisions.

Wilson, one observer noted, put "his enemies in office and his friends in jail."[51] As liberal journalist Oswald Garrison Villard observed, "At the very moment of [Wilson's] extreme trial our liberal forces are by his own act, scattered, silenced, disorganized, some in prison. If he loses his great fight for humanity, it will be because he was deliberately silent when freedom of speech and the right of conscience were struck down in America."[52] Even the CPI's George Creel, mastermind of war propaganda, acknowledged the carnage of the repression Wilson sanctioned. In a letter to Wilson after the 1918 election disaster, Creel observed: "When you raised it to the level of a war for democracy, you rallied to the support of the war all the progressive and democratic elements. The Big Business patriots went with you, ostensibly on your own terms, because they saw that only on your terms could the war be won. . . . All the radical or liberal friends of your anti-imperialist war policy were either silenced or intimidated. The Department of Justice and the Post Office were allowed to silence or intimidate them. There was no voice left to argue for your sort of peace."[53]

After the war, the assault on free speech by Wilson and his subordinates spun out of control. Fearing that the revolution might spread to America—in Russia, communists seized the country in the October 1917 Bolshevik uprising—federal officials and many Americans backed even more repressive measures to quell dissent. In January 1919, thirty-five thousand shipyard workers brought Seattle to a standstill when they went on strike to demand higher wages and shorter work hours. The city's mayor denounced the action as a communist plot to spark an American revolution. With emotions running high, in May 1919, some person or group mailed thirty bombs from New York to various government officials, armed to explode when opened. While only one bomb detonated (blowing off the hand a domestic employee of Georgia Senator Thomas Hardwick), federal officials identified the conspiracy as the work of an alliance between the Bolsheviks and the IWW. Near riots broke out across the country in response to the alleged plot, as mobs attacked those attending mass meetings and rallies of groups identified as radical.[54]

A month later, another bomb severely damaged the home of Attorney General A. Mitchell Palmer. The attorney general was not injured, but was persuaded, despite a lack of evidence, that the culprits were foreign radicals dedicated to overthrowing the government. "If I had my way," popular evangelist Billy Sunday declared, "I'd fill the jails so full of them [Bolsheviks] that their feet would stick out the windows."[55]

Palmer persuaded Congress to appropriate money to investigate and suppress the nation's growing radical movement. In January 1920, with Palmer's permission and under the direction of his twenty-four-year-old aide J. Edgar Hoover, federal agents in thirty major cities stormed union offices and the headquarters of the American communist and socialist parties, arresting about four thousand radicals and aliens. Palmer vowed to deport more than 2,700 of those he arrested. Federal officials deported 591 aliens for their political beliefs and activities. "Out of the sly and crafty eyes of many of them," Palmer said, "leap cupidity, cruelty, insanity, and crime; from their lopsided faces, sloping brows, and misshapen features may be recognized the unmistakable criminal type."[56]

Palmer went too far. Instead of simply investigating and arresting those responsible for the bombings, the Justice Department declared war on much of the nation's radical movement. By the summer of 1920, court challenges ended the deportations and the public's fears of an alien-inspired revolution subsided. But the damage was done. It was one of the darkest chapters in American history. As former Supreme Court Justice Charles Evans Hughes told an audience at Harvard Law School in June 1920, "we may well wonder in view of the precedents now established whether constitutional government as heretofore maintained in this republic could survive another great war even victoriously waged."[57]

EMMA GOLDMAN (1869–1940)

A Lithuanian-born anarchist, Emma Goldman immigrated to the United States with her parents in 1885 and worked in the clothing factories in Rochester, New York. By 1889 she moved to New York City, where she met her eventual companion and political associate, Russian anarchist Alexander Berkman. In 1892, when Berkman shot and wounded an executive of the Carnegie Steel company, Goldman avoided prison, although she had been part of the plot. The next year, however, authorities arrested her for urging unemployed people to steal food. Goldman's radical speeches often earned her scorn, particularly in 1901 when the assassin of President William McKinley claimed that her speeches had influenced his crime.

After Berkman's prison term, he and Goldman began collaborating on Goldman's periodical, Mother Earth, *in which she and others advocated for civil liberties and women's rights. In 1917 her antiwar activities—she spent considerable time on the lecture circuit—earned her prosecution for allegedly obstructing the Conscription Act. A federal judge sentenced her and Berkman to two years in prison. In 1919 U.S. authorities stripped her of citizenship and deported her to Russia.[58]*

PROMOTERS OF THE WAR MANIA
In Mother Earth, *March 1917*

At this most critical moment it becomes imperative for every liberty-loving person to voice a fiery protest against the participation of this country in the European mass murder. If the opponents of war, from the Atlantic to the Pacific, would immediately join their voices into a thunderous No!, then the horror that now menaces America might be yet averted. Unfortunately it is only too true that the people in our so-called Democracy are to a large extent a dumb, suffering herd rather than thinking beings who dare to give expression to a frank, earnest opinion.

Yet it is unthinkable that the American people should really want war. During the last thirty months they have had ample opportunity to watch the frightful carnage in the warring countries. They have seen universal murder, like a devastating pestilence, eat into the very heart of the peoples of Europe. They saw cities destroyed, entire countries wiped off the map, hosts of dead, millions of wounded and maimed. The American people could not help witnessing the spread of insane, motiveless hatred among the peoples of Europe. They must realize the extent of the famine, the suffering and anguish gripping the war-stricken countries. They know, too, that while the men were killed off like vermin, the women and children, the old and the decrepit remained behind in helpless and tragic despair. Why then, in the name of all that is reasonable and humane, should the American people desire the same horrors, the same destruction and devastation upon American soil?

We are told that the "freedom of the seas" is at stake and that "American honor" demands that we protect that precious freedom. What a farce! How much freedom of the seas can the masses of toilers or the disinherited and the unemployed ever enjoy? Would it not be well to look into this magic thing: "the freedom of the seas," before we sing patriotic songs and shout hurrah?

The only ones that have benefitted by the "freedom of the seas" are the exploiters, the dealers in munition and food supplies. The "freedom of the seas" has served these unscrupulous American robbers and monopolists as a pretext to pilfer the unfortunate people of both Europe and America. Out of international carnage they have made billions; out of the misery of the people and the agony of women and children the American financiers and industrial magnates have coined huge fortunes. . . .

President Wilson and other officials of the administration assure us that they want peace. If that claim held even one grain of truth, the government would have long ago carried out the suggestion of many true lovers of people to put a stop to the export of munitions and food stuffs. Had this shameful trade with the implements of slaughter been stopped at the beginning of the war, the good results for peace would have been manifold.

First, the war in Europe would have been starved out through the stoppage of food exports. Indeed, it is no exaggeration when I say that the war would have been at an end long ago had the American financiers been prevented from investing billions in war loans and had the American munition clique and food speculators not been given the opportunity to supply warring Europe with the means to keep up the slaughter.

Second, an embargo on exports would have automatically taken out American ships from the war and submarine zones and would have thus eliminated the much discussed "reason" for war with Germany.

Third, and most important of all, the brazen, artificial increase in the cost of living, which condemns the toiling masses of America to semistarvation, would be an impossibility were not the great bulk of American products shipped to Europe to feed the fires of war. . . .

Militarism and reaction are now more rampant in Europe than ever before. . . . The same is bound to take place in America should the dogs of war be let loose here. Already the poisonous seed has been planted. All the reactionary riffraff, propagandists of jingoism and preparedness, all the beneficiaries of exploitation represented in the Merchants and Manufacturers' Association, the Chambers of Commerce, the munition cliques, etc., etc., have come to the fore with all sorts of plans and schemes to chain and gag labor, to make it more helpless and dumb than ever before. . . .

Hand in hand with this military preparedness and war mania goes the increased persecution of the workers and their organizations. Labor went wild with enthusiasm and gratitude to the President for his supposed humanity in proclaiming the eight-hour law before election, and now it develops that the law was merely a bait for votes and a shackle for labor. It denies the right to strike and introduces compulsory arbitration. Of course it is common knowledge that strikes have long since been made ineffective by antipicketing injunctions and the prosecution of strikers, but the federal eight-hour law is the worst parody on the right to organize and to strike, and it is going to prove an additional fetter on labor. In connection with this arbitrary measure goes the proposition to give the President full power in case of war to take control of the railroads and their employees, which would mean nothing less than absolute subserviency and industrial militarism for the workers. . . .

It is still time to stem the bloody tide of war by word of mouth and pen and action. The promoters of war realize that we have looked into their cards and that we know their crooked, criminal game. We know they want war to increase their profits. Very well, let them fight their own wars. We, the people of America, will not do it for them. Do you think war would then come or be kept up? Oh, I know it is difficult to arouse the workers, to make them see the truth back of the nationalistic, patriotic lie. Still we must do our share. At least we shall be free from blame should the terrible avalanche overtake us in spite of our efforts.[59]

JOHN REED (1887–1920)

A radical poet and war correspondent, John Reed had a passion for covering revolutions. In 1914, as a reporter for Metropolitan Magazine, *Reed covered the Mexican Revolution and followed Pancho Villa's army for more than four months, so ingratiating himself with Villa and his soldiers that the Mexican revolutionary leader reportedly appointed Reed a staff officer with the honorary rank of brigadier general. Reed went next to Europe to cover a war he vehemently opposed, where he reported on the conflict from behind Allied and German lines.*

In 1917 he completed his evolution from radical to revolutionary when he and his wife sailed to Russia to chronicle the Bolshevik Revolution. His friendship with Vladimir I. Lenin and the access that relationship provided resulted in his critically acclaimed account of the revolution, Ten Days that Shook the World. *Reed's communist sympathies earned him a sedition charge in the United States and precluded his return home. Instead, he settled in Russia, where he died of typhus at the age of thirty-three, and was buried in the Kremlin wall, the only American ever accorded that honor.*

WHOSE WAR?
In The Masses, *April 1917*

I know what war means. I have been with the armies of all the belligerents except one, and I have seen men die, and go mad, and lie in hospitals suffering hell; but there is a worse thing than that. War means an ugly mob-madness, crucifying the truth-tellers, choking the artists, side-tracking reforms, revolutions, and the working of social forces. Already in America those citizens who oppose the entrance of their country into the European melee are called "traitors," and those who protest against the curtailing of our meagre [*sic*] rights of free speech are spoken of as "dangerous lunatics." We have had a forecast of the censorship—when the naval authorities in charge of the Sayville wireless cut off American news from Germany, and only the wildest fictions reached Berlin via London, creating a perilous situation. . . . The press is howling for war. The church is howling for war. Lawyers, politicians, stock-brokers, social leaders are all howling for war. . . .

Whose war is this? Not mine. I know that hundreds of thousands of American workingmen employed by our great financial "patriots" are not paid a living wage. I have seen poor men sent to jail for long terms without trial, and even without any charge. Peaceful strikers, and their wives and children, have been shot to death, burned to death, by private detectives and militiamen. The rich have steadily become richer, and the cost of living higher, and the workers proportionally poorer. These toilers don't want war—not even civil war. But the speculators, the employers, the plutocracy— they want it, just as they did in Germany and in England; and with lies and sophistries they will whip up our blood until we are savage—and then we'll fight and die for them.

I am one of a vast number of ordinary people who read the daily papers, and occasionally *The New Republic*, and want to be fair. We don't know much about international politics; but we want our country to keep off the necks of little nations, to refuse to back up American beasts of prey who invest abroad and get their fingers burned, and to stay out of quarrels not our own. We've got an idea that international law is the crystallized common-sense of nations, distilled from their experiences with each other, and that it holds good for all of them, and can be understood by anybody.

We are simple folk. Prussian militarism seemed to us insufferable; we thought the invasion of Belgium a crime; German atrocities horrified us, and also the idea of German submarines exploding ships full of peaceful people without warning. But then we began to hear about England and France jailing, fining, exiling and even shooting men who refused to go out and kill; the Allied armies invaded and seized a part of neutral Greece, and a French admiral forced upon her an ultimatum as shameful as Austria's to Serbia; Russian atrocities were shown to be more dreadful than German; and hidden mines sown by England in the open sea exploded ships full of peaceful people without warning.

Other things disturbed us. For instance, why was it a violation of international law for the Germans to establish a "war-zone" around the British Isles, and perfectly legal for England to close the North Sea? Why is it we submitted to the British order forbidding the shipment of non-contraband to Germany, and insisted upon our right to ship contraband to the Allies? If our "national honor" was smirched by Germany's refusal to allow war materials to be shipped to the Allies, what happened to our national honor when England refused to let us ship non-contraband food and even *Red Cross hospital supplies to Germany*? Why is England allowed to attempt the avowed starvation of German civilians, in violation of international law, when the Germans cannot attempt the same thing without our horrified protest? How is it that the British can arbitrarily regulate our commerce with neutral nations, while we raise a howl whenever the Germans "threaten to restrict our merchant ships going about their business?" Why does our Government insist that Americans should not be molested while traveling on Allied ships armed against submarines? . . .

Those of us who voted for Woodrow Wilson did so because we felt his mind and his eyes were open, because he had kept us out of the mad-dogfight of Europe, and because the plutocracy opposed him. We had learned enough about the war to lose some of our illusions, and we wanted to be neutral. We grant that the President, considering the position he'd got himself into, couldn't do anything else but answer the German note [the Zimmerman telegram] as he did—but if we had been neutral, that note wouldn't have been sent. The President didn't ask us; he won't ask us if we want war or not. The fault is not ours. It is not our war.

ROBERT M. LA FOLLETTE (1855–1925)

A Republican U.S. senator and former three-term governor of Wisconsin, Robert La Follette opposed the 1917 war declaration against Germany and attributed President Woodrow Wilson's support for war to "the glorious group of millionaires who are making such enormous profits" from the conflict. A fearless and visionary progressive—he proposed much of the reform legislation passed in the early years of Wilson's presidency—La Follette endured vicious attacks for his dissent. Former President Theo-dore Roosevelt fumed that he was "an unhung traitor, and if the war should come, he ought to be hung."⁶⁰ In anger, one Senate colleague said La Follette was "pro-German, pretty nearly pro-Goth, and pro-Vandal." A cartoon in the Los Angeles Times *in April 1917—captioned "For services rendered"—pictured the Kaiser awarding La Follette the Iron Cross.⁶¹*

At the end of his Senate speech opposing the war, one observer wrote, La Follette "stood in silence, tears running down his face . . . the grief of this despairing man like that of a person who had failed to keep his child from doing itself irreparable harm." Later, after a reporter misquoted him as having said that "we had no grievance against Germany," two of his Senate colleagues filed petitions calling for his expulsion.⁶²

SPEECH TO THE U.S. SENATE
April 4, 1917

If we are to enter upon this war in the manner the President demands, let us throw pretense to the winds, let us be honest, let us admit that this is a ruthless war against not only Germany's Army and her Navy but against her civilian population as well, and frankly state that the purpose of Germany's hereditary European enemies has become our purpose.

Again, the President says "we are about to accept the gauge of battle with this natural foe of liberty and shall, if necessary, spend the whole force of the nation to check and nullify its pretensions and its power." That much, at least, is clear; that program is definite. The whole force and power of this nation, if necessary, is to be used to bring victory to the Entente Allies,⁶³ and to us as their all in this war. Remember, that not yet has the "whole force" of one of the warring nations been used.

Countless millions are suffering from want and privation; countless other millions are dead and rotting on foreign battlefields; countless other millions are crippled and maimed, blinded, and dismembered; upon all and upon their children's children for generations to come has been laid a burden of debt which must be worked out in poverty and suffering, but the "whole force" of no one of the warring nations has yet been expended; but our "whole force" shall be expended, so says the President. We are pledged by the President, so far as he can pledge us, to make this fair, free, and happy land of ours the same shambles and bottomless pit of horror that we see in Europe today.

Just a word of comment more upon one of the points in the President's address. He says that this is a war "for the things which we have always carried nearest to our hearts—for democracy, for the right of those who submit to authority to have a voice in their own government." In many places throughout the address is this exalted sentiment given expression.

It is a sentiment peculiarly calculated to appeal to American hearts and, when accompanied by acts consistent with it, is certain to receive our support; but in this same connection, and strangely enough, the President says that we have become convinced that the German government as it now exists—"Prussian autocracy" he calls it—can never again maintain friendly relations with us. His expression is that "Prussian autocracy was not and could never be our friend," and repeatedly throughout the address the suggestion is made that if the German people would overturn their government, it would probably be the way to peace. So true is this that the dispatches from London all hailed the message of the President as sounding the death knell of Germany's government.

But the President proposes alliance with Great Britain, which, however liberty-loving its people, is a hereditary monarchy, with a hereditary ruler, with a hereditary House of Lords, with a hereditary landed system, with a limited and restricted suffrage for one class and a multiplied suffrage power for another, and with grinding industrial conditions for all the wageworkers. The President has not suggested that we make our support of Great Britain conditional to her granting home rule to Ireland, or Egypt, or India. We rejoice in the establishment of a democracy in Russia, but it will hardly be contended that if Russia was still an autocratic government, we would not be asked to enter this alliance with her just the same. . . .

Is it not a remarkable democracy which leagues itself with allies already far overmatching in strength the German nation and holds out to such beleaguered nation the hope of peace only at the price of giving up their Government? I am not talking now of the merits or demerits of any government, but I am speaking of a profession of democracy that is linked in action with the most brutal and domineering use of autocratic power. Are the people of this country being so well represented in this war movement that we need to go abroad to give other people control of their governments? Will the President and the supporters of this war bill submit it to a vote of the people before the declaration of war goes into effect? Until we are willing to do that, it ill becomes us to offer as an excuse for our entry into the war the unsupported claim that this war was forced upon the German people by their Government without their knowledge or approval."

Who has registered the knowledge or approval of the American people on the course this Congress is called upon in declaring war upon Germany? Submit the question to the people, you who support it. You who support it dare not do it, for you know that by a vote of more than ten to one the American people as a body would register their declaration against it.

In the sense that this war is being forced upon our people without their knowing why and without their approval, and that wars are usually forced upon all peoples in the same way, there is some truth in the statement; but I venture to say that the response which the German people have made to the demands of this war shows that it has a degree of popular support which the war upon which we are entering has not and never will have among our people. The espionage bills, the conscription bills, and other forcible military measures which we understand are being ground out of the war machine in this country is the complete proof that those responsible for this war fear that it has no popular support and that armies sufficient to satisfy the demand of the Entente Allies can not be recruited by voluntary enlistments.[64]

EUGENE V. DEBS (1855–1926)

A long-time union organizer and former president of the American Railway Union, Eugene Debs was one of the principal founders of the IWW and ran for president five times as the candidate of the Socialist Party of America. A charismatic leader and powerful speaker, Debs converted to socialism while serving a six-month prison term in 1895 for his role in a railway strike. "The issue is Socialism versus Capitalism," Debs said in 1897. "I am for Socialism because I am for humanity. We have been cursed with the reign of gold long enough. Money constitutes no proper basis of civilization." Debs went to prison again in 1919, at age sixty-four, for speaking out against the war in the following speech in Canton, Ohio. President Warren G. Harding ordered Debs and twenty-three other political prisoners released in December 1921.[65]

THE CANTON, OHIO, ANTIWAR SPEECH
June 16, 1918

I have just returned from a visit over yonder, where three of our most loyal comrades are paying the penalty for their devotion to the cause of the working class. They have come to realize, as many of us have, that it is extremely dangerous to exercise the constitutional right of free speech in a country fighting to make democracy safe in the world.

I realize that, in speaking to you this afternoon, there are certain limitations placed upon the right of free speech. I must be exceedingly careful, prudent, as to what I say, and even more careful and prudent as to how I say it. I may not be able to say all I think; but I am not going to say anything that I do not think. I would rather a thousand times be a free soul in jail than to be a sycophant and coward in the streets. They may put those boys in jail—and some of the rest of us in jail—but they can not put the Socialist movement in jail. Those prison bars separate their bodies from ours, but their souls are here this afternoon. They are simply paying the penalty that all men have paid in all the ages of history for standing erect, and for seeking to pave the way to better conditions for mankind. . . .

They tell us that we live in a great free republic; that our institutions are democratic; that we are a free and self-governing people. This is too much, even for a joke. But it is not a subject for levity; it is an exceedingly serious matter.

To whom do the Wall Street Junkers in our country marry their daughters? After they have wrung their countless millions from your sweat, your agony and your life's blood, in a time of war as in a time of peace, they invest these untold millions in the purchase of titles of broken-down aristocrats, such as princes, dukes, counts and other parasites and no-accounts. Would they be satisfied to wed their daughters to honest workingmen? To real democrats? Oh, no! They scour the markets of Europe for vampires who are titled and nothing else. And they swap their millions for the titles, so that matrimony with them becomes literally a matter of money.

These are the gentry who are today wrapped up in the American flag, who shout their claim from the housetops that they are the only patriots, and who have their magnifying glasses in hand, scanning the country for evidence of disloyalty, eager to apply the brand of treason to the men who dare to even whisper their opposition to

Junker rule in the United Sates. No wonder Sam Johnson[66] declared that "patriotism is the last refuge of the scoundrel." He must have had this Wall Street gentry in mind, or at least their prototypes, for in every age it has been the tyrant, the oppressor and the exploiter who has wrapped himself in the cloak of patriotism, or religion, or both to deceive and overawe the people. . . .

They have always taught and trained you to believe it to be your patriotic duty to go to war and to have yourselves slaughtered at their command. But in all the history of the world you, the people, have never had a voice in declaring war, and strange as it certainly appears, no war by any nation in any age has ever been declared by the people.

And here let me emphasize the fact—and it cannot be repeated too often—that the working class who fight all the battles, the working class who make the supreme sacrifices, the working class who freely shed their blood and furnish the corpses, have never yet had a voice in either declaring war or making peace. It is the ruling class that invariably does both. They alone declare war and they alone make peace.

> *Yours not to reason why;*
> *Yours but to do and die.*

That is their motto and we object on the part of the awakening workers of this nation.

If war is right let it be declared by the people. You who have your lives to lose, you certainly above all others have the right to decide the momentous issue of war or peace.[67]

CHAPTER 7

WORLD WAR II

"STOP ASKING FOR WAR"

"THESE ARE OMINOUS DAYS," A SOLEMN PRESIDENT FRANKLIN D. Roosevelt told Congress on May 16, 1940. In Europe, the Battle of France raged. German forces had smashed into Holland, Belgium, and Luxembourg. The Germans were shoving more than three hundred thousand British, French, and Belgian troops toward the English Channel at the French town of Dunkirk. To Roosevelt, these developments meant peril for the United States. "The Atlantic and Pacific oceans were reasonably adequate defensive barriers when fleets under sail could move at an average speed of five miles an hour," the president said, adding that "the new element—air navigation—steps up the speed of possible attack to 200 to 300 miles an hour." In response, Roosevelt asked Congress to drastically increase and modernize the nation's defense capabilities, especially its air force. He set a goal of fifty thousand new airplanes a year.[1] The speech was effective. By week's end, Congress approved everything he asked for—and more.[2]

Not every American agreed. "Our danger in America is an internal danger," Charles Lindbergh, the legendary aviator, told a nationwide radio audience several days later. "We need not fear a foreign invasion unless American peoples bring it on through their own quarrelling and meddling with affairs abroad." Without naming Roosevelt, Lindbergh attacked "this hysterical chatter of calamity and invasion." Peace required only that the nation "stop asking for war. No one wishes to attack us, and no one is in a position to do so."[3] To Democratic Senator Bennett Champ Clark of Missouri, Lindbergh's speech was "magnificent." Democratic Representative John Rankin of Mississippi called it "the finest advice I have heard in many a day."[4] In his speech to Congress, Roosevelt cited a "Fifth Column" of subversives threatening the nation. Reacting to Lindbergh's speech, Representative George Holden of Massachusetts praised the aviator for "expos[ing] the American 'Fifth Column' who are using every energy and art to have the United States enter the war in Europe or Asia."[5]

Lindbergh was the nation's most prominent spokesman for Americans opposed to U.S. participation in the European war. Since 1935, these Americans had pushed Congress to enact a series of neutrality laws to keep the United States out of the war. This "isolationist" legislation reflected the popular view, most prevalent in the Midwest, that loans and trade with the Allies had drawn the nation into

World War I. "Do what we might," Republican Senator William Borah of Idaho said in 1939 during debate over the repeal of the arms embargo legislation," it seemed clear to the people of this country . . . that it was not within our power to right the wrongs of that continent . . . as had been hoped and prayed for when we entered the World War."[6]

"This is a war over the balance of power in Europe," Lindbergh told a national radio audience in October 1939, a month before Congress helped a beleaguered Great Britain by substituting the arms embargo with a cash-and-carry program.[7] Lindbergh's speeches infuriated Roosevelt. "If I should die tomorrow," he told a Cabinet member in May 1939, "I want you to know this. I am convinced Lindbergh is a Nazi."[8] Lindbergh further angered Roosevelt in September when he questioned American military strength. "We are on the verge of a war for which we are still unprepared, and for which no one has offered a feasible plan for victory—a war which cannot be won without sending our soldiers across the ocean to force a landing on a hostile coast against armies stronger than our own."[9]

At a press conference in April 1941, Roosevelt seemed to compare Lindbergh to Clement Vallandigham, the Ohio congressman and leader of the Civil War–era Copperheads. Without using Lindbergh's name, the president said, "There are some people in this country . . . [who] say out of one side of the mouth, 'No, I don't like it. I don't like dictatorship,' and then out of the other side of the mouth, 'Well, it's going to beat democracy, it's going to defeat democracy, therefore I might as well accept it.' Now, I don't call that good Americanism."[10]

For some time, public opinion had appeared to be with Lindbergh and other isolationists. From early 1940 through March 1941, public support for war with Germany was never above 20 percent. In fact, because of its bellicose rhetoric and aggressive actions in the Pacific, Japan sparked far more public outrage. In November 1941, just prior to the Japanese attacks on U.S. naval forces at Pearl Harbor, more than 70 percent of Americans polled were willing to risk war with Japan. Only 30 percent were willing to go war against Germany.[11] For Roosevelt, however, the struggle was not to prod the nation to war, but to persuade Congress to help Britain.[12] Standing foursquare against more help for England was the America First Committee, with sixty thousand members who believed defending American democracy required staying out of the war and strengthening national defenses. Roosevelt took to the radio airwaves in December 1940 to argue for his lend-lease proposal and directly rebutted the arguments of his isolationist opponents:

> These people not only believe that we can save our own skins by shutting our eyes to the fate of other nations. Some of them go much further than that. They say that we can and should become the friends and even the partners of the Axis powers. Some of them even suggest that we should imitate the methods of the dictatorships. Americans never can and never will do that.
>
> The experience of the past two years has proven beyond doubt that no nation can appease the Nazis. No man can tame a tiger into a kitten by stroking it. There can be no appeasement with ruthlessness. There can be no reasoning with an incendiary bomb. We know now that a nation can have peace with the Nazis only at the price of total surrender.[13]

Fighting Roosevelt's lend-lease proposal in a speech two days later, Democratic Senator Burton Wheeler of Montana argued that peace would come, in any event. "At some time [England and Germany] will sit around a table," he said in a radio address. "Some time they will agree upon peace, and until that day the world suffers." In the meantime, he said, "America's war ought to be a war against industrial unemployment and low farm prices."[14]

As Nazi Germany conquered much of Europe, leaving Great Britain exposed as one of America's last lines of defense, Roosevelt and his congressional allies moved to eliminate or modify the nation's neutrality laws, finally repealing them in November 1941, less than a month before the Japanese attack on Pearl Harbor. As the nation gradually shed its neutrality, Roosevelt became more combative with the isolationists. Moreover, he and others lost some of their tolerance for dissent.

In the years since the government's appalling lack of regard for civil liberties and free speech during and after World War I, many Americans had adopted, in the words of legal scholar Geoffrey R. Stone, "a more expansive view of free expression." Passionate public debate over a wide range of issues, including Prohibition, women's rights, evolution, labor reform, and federal economic and social reforms, Stone observed, "gradually fostered a new social awareness and a heightened understanding of the earlier suppression of dissent."[15] In addition, the Supreme Court, which had upheld the attacks on civil liberties during World War I, began adopting a broader interpretation of free speech. As Justice Louis Brandeis wrote in an opinion in 1927, "public discussion is a political duty . . . [and] should be a fundamental principle of the American government."[16]

Many Americans now realized what historian Henry Steele Commager argued in a *New York Times* article in April 1939, "The heritage of intolerance and lawlessness which such [World War I–era] legislation left us did infinite injury to the cause of democracy, for which the war was ostensibly fought."[17] While not eager to repeat that repression, Roosevelt was not among the enthusiastic champions of civil liberties, especially during wartime. In 1936, responding to complaints by the American Civil Liberties Union (ACLU) about military intelligence investigations into the activities of pacifist and leftist organizations, Roosevelt argued that some groups "disseminate false information and false teaching which are contrary to our democratic ideals and the objectives of a republican form of government."[18] Undoubtedly adding to Roosevelt's ire was his critics' incendiary and anti-Semitic attacks. Referring to the November 1940 presidential election in which voters reelected Roosevelt to an unprecedented third term, Lindbergh said in May 1941, "We had no more chance to vote on the issue of peace and war last November than if we had been in a totalitarian state ourselves."[19]

Shortly after Lindbergh's statement, in a radio fireside chat to the nation, Roosevelt went on the attack, without naming Lindbergh and his allies in Congress:

There is, of course, a small group of sincere, patriotic men and women whose real passion for peace has shut their eyes to the ugly realities of international banditry and to the need to resist it at all costs. I am sure they are embarrassed by the sinister support they are receiving from the enemies of democracy in our midst—the Bundists, the Fascists, and Communists, and every group devoted to bigotry and racial and religious intolerance. . . . Those same words have been used before in other countries—to scare them, to divide them, to soften them up. Invariably, those same words have formed the advance guard of physical attack. . . . Your Government has the right to expect of all citizens that they take part in the common work of our common defense, take loyal part from this moment forward.[20]

How would Roosevelt ensure the loyalty of the nation's citizens? In June 1940 he had signed the Alien Registration Act (also known as the Smith Act), legislation that restricted the free speech of every American. It required not only the registration of aliens and streamlined the deportation process, but made it a crime for "any person" to advocate the government's overthrow or to "urge, or in any manner cause insubordination, disloyalty, mutiny, or refusal of duty by any member of the military." Furthermore, it prohibited distribution of "any written or printed matter which . . . urges insubordination, disloyalty . . . by any member of the military."[21]

It was not just Roosevelt and his administration that intimidated dissenters and suppressed free speech. Some prominent liberals proclaimed the threats of communism and Fascism were too serious to permit unfettered speech. The liberal publication, the *New Republic*, advocated an investigation of the America First organization for "waging war against the whole American democratic heritage." Liberal journalist Dorothy Thompson, expelled from Germany in 1934, advocated suspending the Bill of Rights for the duration of the war. Freedoms of speech and assembly, she told a large gathering in New York, "were the very instruments by which the Nazis came to power."[22]

Liberals who wanted to suspend civil liberties had no reason to worry that Roosevelt or Congress would go soft on "subversive" organizations. The House Un-American Activities Committee, created in 1938 and chaired by Congressman Martin Dies of Texas, took seriously its charge to investigate "the extent, character and objects of un-American propaganda activities in the United States." While it first went after members of the pro-Nazi German-American Bund, it eventually devoted more attention to recklessly identifying various groups—including the Boy Scouts and the Camp Fire Girls—as "Communistic" organizations. Dies's committee even found communist sympathies in Roosevelt's cabinet, demanding the resignation of Interior Secretary Harold Ickes and Labor Secretary Frances Perkins for subversive tendencies. In 1941 the committee asserted that 1,121 federal employees were "either communists or affiliates of subversive organizations" and that there were "six million Communist and Nazi sympathizers" the United States. Although an FBI investigation turned up nothing of consequence, a frightened public generally supported the committee. The committee was not hunting alone for subversives. Since 1936, on orders from Roosevelt, the Federal Bureau of Investigation (FBI) had investigated people suspected of fascist or communist beliefs. This included, FBI Director J. Edgar Hoover told his agents, "the distribution of literature . . . opposed to the American way of life."[23]

It was the devastating December 7, 1941, attack on Pearl Harbor by the Japanese that ended isolationism in the United States. "American soil has been treacherously attacked by Japan," former President Herbert Hoover, a prominent isolationist declared. "Our decision is clear. It is forced upon us. We must fight with everything we have." Prominent isolationist Republican Senator Arthur Vandenberg of

Michigan called the White House and told an aide to tell Roosevelt that "he would support him without reservation." Even Republican Representative Hamilton Fish of New York, among the most implacable critics of Roosevelt and his war policies, asked the public "to present a united front in support of the President."[24] Overnight, public opinion shifted. With only the dissenting vote of Representative Jeanette Rankin of Montana (the only member of Congress to have also voted against war in 1917), Congress quickly declared war on Japan and, days later, on Germany.

At the Justice Department, Attorney General Robert Jackson resolved to prevent a recurrence of the repression of World War I. Appointed by Roosevelt in 1940, Jackson promptly prohibited prosecution of individuals for "so-called 'subversive activity.'" He forbade prosecutions on matters of speech or opinion. Next, he created a Neutrality Laws Division and ordered no arrests by federal agents for suspected internal security violations without the approval of the new division. Jackson also worked to ensure that state and local governments would not prosecute internal security cases, as many had during World War I.[25]

In time, however, Jackson succumbed to intense pressure from Roosevelt and members of Congress who demanded a more vigorous fight against internal subversion. He could not prevent passage of the 1940 Smith Act and its great potential for repression. Given the domestic concern that followed Germany's sudden invasion of much of Western Europe in the fall of 1939 and the spring of 1940, Jackson's commitment to civil liberties appeared, to some, a quaint relic of the past. In the heat of the moment, Congress had overwhelmingly, in the words of one historian, "put into the statute books the peacetime anti-sedition act that A. Mitchell Palmer [Woodrow Wilson's attorney general] had sought in vain."[26]

When Roosevelt appointed Jackson to the Supreme Court in 1940, Solicitor General Francis Biddle, an ACLU member devoted to free-speech rights, became acting attorney general and later won the job permanently. Like Jackson, Biddle wanted to avoid repeating the mistakes of World War I. A week after Pearl Harbor, in a speech commemorating the 152nd anniversary of the Bill of Rights, Biddle recalled "periods of gross abuse, when hysteria and fear and hate ran high, and minorities were unlawfully and cruelly abused." Calling for tolerance, he added, "Every man . . . who cares about freedom must fight [to protect it] for the *other* man with whom he disagrees."[27] Biddle told U.S. attorneys they could not prosecute individuals for "alleged seditious utterances" without his consent. Biddle backed up his words. When federal officials arrested several men in Los Angeles for allegedly praising Hitler and Imperial Japan and calling for Roosevelt's impeachment, Biddle dropped the charges.[28]

Like Jackson before him, Biddle's expansive view of the First Amendment angered Roosevelt and some in Congress. Biddle later said that Roosevelt "was not much interested in the theory of sedition, or in the constitutional right to criticize the government in wartime. He wanted this anti-war talk stopped." Biddle recalled that at a cabinet meeting, a stern-faced Roosevelt turned to him and said, "When are you going to indict the seditionists?" A frustrated president would fire the same question at Biddle for weeks. Finally, in January 1942, Roosevelt asked FBI Director J. Edgar Hoover to handle the matter, particularly the case of William Dudley Pelley. Once a successful novelist and screenwriter, Pelley turned to mysticism and fascism in the early 1930s, forming a fascist organization, the Silver Legion of

America, and publishing a weekly newsletter in which he attacked Jews for, among other things, causing the Great Depression. He also praised the German regime, arguing, in 1935, "the time has come for an American Hitler."[29] Roosevelt believed that Pelley's writing came "pretty close to being seditious." To Roosevelt it seemed that "now that we are in the war, it looks like a good chance to clean up a number of . . . vile publications."[30] In March 1942, Pelley wrote in his publication, the *Galilean*, that Roosevelt had deceived the American people by claiming the Pacific fleet had largely survived the attack on Pearl Harbor. Indeed, Pelley's evaluation was accurate, a fact that the government concealed from the American public until after the war. Roosevelt's anger over Pelley's assertion boiled over in April when he confronted Biddle again with the pointed question, "When are you going to indict the seditionists?" Finally, Biddle relented.[31]

In February 1942, federal authorities ordered Pelley to submit all new issues of his magazine to U.S. Post Office officials for review. Pelley, instead, stopped publishing the *Galilean*. On April 4, FBI agents caught up with Pelley in Connecticut, arresting him on charges of seditious activities under the 1917 Espionage Act. The government's case relied on the very flimsy evidence of a single copy of the *Galilean* found in a soldier's duffle bag. Pelley's trial that summer, marred by an incompetent defense, ended in a conviction on eleven counts of sedition and an eleven-year prison sentence.[32]

Pelley's indictment and trial did little to quell the appetite for a more vigorous attack on internal subversion and sedition. *Life*, read by millions of Americans every week, amplified the public demand for a more muscular federal crackdown on seditious speech with a prominent article in April 1942, "Voices of Defeat." The article quoted Ellis O. Jones, the "self-styled chief of the National Copperheads," "The Japanese have a right to Hawaii. . . . I would rather be in the war on the side of Germany than on the side of the British." The magazine also quoted Robert Noble, a Copperhead leader who reportedly claimed, "I am for the Axis powers because they are the liberators of the world." *Life* provided examples of what it considered seditious speech by American citizens across the country, in Southern California, Chicago, Detroit, the Midwest, New York City, and Boston.

Much of the criticism of the war and Roosevelt quoted by *Life* was, by the magazine's own admission, "crackpot talk." Nonetheless, the article noted that "in time of war, especially an all-out war for national existence, crackpots who spread enemy propaganda are a dangerous luxury." Among those quoted were the group, We, The Mothers, Mobilize for America Inc., which boasted of fifteen thousand members in thirty-two states. The national president of the organization, Lyrl Van Hyning, stressed the privations of war. "Your automobiles are being taken away from you—that means you are going back to peasantry." Lease-Lend to America, based in Chicago, was singled out for promoting "negotiated peace" with the Axis powers and for holding "'peace meetings' all over Chicago." The most prominent "voice of defeat" in Chicago, however, was Colonel Robert R. McCormick, publisher of the *Chicago Tribune*, who advocated Roosevelt's impeachment.

Among the article's other major targets were Pelley and Father Charles E. Coughlin, a well-known Catholic priest from Detroit who had gained fame in the early 1930s with his nationwide radio broadcasts attacking the New Deal and the labor movement. At his zenith, Coughlin's Sunday afternoon radio sermons commanded an audience estimated at as many as forty million.[33] Eventually, however, Coughlin's message turned ugly and anti-Semitic, first in his newspaper, *Social Justice*, and then on his radio show. Coughlin argued the Jews were to blame for the war in Europe. "Soon nine years will have elapsed since a worldwide 'sacred war' was declared on Germany, not by the U.S., not by Great Britain, not by France, not by any nation, but by the race of Jews." While *Life* never made a credible case for why the "crackpot" voices were a danger to American security, it ended its lengthy expose with this call to action, "All that is really required are spontaneous demands by local citizens and their patriotic organizations upon their public officials to silence these discordant voices of defeat."[34]

The article had its intended impact. In late April, Attorney General Biddle announced that his department would begin convening grand juries to investigate many of the individuals identified by *Life* and those in a separate investigation by the *Washington Post*. The inquiry, he said, would begin in Chicago and continue by weekly intervals in other cities where the alleged seditionists lived. In July, Biddle announced indictments of twenty-eight prominent pro-German fascists—many of them targets of the *Life* article. He charged them with attempting to undermine the morale of armed forces personnel, in violation of the Espionage Act of 1917 and the Smith Act of 1940. The Justice Department said the group engaged in "the systematic campaign of personal vilification and defamation of public officials of the United States."[35]

The public and the press appeared generally to support the prosecutions. Calling them "morale indictments," *Newsweek* said the case "constituted a warning from the Justice Department that it was going to quit fooling" and end its "easygoing course." There was also skepticism and criticism. The *New York Daily News*, long an opponent of Roosevelt's war policy, gingerly suggested "the newspapers of the nation watch these trials closely" because they "may be aimed at setting some precedents." More vexed was the *Christian Century*, "To whom does the Constitution contain guarantees of freedom of speech, press and assemblage if not to unpopular minorities and even to fools, so long as they confine their activities to the expression of opinion?"[36]

The November congressional elections saw many of Roosevelt's fiercest critics, some of them former isolationists, elected to Congress in a lopsided election in which Republicans gained forty-four seats in the House and seven in the Senate. Emboldened, Roosevelt's detractors saw the indictments and impending trials as the president's attempt to silence his critics, which was largely the case. Republican Senator Robert Taft of Ohio, an isolationist before the war, declared that the case resembled the "'witch hunting' of the first war, except that this witch hunt is more dangerous, more calculated and vicious than that of '17."[37] Another former isolationist, Republican Senator Gerald P. Nye of North Dakota, told the Senate that the defendants "are no more guilty of conspiracy than I am."[38] Senator Burton K. Wheeler—enraged that grand jury witnesses were apparently asked if they knew the Montana Democrat—responded by suggesting that he and several other senators might demand an investigation of the Justice Department.[39]

In January 1943, the Justice Department indicted five new defendants, bringing the total of alleged seditionists to thirty-three. Arrested and brought to Washington to await trial, the group waited for almost two years. When the trial finally opened in the spring of 1944, it devolved into a circus. The rowdy defendants routinely interrupted the trial with moans, groans, and laughter. One day, they mocked the proceedings by wearing Halloween masks.[40]

Further undermining the trial was a series of Supreme Court rulings that expanded free-speech rights and suggested that, even if successful, the department's case would not survive an appeal. In the 1943 case *Schneiderman v. United States*, the court rejected the government's practice of denaturalizing an American citizen because of his membership in the Communist Party unless there was proof that the individual had endorsed "present violent action which creates a clear and present danger." The following year, in *Baumgartner v. United States*, the court expanded on the *Schneiderman* ruling and ended the government's program to denaturalize former members of the German-American Bund. In a 1943 case, *Taylor v. Mississippi*, the Court overturned a Mississippi law that made it a felony to "preach, teach, or disseminate any teachings . . . [or] set of alleged principles . . . designed and calculated to encourage violence, sabotage, or disloyalty to the government of the United States, or the state of Mississippi."[41]

In *Hartzel v. United States*, justices in 1944 overturned the conviction of a virulent anti-Semite who had written, among other things, that only a German victory would bring "increased stability and safety for the West." Writing for the majority, Justice Owen Roberts argued, "an American citizen has the right to discuss these matters either by temperate reasoning or by immoderate and vicious invective without running afoul of the Espionage Act of 1917."[42] Perhaps the most decisive Court decision in this realm was the 1943 case *West Virginia State Board of Education v. Barnette*, in which the Court ruled that school districts could not force students to pledge allegiance to the flag. Overturning a 1940 decision, the Court's majority said, "If there is any fixed star in our constitutional constellation, it is that no official, high or petty, can prescribe what shall be orthodox in politics, nationalism, religion, or other matters of opinion or force citizens to confess by word or act their faith therein.[43]

Despite these setbacks, the Justice Department persisted with its sedition case— even after the trial judge died in December 1944, causing a mistrial, and after the Supreme Court overturned the convictions of twenty-four German-American Bund leaders charged with advising the organization's members to evade the draft. Even Biddle's departure as attorney general in June 1945 did not immediately affect the case, as the new attorney general, Thomas Clark, initially refused to dismiss the charges, despite the war's end.

Finally, with Nazism defeated and the cold war dawning, the Justice Department turned its attention to fighting the suspected international communist conspiracy. The Justice Department dismissed charges against the American Nazis in December 1946. While Roosevelt and compliant Justice Department officials had waged war on free speech, their attacks and repressive actions were nothing compared to the outrageous abuses of a previous generation. Congress, for wise and sometimes politically expedient reasons, usually resisted efforts to pass tougher antisedition laws. Most important, the Supreme Court, in issuing a series of important rulings in 1943 and 1944, established and expanded free-speech rights. "In the end," as one historian of the era concluded, "the system worked, though just barely."[44]

WILLIAM E. BORAH (1865–1940)

Often labeled as isolationist, William Borah's opposition to U.S. participation in the European conflict was more complex than simple isolationism. He believed in economic engagement with other nations, but was deeply suspicious of military alliances. A respected progressive Republican senator from Idaho who served as Senate Foreign Relations Committee chair from 1925 to 1933, Borah opposed the League of Nations treaty in 1919 and was a prime mover behind the "Outlawry of War" international treaty in the late 1920s. Borah and several Senate colleagues—primarily Burton K. Wheeler of Montana, Gerald Nye of North Dakota, and Hiram Johnson of California—were the leading congressional opponents of American entry into the European war. As demonstrated in the following speech, Borah and his colleagues believed it was folly to embroil the United States in the incessant conflicts and sly diplomatic maneuverings of Europe. Unlike his colleagues, Borah did not live to see his anti-interventionist views repudiated by the December 1941 Japanese attack on Pearl Harbor. He died in January 1940.[45]

SPEECH TO THE U.S. SENATE
October 2, 1939

When this Nation solemnly resolved and wrote into its laws that it would never again furnish arms, munitions, and implements of war to any nation engaged in war [the Neutrality Act of 1935] it was almost universally believed that not only here but abroad we had marked an epoch in the cause of peace, that we had offered a challenge to the reign of force which would in time break its hold on the people of the world.

When 130,000,000 people—taken as a whole the most enlightened in the world—with their code of free press, free speech, and personal liberty, not in groups but to all, incorporated in their code of freedom and humanity the pledge never again to furnish warring nations the instrumentalities of mass murder it was hoped, and by millions believed, that the cause of peace had received a most substantial and permanent advance. The only question was, Could we hold our ground? The only element of doubt among those who realized how soon and how powerfully our policy would be assailed was, Could we maintain our position in time of test and trial?

When we as a nation took this position and declared our policy, there was great unanimity among all our people. The Congress, the Executive, and the people were practically in accord to the effect that we would close our markets to all arms for belligerent nations.

Why was the law enacted? What was it which gave support and direction to its enactment? Doubtless different reasons appealed to different persons. Two outstanding reasons held sway with practically all our people. First, we wanted to keep out of and remain aloof from the controversies, embroilments, and wars of the Old World. We had had our experience. We had suffered greatly in the European cause, and from the highest motives, without accomplishing anything substantial in the cause of peace.

We had observed that after the great war Europe had slipped back, as evidenced by the Versailles Treaty and by the current history of Europe, to the ways and the deeds of Europe through the centuries. Do what we might, it seemed clear to the people of this country—it seemed conclusive—that it was not within our power to right the wrongs of that continent, to wipe out its racial bitterness and religious persecutions, to adjust with satisfaction its boundary lines, or to bring happiness and contentment to the masses, as had been hoped and prayed for when we entered the World War. Our task, it seemed to us all, was to maintain liberty, freedom, and free institutions upon the western continent. By doing so we could render greater service to humanity everywhere than by joining in Europe's wars and taking part in her everlasting imperial contests.

We felt that a step in this direction was to embargo arms, to give neither encouragement, nor help, nor moral support, nor means to carry on European wars.

Arms are the source of conflict. They are the symbol of war, the cause of fear and hatred. We were not to place ourselves in a position in which bitterness and retaliation might be engendered, or millions might be slaughtered by means of instruments furnished by a nation professing peace.

There was another moving cause, a cause which permeated our legislative halls and doubtless had its effect upon our executive department. It was a deep humanitarian sentiment against manufacturing and selling to warring nations, for profit, arms with which they might destroy one another. We do not now hear so much about that sentiment, because war is abroad. Nevertheless, I venture to say that it is well implanted in the hearts of the American people this day. The question was constantly presented to the minds and thoughts of our people, Shall this Nation, with all its professions of peace and its Christian teachings, manufacture and sell, purely for gain, vast armaments fit only for the destruction of human life? . . .

Has not the law worked? One of the prime purposes of the enactment of the law was to prevent the sale of arms and munitions to people engaged in war. Has it not accomplished that end? Are we or not preventing the sale of arms, munitions, and implements of war to the warring nations? The Neutrality Act is now the law of the land. It is being enforced by the Chief Executive. The proclamations have gone forth; and no arms, munitions, or implements of war are going to the warring nations of Europe. Has not the law worked in that respect. Was not that one of the prime objects? . . .

We are not here today to repeal the embargo law because of any injury it is doing to the people of the United States. We are here seeking to repeal it because certain nations feel that they want the arms and munitions; yet that is the very reason why we passed the law, to see that neither they nor anyone else got them. Is it working? If it were not working, they would not be complaining. It is the fact that it is working that causes the complaint.[46]

CHARLES LINDBERGH (1902–1974)

The first person to complete a solo, nonstop trans-Atlantic airplane flight, Charles Lindbergh became an international celebrity after his historic feat in 1927. By the late 1930s, he was still America's most respected aviator and had gained considerable knowledge about German air power after several high-profile visits to prewar Germany. When he returned to the United States, he became the leading spokesman for the isolationist (and anti-Semitic) America First Committee and trumpeted its opposition to American participation in the European war.

Lindbergh argued that instead of joining the fight in Europe—a war he believed American might not win—the wiser course was to strengthen the nation's defenses and therefore eliminate the likelihood of German attack. A Congressional Medal of Honor recipient, Lindbergh tried to enlist in the military after the Japanese attacks on Pearl Harbor, but President Roosevelt—who considered Lindbergh a Nazi sympathizer—objected. Lindbergh later flew several combat missions in the Pacific theater as a civilian consultant. In the following excerpt, Lindbergh testifies before the U.S. House Foreign Affairs Committee and answers questions from a senior committee member, Democratic Representative Luther Johnson of Texas.[47]

TESTIMONY ON THE LEND-LEASE BILL
Committee on Foreign Affairs, U.S. House, January 23, 1941

Our position is greatly strengthened for defense and greatly weakened for attack. I base this statement upon two facts. First, that an invading army and its supplies must still be transported by sea. Second, that aviation makes it more difficult than ever before for a navy to approach a hostile shore.

In support of these facts, I cite, for the first, the minute carrying capacity of aircraft in relation to the weight of equipment and supplies required for a major expeditionary force; and for the second, the experience of the British Navy off the Norwegian coast and in the North Sea.

I do not believe there is any danger of an invasion of this continent, either by sea or by air, as long as we maintain an Army, Navy, and Air Force of reasonable size and in modern condition, and provided we establish the bases essential for defense. . . .

There has never been an invasion of enemy territory by air alone. The two outstanding examples of what might be called a partial air invasion were furnished by the German occupations of Norway and Holland. But in each of these instances, the landing of troops by air was carried on simultaneously with a ground army invasion on a major scale. The maximum number of troops that could have been transported and supplied by air would have been ineffective without the immediate support of a ground army. If air invasion alone could be successful, it would have been used by the Germans against England many months ago.

It is important to note that the transport of troops by air in Europe has been over a distance of a few hundred miles at most. An air invasion across the ocean is, I believe, absolutely impossible at this time, or in any predictable future. To be effective in America, enemy aircraft would have to operate from bases in America, and those bases would have to be established and supplied by sea. Aircraft alone are not capable of carrying a sufficient quantity of material. . . . The cost of transoceanic bombing would be extremely high, enemy losses would be large, and the effect on our military position negligible. Such bombing could not begin to prepare the way for an invasion of this continent. . . .

MR. [LUTHER] JOHNSON: You also said . . . that the war that has broken out in Europe was a war over the balance of power in Europe. You used that expression?

LINDBERGH: I believe it is primarily; yes.

JOHNSON: And you also used the language that it was just a quarrel within the family of nations?

LINDBERGH: Not just, sir. I said it was a quarrel.

JOHNSON: A quarrel?

LINDBERGH: Right.

JOHNSON: You did not in any of those speeches express any opinion as to being with one belligerent or the other, or one set of belligerents or the other?

LINDBERGH: No.

MR. JOHNSON: Have you ever done that?

LINDBERGH: No, sir; I have not. I believe the fault of the war is about evenly divided in Europe, and the causes of it.

JOHNSON: Which side do you want to win?

LINDBERGH: I prefer to see neither side win. I would like to see a negotiated peace. I believe a complete victory on either side would result in prostration in Europe such as we have never seen.

JOHNSON: You have no desire one way or the other. Naturally, in every contest, we have a feeling for one side or the other, but you have none; you are absolutely neutral?

LINDBERGH: I feel it would be better for us, and for every nation in Europe, to have this war end without a conclusive victory.

JOHNSON: I was not asking you about that.

LINDBERGH: I am sorry, sir, I must have missed your question.

JOHNSON: Your feelings about this war are on which side? Which side are you on?

LINDBERGH: On neither side, except our own.

JOHNSON: Do you think it would be to the best interests of the United States for Hitler to be defeated?

LINDBERGH: No. I think a negotiated peace would be to the best interests of this country, sir.

JOHNSON: What kind of a negotiated peace?

LINDBERGH: That would have to depend upon negotiations.

JOHNSON: That would depend upon Mr. Hitler at this time, his will, would it not?

LINDBERGH: Partially.

JOHNSON: Entirely, since he is in control, would it not?

LINDBERGH: No; I do not believe so, sir. Negotiation implies discussion from two standpoints.

JOHNSON: What two standpoints?

LINDBERGH: Both sides of the war, sir.

JOHNSON: One side does not have much voice in the terms of peace when they are on the bottom, do they?

LINDBERGH: That has been one of my concerns, sir, from the time that this war was first considered. I believe that negotiation becomes more and more difficult and the British position more and more desperate. That is one of the reasons I believe in a negotiated peace.

JOHNSON: You are not, then, in sympathy with England's efforts to defeat Hitler?

LINDBERGH: I am in sympathy with the people on both sides, but I think that it would be disadvantageous for England herself, if a conclusive victory is sought.

JOHNSON: I think you are evading the question—not intentionally; but the question is very simple, whether or not you are in sympathy with England's defense against Hitler?

LINDBERGH: I am in sympathy with the people and not with their aims.

JOHNSON: You do not think that it is to the best interests of the United States economically as well as in the matter of defense for England to win?

LINDBERGH: No, sir. I think that a complete victory, as I say, would mean prostration in Europe, and would be one of the worst things that could happen there and here.

JOHNSON: Do you think the fall and the destruction of the British Empire would menace the United States in her defense against attack?

LINDBERGH: Not seriously.

JOHNSON: Not seriously?

LINDBERGH: No, sir.

JOHNSON: It would be just a small matter?

LINDBERGH: I believe this Nation is in itself impregnable, sir, if we maintain reasonable forces.

JOHNSON: If the representatives of the Army and Navy—and I understood you to say a little while ago you deferred to their judgment on matters with which they are familiar—if they thought it was dangerous to the United States for the British Navy to fall, would that change your opinion?

LINDBERGH: Most of the representatives of the Army and Navy that I know, sir, are not of that opinion.

JOHNSON: I think we have had some contacts with some of those representatives that are of that opinion, Colonel Lindbergh.

LINDBERGH: I am sorry, sir; I disagree.

JOHNSON: You think the United States has no interest whatever in the outcome of the war?

LINDBERGH: I did not say that, sir. I believe we have an interest in the outcome of the war.

JOHNSON: On which side?

LINDBERGH: In a negotiated peace; we have the greatest interest.

JOHNSON: Peace is in the future. I am talking about a contest that is going on now. You do not think we will be affected by the result of the war one way or the other?

LINDBERGH: I think we are very much affected by the result of the war.

JOHNSON: Which side would it be to our interest to win?

LINDBERGH: Neither.[48]

ROBERT M. HUTCHINS (1899–1977)

The iconoclastic president and chancellor of the University of Chicago from 1929 to 1945, Robert Hutchins was one of the nation's most prominent and controversial educational leaders. He became dean of Yale Law School only two years after receiving his law degree. At age thirty he took over the University of Chicago and began a radical overhaul of the school's undergraduate curriculum that emphasized a classics-based humanities education. Although a pacifist, Hutchins served as an ambulance driver in Italy during World War I. As World War II approached, Hutchins was outspoken in his opposition to American involvement, but later his strong sense of patriotic duty led him to marshal his university's resources to support the war, which included the testing—the earliest controlled nuclear chain reaction—that led to the development of the atomic bomb. In 1954 Hutchins took over the Ford Foundation's Fund for the Republic, an institution dedicated to protecting civil liberties.[49]

THE PATH TO WAR—WE ARE DRIFTING INTO SUICIDE
National Radio Address, January 23, 1941

I speak tonight because I believe that the American people are about to commit suicide. We are not planning to. We have no plan. We are drifting into suicide. Deafened by martial music, fine language, and large appropriations, we are drifting into war.

I address you simply as an American citizen. I do not represent any organization or committee. I do not represent the University of Chicago. I am not a military expert. It is true that from the age of eighteen to the age of twenty I was a private in the American Army. I must have somewhere the very fine medal given me by the Italian government of that day in token of my cooperation on the Italian front. But this experience would not justify me in discussing tactics, strategy, or the strength to which our armed forces should now attain.

I wish to dissociate myself from all Nazis, Fascists, Communists and appeasers. I regard the doctrine of all totalitarian regimes as wrong in theory, evil in execution, and incompatible with the rights of man.

I wish to dissociate myself from those who want us to stay out of war to save our own skins or our own property. I believe that the people of this country are and should be prepared to make sacrifices for humanity. National selfishness should not determine national policy.

It is impossible to listen to Mr. Roosevelt's recent speeches, to study the lease-lend bill, and to read the testimony of cabinet officers upon it without coming to the conclusion that the President now requires us to underwrite a British victory and apparently a Chinese and a Greek victory, too. We are going to try to produce the victory by supplying our friends with the materials of war. But what if this is not enough? We have abandoned all pretense of neutrality. We are to turn our ports into British naval bases. But what if this is not enough? Then we must send the Navy, the Air Force, and, if Mr. Churchill wants it, the Army. We must guarantee the victory. . . .

I have supported Mr. Roosevelt since he first went to the White House. I have never questioned his integrity or his good will. But under the pressure of great responsibilities, in the heat of controversy, in the international game of bluff, the President's speeches and recommendations are committing us to obligations abroad which we cannot perform. The effort to perform them will prevent the achievement of the aims for which the President stands at home.

If we go to war, what are we going to war for? This is to be a crusade, a holy war. Its object is moral. We are seeking, the President tells us, "a world founded on freedom of speech, freedom of worship, freedom, from want, and freedom from fear." We are to intervene to support the moral order. We are to fight for "the supremacy of human rights everywhere."

With the President's desire to see freedom of speech, freedom of worship, freedom from want, and freedom from fear flourish everywhere we must all agree. Millions of Americans have supported the President because they felt that he wanted to achieve these four freedoms for America. Others, who now long to carry these blessings to the rest of the world, were not conspicuous on the firing line when Mr. Roosevelt called them, eight years ago, to do battle for the four freedoms at home. But let us agree now that we want the four freedoms; we want justice, the moral order, democracy, and the supremacy of human rights, not here alone, but everywhere. The question is whether entrance into this war is likely to bring us closer to this goal.

How can the United States better serve suffering humanity everywhere; by going into this war, or by staying out? I hold that the United States can better serve suffering humanity everywhere by staying out. . . .

We have it on the highest authority that one-third of the nation is ill-fed, ill-clothed, and ill-housed. The latest figures of the National Resources Board show that almost precisely 55 percent of our people are living on family incomes of less than $1,250 a year. This sum, says *Fortune* magazine, will not support a family of four. On this basis more than half our people are living below the minimum level of subsistence. More than half the army which will defend democracy will be drawn from those who have had this experience of the economic benefits of "the American way of life."

We know that we have had until lately nine million unemployed and that we should have them still if were not for our military preparations. When our military preparations cease we shall, for all we know, have nine million unemployed again. In his speech on December twentieth, Mr. Roosevelt said, "After the present needs of our defense are past, a proper handling of the country's peacetime needs will require all of the new productive capacity—if not still more." For ten years we have not known how to use the productive capacity we had. Now suddenly we are to believe that by some miracle, after the war is over, we shall know what to do with our old productive capacity and what to do in addition with the tremendous increases which are now being made. We have want and fear today. We shall have want and fear "when the present needs of our defense are past." . . .

The path of war is a false path to freedom. A new moral order for America is the true path to freedom. A new moral order for America means new strength for America, and new hope for the moral reconstruction of mankind. We are turning aside from the true path to freedom because it is easier to blame Hitler for our troubles than to fight for democracy at home. As Hitler made the Jews his scapegoat, so we are making Hitler ours. But Hitler did not spring full-armed from the brow of Satan. He sprang from the materialism and paganism of our times. In the long run we can beat what Hitler stands for only by beating the materialism and paganism that produced him. We must show the world a nation clear in purpose, united in action, and sacrificial in spirit. The influence of that example upon suffering humanity everywhere will be more powerful than the combined armies of the Axis.[50]

FRANK MURPHY (1890–1949)

In a 1944 dissent, U.S. Supreme Court Justice Frank Murphy sharply rebuked his fellow justices for their decision to affirm the constitutionality of President Franklin Roosevelt's imprisonment of approximately 110,000 Japanese nationals and American citizens of Japanese descent. Supported and carried out by military officials in early 1942 following the Japanese attacks on Pearl Harbor, Roosevelt's Executive Order 9066 labeled Japanese individuals (most of them American citizens) as "enemy aliens" and authorized their removal from the West Coast into War Relocation Camps. Despite large numbers of German and Italian Americans, military authorities singled out the Japanese for persecution and sent them to the camps without trial or evidence of disloyalty.

Among those ordered into the camps was a twenty-three-year-old welder from Oakland, California, Fred Korematsu. An American citizen, but also the son of Japanese immigrants, Korematsu refused to follow his parents into the camp. He fled and underwent plastic surgery to alter the shape of his eyes. Nonetheless, authorities tracked him down and sent him to jail. When an official of the American Civil Liberties Union of Northern California contacted Korematsu about challenging his internment, he readily agreed. Korematsu's case went the U.S. Supreme Court, which rejected his appeal in a six-to-three decision in December 1944. For his dissent, Korematsu's friends and neighbors shunned him during and after the war. "All of them turned their backs on me at that time because they thought I was a troublemaker," he later said.

In 1981 Korematsu finally received justice when a legal historian uncovered evidence of misconduct by U.S. government officials during his Supreme Court appeal. Back in federal court, Korematsu turned down a pardon, insisting on complete vindication. "As long as my record stands in federal court," he said, "any American citizen can be held in prison or concentration camps without a trial or a hearing." Agreeing with Korematsu, the judge vacated the conviction and wiped his record clean.

Thirty-seven years earlier, three justices of the Supreme Court had sided with Korematsu, each writing a separate dissent to the decision that affirmed his conviction. The most passionate and straightforward was by Murphy, Roosevelt's former attorney general, who believed strongly in protecting civil liberties. In his dissent, Murphy attacked the ruling, which he called "legalization of racism."[51]

DISSENTING OPINION IN KOREMATSU V. UNITED STATES
United States Supreme Court, December 18, 1944

This exclusion of "all persons of Japanese ancestry, both alien and non-alien," from the Pacific Coast area on a plea of military necessity in the absence of martial law ought not to be approved. Such exclusion goes over "the very brink of constitutional power," and falls into the ugly abyss of racism.

In dealing with matters relating to the prosecution and progress of a war, we must accord great respect and consideration to the judgments of the military authorities who are on the scene and who have full knowledge of the military facts. The scope of their discretion must, as a matter of necessity and common sense, be wide. And their judgments ought not to be overruled lightly by those whose training and duties ill-equip them to deal intelligently with matters so vital to the physical security of the nation.

At the same time, however, it is essential that there be definite limits to military discretion, especially where martial law has not been declared. Individuals must not be left impoverished of their constitutional rights on a plea of military necessity that has neither substance nor support. Thus, like other claims conflicting with the asserted constitutional rights of the individual, the military claim must subject itself to the judicial process of having its reasonableness determined and its conflicts with other interests reconciled. . . .

The judicial test of whether the Government, on a plea of military necessity, can validly deprive an individual of any of his constitutional rights is whether the deprivation is reasonably related to a public danger that is so "immediate, imminent, and impending" as not to admit of delay and not to permit the intervention of ordinary constitutional processes to alleviate the danger. . . . Civilian Exclusion Order No. 34, banishing from a prescribed area of the Pacific Coast "all persons of Japanese ancestry, both alien and non-alien," clearly does not meet that test. Being an obvious racial discrimination, the order deprives all those within its scope of the equal protection of the laws as guaranteed by the Fifth Amendment. It further deprives these individuals of their constitutional rights to live and work where they will, to establish a home where they choose and to move about freely. In excommunicating them without benefit of hearings, this order also deprives them of all their constitutional rights to procedural due process. Yet no reasonable relation to an "immediate, imminent, and impending" public danger is evident to support this racial restriction, which is one of the most sweeping and complete deprivations of constitutional rights in the history of this nation in the absence of martial law.

It must be conceded that the military and naval situation in the spring of 1942 was such as to generate a very real fear of invasion of the Pacific Coast, accompanied by fears of sabotage and espionage in that area. The military command was therefore justified in adopting all reasonable means necessary to combat these dangers. In adjudging the military action taken in light of the then apparent dangers, we must not erect too high or too meticulous standards; it is necessary only that the action have some reasonable relation to the removal of the dangers of invasion, sabotage and espionage. But the exclusion, either temporarily or permanently, of all persons with Japanese blood in their veins has no such reasonable relation. And that relation is lacking because the exclusion order necessarily must rely for its reasonableness upon the assumption that all persons of Japanese ancestry may have a dangerous tendency to commit sabotage and espionage and to aid our Japanese enemy in other ways. It is difficult to believe that reason, logic, or experience could be marshaled in support of such an assumption. . . .

The main reasons relied upon by those responsible for the forced evacuation, therefore, do not prove a reasonable relation between the group characteristics of Japanese Americans and the dangers of invasion, sabotage and espionage. The reasons appear, instead, to be largely an accumulation of much of the misinformation, half-truths and insinuations that for years have been directed against Japanese Americans by people with racial and economic prejudices—the same people who have been among the foremost advocates of the evacuation. . . .

I dissent, therefore, from this legalization of racism. Racial discrimination in any form and in any degree has no justifiable part whatever in our democratic way of life. It is unattractive in any setting, but it is utterly revolting among a free people who have embraced the principles set forth in the Constitution of the United States. All residents of this nation are kin in some way by blood or culture to a foreign land. Yet they are primarily and necessarily a part of the new and distinct civilization of the United States. They must, accordingly, be treated at all times as the heirs of the American experiment, and as entitled to all the rights and freedoms guaranteed by the Constitution.[52]

CHAPTER 8

THE COLD WAR

"HURTLING TOWARD WAR AGAIN"

HARRY TRUMAN HAD NOT BEEN PRESIDENT FOR A FULL twenty-four hours before he asserted to his Secretary of State, Edward Stettinius, "We must stand up to the Russians," and suggested that President Franklin Roosevelt had been too easy on them.[1] Perhaps Roosevelt had decided the same before his death in April 1945. The agreement concerning postwar Europe—negotiated at the Crimean Black Sea resort of Yalta in February 1945—had quickly disintegrated over Russia's refusal to allow pro-Western Poles meaningful participation in Poland's government. American officials interpreted Russian intentions ominously, concluding, in the words of the then-Navy secretary, that the "aim of Soviet foreign policy is Russian domination of a communist world."[2]

Barely a week before Roosevelt's death—as U.S. and Russian allies battled Nazi Germany—the U.S. ambassador to Russia warned officials in Washington about the dangers of allowing Josef Stalin to rule in the regions of Europe then occupied by Russia. "Unless we are prepared to live in a Soviet-dominated world," Averill Harriman wrote, "we must use our economic power to assist countries naturally friendly to us."[3] In the early days of Truman's administration, it was Harriman, the hardliner, who best articulated and exploited Truman's innate distrust of the Soviets. Harriman warned of a "barbarian invasion of Europe" and argued that the U.S. relationship with Russia hinged on its willingness to loosen its stranglehold on Poland and the rest of Eastern Europe.

In an April 23 meeting, Truman berated the Soviet foreign minister for his country's perceived deceit at Yalta. Stalin eventually allowed more pro-Western Poles into the government, but the U.S.-Russian alliance was frayed. The two nations were drifting into a forty-five-year era of mutual distrust, antagonism, and proxy wars. Soviet domination of Eastern Europe—plus forays into Africa, Latin America, and Afghanistan—would be countered by the North Atlantic Treaty Organization (NATO). Each side would arm itself until overflowing with nuclear weapons. Russia zealously defended its sphere of influence by tightening its grip on most of Eastern Europe. The United States had its own sphere of military and economic influence in Western Europe (at the July 1945 Potsdam conference, the United States, Britain, and Russia agreed on a postwar division of Europe leaving Germany split into east and west), but consistently downplayed that less-altruistic reality in favor of lofty rhetoric about democracy, capitalism, and the defense of freedom.

By February 1946, Truman and his advisors were increasingly fearful U.S.-Soviet relations were beyond repair. "There will be another war," General George Patton flatly predicted, echoing the private fears of many.[4] Stalin seemed to confirm these fears in a speech early that year in which he identified "monopoly capitalism" as the cause of World War II and attacked an economic system that he said must be replaced to avoid future wars. As if to make the Soviet threat undeniable, Canada arrested twenty-two people on charges of trying to steal nuclear weapons secrets on behalf of Russia during and after the war.[5]

Into this volatile mix of acrimony and confusion over Soviet actions and intentions arrived a lengthy and influential diplomatic message from George F. Kennan, the forty-four-year-old minister-counselor at Moscow's American embassy and an acknowledged expert on Russian history and politics. Published the following year in *Foreign Affairs* under the pseudonym "X," Kennan's widely circulated article articulated a view of the Soviet Union that would guide the American-led response for much of the cold war. Kennan wrote that the Soviet approach was one in which "no opposition to them can be officially recognized as having any merit or justification whatsoever. Such opposition can flow, in theory, only from the hostile and incorrigible forces of dying capitalism." The U.S.-led response, he argued, should be "long-term, patient but firm and vigilant containment of Russian expansive tendencies."[6]

A few weeks later, American officials were still pondering Kennan's then-secret cable when former British Prime Minister Winston Churchill, speaking at Westminster College in Missouri, painted a grim portrait of Soviet intentions. "From Stettin in the Baltic to Trieste in the Adriatic, an iron curtain has descended across the continent. From what I have seen of our Russian friends and allies during the war, I am convinced that there is nothing they admire so much as strength, and there is nothing for which they have less respect than weakness, especially military weakness."[7] Because Truman accompanied Churchill to Missouri and applauded several times during his speech, some believed that he agreed with Churchill's harsh assessment of Soviet intentions and the recommended response.[8]

In truth, the new president was still weighing his options. For his part, Stalin was greatly alarmed by Churchill's words and Truman's supposed acquiescence. Indeed, Truman's subsequent actions demonstrated that he regarded Soviet behavior with alarm.[9] Pursuing the "containment" strategy that Kennan had recommended, Truman challenged Soviet influence in the eastern Mediterranean by dispatching the Sixth Fleet, which some believed prompted the Soviet troop withdrawal from northern Iran and a lessening of pressure on Turkey. Truman also blocked Russia from a significant role in postwar Japan and prevented the Soviet-backed unification of the two Koreas under North Korean rule. In China, Truman approved billions in military support for the Chinese nationalist government of Chiang Kai-shek in his struggle against the communist forces of Mao Zedong.[10]

As Truman and his aides labored to create a coherent strategy to blunt Soviet expansionism, there were prominent dissenters who believed that Russian actions would be guided largely by the degree to which they were threatened by the U.S.

monopoly of nuclear weapons. In other words, these dissenters argued, it was reasonable to assume that Stalin expected the United States eventually to use its nuclear status for blackmail. To calm those perceived fears, Secretary of War Henry Stimson believed that Truman should share atomic secrets with the Soviet Union, explaining in a September 1945 memorandum, "the only way you make a man trustworthy is to trust him." Like others, Stimson worried about the consequences of negotiating with nuclear weapons "rather ostentatiously on our hip," which he feared would increase the Soviets' "distrust of our purposes."[11]

While Stimson's dissent was cautionary advice, not outright dissent, Secretary of Commerce Henry A. Wallace's criticism was far more pointed; he argued that Russian desires for a sphere of influence were legitimate. Vice president during Franklin Roosevelt's third term, Wallace was still enormously popular among liberals and union members. His first dissent—submitted in a private letter in July 1946—assailed Truman's military policies and recommended military spending cuts to achieve a "reasonable Russian guarantee of security." Like Stimson, Wallace wanted to share nuclear technology with the Soviets. "How would it look to us if Russia had the atomic bomb and we did not?" Wallace asked.[12]

In September, Wallace enraged Truman by taking his dissent public at a rally of liberal Democratic organizations. "For our part," Wallace said, "we should recognize that we have no more business in the political affairs of Eastern Europe than Russia has in the political affairs of Latin America." Wallace also criticized Truman's "excessive expenses for military purposes."[13] Truman had actually given Wallace permission to deliver the speech (although he weakly protested that he had not read it), but congressional leaders and his own secretary of state forced him to deal with the controversy. A week after the speech, Truman demanded Wallace's resignation.[14]

Wallace was not the only prominent Democrat to publicly voice concerns about the growing hostilities between the two countries. Florida Senator Claude Pepper—a liberal Democrat who admired Wallace and had met with Stalin in Moscow in the fall of 1945—had long argued for reducing tensions between the two nations. In the days following Churchill's "Iron Curtain" speech, Pepper and two Senate colleagues assailed Churchill for damaging the wartime alliance of the United States, Britain, and Russia. In a Senate speech in late March 1946, Pepper warned that the world was "hurtling toward war again" and argued that U.S. atomic weaponry represented a threat to Russia's security and its elimination would help lead the world "out of this web of fear." Proposing a meeting of the so-called Big Three, Pepper suggested that the United States beforehand "destroy every atomic bomb we have."

Like Wallace, Pepper empathized with the Russians' postwar desire for greater protection from invasion and argued that they were justifiably fearful. "If we, with our atomic bomb, with the greatest navy in the world, the largest air force, and the most superbly equipped army, are fearful," Pepper asked the Senate, "is there any real wonder that Russia, knowing the horrors of war as we never have know them, as even the British have not known them, is determined that never again shall the cruel assault which she has experienced twice in one generation come to curse her?"[15] Influential author and syndicated newspaper columnist Walter Lippmann shared Pepper's views about Russia's desire for domestic security. "The realm in which each state has the determining influence is limited by geography and circumstances," Lippmann observed in a column in

1945. "Beyond that realm it is possible to bargain and persuade but not to compel, and no foreign policy is well conducted which does not recognize these invisible realities."[16]

That empathetic—or realistic—approach to U.S.-Russian relations carried little weight with Truman's conservative critics in Congress, the most vocal being Ohio Senator Robert Taft, son of the late President William Howard Taft. Among the most respected Senate Republicans, Taft led a bloc of midwestern Republicans who opposed a large postwar U.S. military presence in Europe. Taft leaned heavily toward isolationism in the years leading up to World War II and now worried that U.S. wartime and postwar foreign policy goals were too broad and potentially involved the nation too deeply in other nations' affairs. In 1944, before the war's end, Taft worried about American postwar moral and economic imperialism and wanted to "give up any idea of ruling the world, or telling other countries how to manage their own affairs." To Taft, the primary goal of American military and foreign policy should be, simply, to guarantee liberty for the American people. He therefore opposed Truman's legislative proposal in July 1946 to send U.S. military advisors to allies who requested them, arguing that it was "interference and promoted war." The Republican-controlled Congress never brought the legislation to a vote.[17]

In early 1947 Taft, Pepper, and their respective allies opposed Truman's plan to assume Britain's role in staving off communist encroachment in Turkey and Greece. Truman cast the issue in grave terms, following the advice of Republican Senator Arthur Vandenberg of Michigan, who urged him to "scare the hell out of the American people." Asking Congress for $400 million in military aid for the two countries, Truman articulated the nation's new cold war policy, later known as "the Truman Doctrine," "I believe that it must be the policy of the United States to support free peoples who are resisting attempted subjugation by armed minorities or by outside pressures."[18] From his new perch at the National War College in Washington, DC, George F. Kennan privately informed Truman's advisors that he believed the president was going too far, turning help for Greece and Turkey into a universal principle that would unwisely commit the country to worldwide armed conflicts.[19]

Not surprisingly, Pepper opposed the plan, although he supported economic aid to both countries. Like Taft, Pepper worried about American imperialists "stepping into empty British footprints in the imperial quicksands of the world." Therefore, Pepper argued, the United States could not "expect to carry conviction in our condemnation of the Russians for doing some of the same things." Taft's criticism of the proposal echoed Pepper's. He worried that Truman might try to "secure a special domination over the affairs of these countries." He could not see how Truman's proposal was substantially different from "Russia's demands for domination in her sphere of influence." Furthermore, Taft worried the plan might provoke a war.[20] Others, including Republican Senator Alexander Smith of New Jersey and Democratic Senator Harry Byrd of Virginia, worried aloud that Truman's request for military aid undermined the relatively new United Nations (UN).[21]

Despite their concerns, many members of Congress reluctantly supported Truman. Explained Senator Vandenberg, "They don't like Russia, they don't like the Communists, but still they don't want to do anything to stop it. But they are all put on the spot now, and they all have to come clean." Some members of Congress—including Pepper and Idaho Senator Glen Taylor—were not persuaded. Taft, however, was among the critics who voted for the plan, explaining that the president had committed the nation and "to repudiate it now would destroy his prestige" in negotiations with the Russians. Taft comforted himself with the belief (supported by legislative language) that military assistance would be temporary and the United States would withdraw whenever the host government or the UN determined the assistance was no longer wanted or needed. Taft badly misjudged the temporary nature of Truman's doctrine. It would guide American foreign policy for decades and was the justification for deploying American military might throughout much of the world.[22]

Taft's about-face on military aid to Greece and Turkey reflected the growing fear in Congress and elsewhere of communism's spread and the political peril of appearing "soft." Taft was therefore conflicted when Truman's secretary of state, George C. Marshall, proposed a $17 billion plan in June 1947 to rebuild Europe. While he opposed "an international [Works Progress Administration]" and worried about American imperialism, he admired the plan because he believe it might stop the spread of communism. Although he supported the plan, Taft tried unsuccessfully to reduce it from $5.3 billion in the first year to $4 billion. Other members of Congress were far more skeptical. Democratic Senator Glen Taylor of Idaho—who would join Henry Wallace in a third-party White House campaign in 1948—opposed the Marshall Plan because it bypassed the UN and sought to undermine what Taylor believed was a legitimate Russian desire to maintain a sphere of influence.[23]

Announcing that he would challenge Truman for reelection as a third-party candidate, Wallace lauded the notion of humanitarian aid to Europe, but noted with regret that the United States, not the UN, was implementing the plan. Ultimately, he believed, the Truman Doctrine and the Marshall Plan would "divide Europe into two warring camps. Those whom we buy politically with our food will soon desert us. They will pay us in the basic coin of temporary gratitude and then turn to hate us because our policies are destroying their freedom."[24]

Congress overwhelmingly approved and funded the Marshall Plan, one more sign of a growing bipartisan consensus that Truman built around the view that the Soviet Union's goal was world domination, as opposed to merely security within a more limited sphere of influence. Kennan, whose cable was the containment policy's inspiration, soon lamented how Truman and others used his views from 1945 to reject negotiations with the Soviets. Typical of Truman's attitude was his reaction in February 1948 to a purge of noncommunists from the Czech coalition government—"moral God fearing peoples . . . must save the world from Atheism and totalitarianism."[25]

The following year, after the end of the Berlin blockade—during which the Soviets blocked access to Berlin by train and road and Western nations supplied the city's residents with a massive airlift—the United States and eleven other, mostly European, allies signed treaties forming NATO, a collective security organization, which meant the permanent presence of U.S. troops and arms in Western Europe. In the Senate, only thirteen members opposed NATO. The most prominent and vocal critic was Taft, who believed the treaty might hasten a war with Russia because "they may well decide that if war is the certain result, that war might better occur now rather than after the arming of Europe is completed."[26]

Taft's fears about rearming Europe were not without merit. Despite assurances to the contrary, by 1950 Truman would propose sending overseas four divisions of

American troops. Several events prompted that change of heart, including the news in August 1949 that the Soviets had detonated a nuclear device. Later that year in China, the loss of nationalist forces to the communist army of Mao Zedong only heightened U.S. fears of a growing worldwide communist plan to dominate the world.

The contours of America's cold war policies were solidifying and the massive remilitarization of the West was beginning in earnest. The approval of the top-secret National Security Council Document 68 (NSC 68) in September 1950 articulated the rationale for drastic increases in U.S. military spending. "We must realize that we are now in a mortal conflict," one of the memorandum's authors wrote, "that we are now in a war worse than any we have experienced."[27] The fear of preemptive attack sparked an accelerated nuclear and conventional arms race by both sides during the cold war. From 1950 to 1953, the U.S. defense budget soared, from $13 billion to almost $50 billion. To Kennan, now a (privately) dissenting State Department official with waning influence, the militarization of the cold war spelled disaster. The United States and its allies had "unconsciously embrace[d] the assumption that a war so much prepared for cannot fail to be eventually fought."[28] It was a fear that would eventually be realized in Korea, Vietnam, Cuba, and other corners of the world, as both nations would pour into the conflict sizable amounts of their wealth and human treasure.

CLAUDE PEPPER (1900–1989)

An outspoken southern liberal, Claude Pepper represented Florida in the U.S. Senate from 1936 to 1950 and in the U.S. House from 1962 until his death in 1989. An advocate of greater preparedness in the years before World War II, Pepper sponsored the lend-lease bill in 1940 that extended military supplies to Great Britain. He traveled to Moscow to meet with Russian leader Josef Stalin in 1945 and returned to advocate better relations with the Soviet Union, arguing that the Marshall Plan should extend postwar aid to Russia. He touted Stalin as "a man Americans can trust."

No ally of President Harry Truman, Pepper tried to persuade Democratic leaders in 1948 to dump Truman in favor of General Dwight D. Eisenhower. In 1950 Truman—who called Pepper an "A-1 demagogue"—backed Pepper's challenger in the Democratic primary. Congressman George Smathers handily defeated Pepper, after branding him "Red Pepper" and telling audiences that "he likes [Stalin] and Joe likes him." Pepper returned to Congress in 1962 as a House member representing southern Florida.[29]

AN AMERICAN POLICY FOR PEACE AND A NEW WORLD
Speech to the U.S. Senate, March 20, 1946

It is time for the Government and the people of this country to step, look, and listen. It is time—yes, it is late—for those millions of American men and women who have just laid down the weapons of war to awaken to the fact that we are hurtling toward war again. It is late for the mothers and fathers of this country who have just got some of their sons home, to be startled, and to realize that they are about to lose them again, and that the monster of war which they thought forever dead is rising once more. . . .

Here, for the first time in modern history, three major powers, all who fought grandly together as allies, stand unchallenged in the world. Their enemy is defeated, and no one save those whose hands they have clasped in the friendship of struggle and sacrifice are capable of threatening them. And yet we live in tension comparable to the days before Munich or on the eve of either of the last wars. Before we throw away this peace we have so dearly won, before we condemn mankind to war suicide, before we thrust back the hand of plenty which the future has hospitably been extending toward us and toward all mankind, is it not time to look with candor and clear sight, and with an earnestness which bespeaks the horror of what we risk if we fail, to try to understand what lies behind all this planning and talking about war.

Of course, there are always national chauvinism, imperial vanity, and the dangerous dregs of unrepentant isolationism loose in the land and in the world. And there is, of course, the infamous influence of fearmongers and warmongers who are promoting their gambles with death and destruction to recapture their industrial or political empires which were destroyed in the defeat of Nazism.

But beyond and behind these sinister forces and people, this tension which threatens war is the reflection of the desperate reaching out of the United States, Great Britain, and the Soviet Union for national security. . . .

Over and above all this, we have the atomic bomb. According to reports we are stock piling atomic bombs as fast as our facilities will allow, notwithstanding the growing resignations and resistance of the scientists who made the bomb possible.

We are on the verge of the most colossal experiment in military history to see what is the real strength and power and behavior of this atomic bomb, so that we may increase its destructive character, and at the same time build perhaps a new type of fleet impervious to the atomic bomb of another—an experiment, incidentally, to which the Security Council of the United Nations Organization has not yet been invited. And we clutch desperately to the atomic bomb and our exclusive control of it like a fearful child clutching the hand of an all-powerful father. . . .

Russia is strong today. But after a bitter yesterday, Russia looks apprehensively to what she may encounter tomorrow. She is suspicious. Denied the atomic bomb, denied warm water outlets, denied the common courtesy of economic negotiations with her greatest ally, believing that her philosophy is such that she will never be accepted by nations dominated by cartelists, reactionaries, or Russophobes, Russia is beset with many fears. . . .

If we, with our atomic bomb, with the greatest navy in the world, the largest air force, and the most superbly equipped army, are fearful; if we, for security, defend a zone which now includes the Western Hemisphere, the Pacific Ocean, Japan, and central China, and the Atlantic Ocean north to Iceland and east to the Azores; if Britain's defense zone embraces western Europe, the Mediterranean, the Near East, Africa, and southwest Asia, as well as the seven seas, is there any real wonder that Russia, knowing the horrors of war as we never have known them, as even the British have not known them, is determined that never again shall the cruel assault which she has experienced twice in one generation come to curse her? . . .

It is senseless to think that there can be a stable and secure world as long as only a part of the major powers have the atomic bomb. It is folly to expect Russia to sit supinely by and not make every desperate effort to provide for its own security this incalculably dangerous and destructive weapon while others have it perfected and are producing bombs for their stockpiles. There can be only a panicky atomic bomb race among the great powers if this question is not satisfactorily resolved. . . .

Let America, therefore, take the lead in proposing a resolution of this most dangerous of issues among the Big Three. I would prefer that we should first, before the convening of such a conference, after calling on Britain and Canada to join us, destroy every atomic bomb which we have, and smash every facility we possess which is capable of producing only destructive forms of atomic energy. . . .

Then we could go into the court of this conference with the cleanest of hands to talk about the future control of atomic power for the purposes of peace and outlawing it for war. . . .

Before us then, is the choice, war or peace, poverty or plenty, hopelessness or hope.[30]

HENRY WALLACE (1888–1965)

Born into a farming and newspaper publishing family in rural Iowa, Henry Wallace followed his father's footsteps—first as editor of the family's paper, Wallace's Farmer, *and then as U.S. agriculture secretary to President Franklin Roosevelt (his father held the same post under President Warren G. Harding). An outspoken and effective advocate for an American role in Europe in the late 1930s, Wallace won the vice presidential nomination in 1940. As vice president during Roosevelt's third term, Wallace used his considerable influence to sell Roosevelt's war policies in the heavily isolationist Midwest and to the American labor movement.*

A reliable New Dealer, Wallace increasingly drifted leftward and advocated stronger postwar ties to Russia. In 1944, alarmed by Wallace's increasingly radical ideology, moderate Democratic leaders forced Roosevelt to replace him with Missouri Senator Harry Truman. Wallace became commerce secretary in Roosevelt's fourth term, a job he continued to hold when Truman became president in April 1945. Under Truman, Wallace became even more outspoken about nurturing closer ties to the Soviets. In July 1946, Wallace wrote Truman a letter bluntly criticizing the president's Soviet policy. In September, after the letter became public and Wallace delivered a speech that echoed many of the letter's points, Truman forced his resignation. Wallace edited The New Republic *until 1948, when he challenged Truman as a third-party candidate for president on the Progressive Party's ticket.[31]*

LETTER TO PRESIDENT HARRY TRUMAN
July 23, 1946

I have been increasingly disturbed about the trend of international affairs since the end of the war, and I am even more troubled by the apparently growing feeling among the American people that another war is coming and the only way that we can head it off is to arm ourselves to the teeth. Yet all of past history indicates that an armaments race does not lead to peace but to war. The months just ahead may well be the crucial period which will decide whether the civilized world will go down in destruction after the five or ten years needed for several nations to arm themselves with atomic bombs. Therefore, I want to give you my views on how the present trend toward conflict might be averted. . . .

How do American actions since V-J Day appear to other nations? I mean by actions the concrete things like $13 billion for the War and Navy Departments, the Bikini tests of the atomic bomb and continued production of bombs, the plan to arm Latin America with our weapons, production of B-29s and planned production of B-36s, and the effort to secure air bases spread over half the globe from which the other half of the globe can be bombed. I cannot but feel that these actions must make it look to the rest of the world as if we were only paying lip service to peace at the conference table.

These facts rather make it appear either (1) that we are preparing ourselves to win the war which we regard as inevitable or (2) that we are trying to build up a predominance of force to intimidate the rest of mankind. How would it look to us if Russia had the atomic bomb and we did not, if Russia had 10,000-mile bombers and air bases within a thousand miles of our coastlines, and we did not?

Some of the military men and self-styled "realists" are saying: "What's wrong with trying to build up a predominance of force? The only way to preserve peace is for this country to be so well armed that no one will dare attack us. We know that America will never start a war."

The flaw in this policy is simply that it will not work. In a world of atomic bombs and other revolutionary new weapons, such as radioactive poison gases and biological warfare, a peace maintained by a predominance of force is no longer possible.

Why is this so? The reasons are clear:

FIRST. Atomic warfare is cheap and easy compared with old-fashioned war. Within a very few years several countries can have atomic bombs and other atomic weapons. Compared with the cost of large armies and the manufacture of old-fashioned weapons, atomic bombs cost very little and require only a relatively small part of a nation's production plant and labor force.

SECOND. So far as winning a war is concerned, having more bombs—even many more bombs—than the other fellow is no longer a decisive advantage. If another nation had enough bombs to eliminate all of our principal cities and our heavy industry, it wouldn't help us very much if we had ten times as many bombs as we needed to do the same to them.

THIRD. And most important, the very fact that several nations have atomic bombs will inevitably result in a neurotic, fear-ridden, itching-trigger psychology in all the peoples of the world, and because of our wealth and vulnerability we would be among the most seriously affected. Atomic war will not require vast and time-consuming preparations, the mobilization of large armies, the conversion of a large proportion of a country's industrial plants to the manufacture of weapons. In a world armed with atomic weapons, some incident will lead to the use of those weapons.

There is a school of military thinking which recognizes these facts, recognizes that when several nations have atomic bombs, a war which will destroy modern civilization will result and that no nation or combination of nations can win such a war. This school of thought therefore advocates a "preventive war," an attack on Russia *now* before Russia has atomic bombs.

This scheme is not only immoral, but stupid. If we should attempt to destroy all the principal Russian cities and her heavy industry, we might well succeed. But the immediate countermeasure which such an attack would call forth is the prompt occupation of all Continental Europe by the Red Army. Would we be prepared to destroy the cities of all Europe in trying to finish what we had started? This idea is so contrary to all the basic instincts and principles of the American people that any such action would be possible only under a dictatorship at home. . . .

In general there are two overall points of view which can be taken in approaching the problem of the United States-Russian relations. The first is that it is not possible to get along with the Russians and therefore war is inevitable. The second is that war with Russia would bring catastrophe to all mankind, and therefore we must find a way of living in peace. It is clear that our own welfare as well as that of the entire world requires that we maintain the latter point of view. . . .

We must recognize that the world has changed and that today there can be no "one world" unless the United States and Russia can find some way of living together. . . . We should ascertain from a fresh point of view what Russia believes to be essential to her own security as a prerequisite to the writing of the peace and to cooperation in the construction of a world order. We should be prepared to judge her requirements against the background of what we ourselves and the British have insisted upon as essential to our respective security. We should be prepared, even at the expense of risking epithets of appeasement, to agree to reasonable Russian guarantees of security. . . .

We should make an effort to counteract the irrational fear of Russia which is being systematically built up in the American people by certain individuals and publications. The slogan that communism and capitalism, regimentation and democracy, cannot continue to exist in the same world is, from a historical point of view, pure propaganda. Several religious doctrines, all claiming to be the only true gospel and salvation, have existed side by side with a reasonable degree of tolerance for centuries. This country was for the first half of its national life a democratic island in a world dominated by absolutist governments.

We should not act as if we too felt that we were threatened in today's world. We are by far the most powerful nation in the world, the only Allied nation which came out of the war without devastation and much stronger than before the war. Any talk on our part about the need for strengthening our defenses further is bound to appear hypocritical to other nations.[32]

ROBERT TAFT (1889–1953)

As the Senate Republicans' ideological leader, Robert Taft was often a vigorous critic of U.S. foreign policy in the years after World War II. The son of a former president and chief justice, William Howard Taft, the younger Taft entered the Senate in 1938. While not an outright isolationist, he was initially skeptical of U.S. involvement in World War II and afterward argued that the United States should resist any imperialist urge and should promptly withdraw its troops from Europe. Before the war, Taft had argued that "even the collapse of England is to be preferred to participation for the rest of our lives in European wars."

When not opposing Harry Truman's foreign policy, Taft often appeared ambivalent. He supported the UN charter, but opposed appointing U.S. delegates because he believed the charter allowed the UN, and not Congress, to make war. After criticizing the Marshall Plan, and trying to reduce its size, Taft supported it. In 1949, Taft strongly opposed creation of the NATO, arguing that the alliance would rearm Europe and make war with Russia more likely.[33]

IN OPPOSITION TO THE NATO TREATY
U.S. Senate Speech, July 11, 1949

I must vote against the [NATO] pact, rather than for it . . . because I think the pact carries with it an obligation to assist in arming, at our expense, the nations of western Europe, because with that obligation I believe it will promote war in the world rather than peace, and because I think that with the arms plan it is wholly contrary to the spirit of the obligations we assumed in the United Nations Charter. I would vote for the pact if a reservation were adopted denying any legal or moral obligation to provide arms. . . .

What is the nature of [the NATO] treaty?

It is obviously, and I do not think it can be questioned, a defensive military alliance between certain nations, the essence of which is an obligation under Article 5 to go to war if necessary with any nation which attacks any one of the signers of the treaty. Such an attack may come from outsiders or it may come from one of the signers of the treaty itself. The obligation is completely binding for a period of 20 years. It imposes an obligation upon the United States to each member nation whether or not there is consultation or joint action by the Council, or a finding by any court that an unjustified armed attack has occurred. Our obligation is self-executing upon the occurrence of an armed attack.

Some doubt will always remain as to whether the Congress must declare war before our armed forces actually take part. I am inclined to think such action is not necessary if the President chooses to use our armed forces when an ally is attacked. But whether it is or not, the obligation to go to war seems to me binding upon the United States as a nation, so that Congress would be obligated to declare war if that were necessary to comply with the provisions of the treaty. It is pointed out that the President could fail to act and Congress could refuse to declare war, but certainly we are not making a treaty on the theory that we expect to violate it in accordance with our own sweet will. . . .

By executing a treaty of this kind, we put ourselves at the mercy of the foreign policies of 11 other nations, and do so for a period of 29 years. The Charter is obviously aimed at possible Russian aggression against western Europe, but the obligation assumed is far broader than that. I emphasize again that the obligation is much more unconditional, much less dependent on legal processes and much less dependent on joint action than the obligation of the United Nations Charter.

And yet in spite of these dangers, I have wanted to vote in favor of the Atlantic Pact for one reason and would still do so if the question of arms were not involved. I fully agree with the effective argument in favor of the pact made by the distinguished Senator from Michigan [Arthur Vandenberg] because of its warning to the U.S.S.R.

I think we should make it clear to the U.S.S.R. that if it attacks western Europe, it will be at war with us. . . .

It is said that the Atlantic Treaty is simply another Monroe Doctrine. I wish it were. That would be much more acceptable to me than the Atlantic pact, arms or no arms. Let me point out the vital differences. The Monroe Doctrine was a unilateral declaration. We were free to modify it or withdraw from it at any moment. This treaty, adopted to deal with a particular emergency today, is binding upon us for 20 years to cover all kinds of circumstances which cannot possibly be foreseen. The Monroe Doctrine left us free to determine the merits of each dispute which might arise and to judge the justice and the wisdom of war in the light of the circumstances at the time. The present treaty obligates us to go to war if certain facts occur. The Monroe Doctrine imposed no obligation whatever to assist any American Nation by giving it arms or even economic aid. We were free to fight the war in such a manner as we might determine, or not at all. This treaty imposes on us a continuous obligation for 20 years to give aid to all the other members of the pact, and, I believe, to give military aid to all the other members of the pact. . . .

And yet, in spite of my belief that the treaty goes much too far and should have been confined to a mere declaration on our part that we would go to war if Russia attacked western Europe, I would still vote for the treaty except for my belief that the pact commits us to the arming of all the other signers of the pact. There is no question that the arms program and the treaty were negotiated together. There is no question in my mind that foreign nations which signed the treaty regarded the providing of arms as an essential part of it. . . .

The pact standing by itself would clearly be a deterrent to war. If Russia knows that if it starts a war it will immediately find itself at war with the United States, it is much less likely to start a war. I see and believe in the full force of that argument. That is why I would favor the extension of the Monroe Doctrine to Europe. But if Russia sees itself ringed about gradually by so-called defensive arms, from Norway and Denmark to Turkey and Greece it may form a different opinion. It may decide that the arming of western Europe, regardless of its present purpose, looks to an attack upon Russia. Its view may be unreasonable, and I think it is. But from the Russian standpoint it may not seem unreasonable. They may well decide that if war is the certain result, that war might better occur now rather than after the arming of Europe is completed. . . .

In any war the result will not come from the battle put up by the western European countries. The outcome will finally depend on the armed forces of America. Let us keep our forces strong. Let us use the money we have for armament in building up the American Army, the American Air Forces, and the American Navy. Let us keep our forces strong, and spend the money that is available for arms for those forces, because in the last analysis, we will win a war only if the United States wins the war, no matter how we assist other nations.[34]

CHAPTER 9

THE KOREAN WAR

"NO SUBSTITUTE FOR VICTORY"

IN THE EARLY MORNING HOURS OF JUNE 25, 1950, communist North Korea staged a surprise invasion of the Republic of Korea. Encountering little resistance from the poorly trained, ill-equipped South Korean military, Soviet-backed communist forces surged south across the thirty-eighth parallel—the arbitrary border created by the United States and the Soviet Union at the end of World War II—and headed for Seoul. Within days, the capital fell and a devastated South Korean army fled in full retreat. In the United States, President Harry Truman and his aides viewed the situation with alarm and concluded the invasion was a Soviet-backed operation designed to test Truman's mettle. Only eleven months earlier, when Truman had ordered most U.S. troops removed from Korea, the Joint Chiefs of Staff and the State Department had given their assent, not viewing the region as strategically important. The events of late June changed that. Truman and Secretary of State Dean Acheson knew that the entire world would be watching their response. Failing to respond decisively to communist aggression in Asia would expose Truman to charges from Republicans that he had allowed two Asian nations to fall into communist hands in nine months' time (China's nationalist government had fallen in October 1949).

Had Truman wavered or refused to assist South Korea in the days following the invasion, it would have irreparably damaged his presidency and may have ended Democratic control of Congress. Truman ordered General Douglas MacArthur, commander of the U.S. occupation forces in Japan, to supply South Korea with weapons and ammunition. He sent the U.S. Seventh Fleet to Taiwan to protect nationalist leader Chiang Kai-shek's forces from Chinese attack.[1] On June 30, after an urgent request from MacArthur, and over strenuous opposition from the Joint Chiefs of Staff, he committed ground, air, and naval forces to the defense of South Korea. By the end of July, more than forty-seven thousand U.S. troops were in Korea.[2]

The first signs of domestic trouble over Korea appeared on June 30, 1950, when Truman met with congressional leaders, not to consult, but to inform them of his decision to deploy U.S. troops. Republican Senator Kenneth Wherry of Nebraska wanted to know, recalled one Truman aide, "if the President was going to advise the Congress before he sent ground troops into Korea." Truman matter-of-factly responded, "I just had to act as Commander-in-Chief, and I did." Should the need arise for a full-scale military action, Truman assured the congressional leaders, he would consult Congress.[3]

Whether Truman had the constitutional right to dispatch U.S. troops to Korea is debatable; but because did not make congressional leaders partners in his decision, the Republicans would share no blame if the conflict went badly. Indeed, they would attack him mercilessly at the first opportunity. As it turned out, that opportunity came early. Republican leaders were seething, not only over their exclusion from the troop decision, but because of administration policies that they believed had encouraged the attack on South Korea.

Secretary of State Acheson had seemed to say as much in a speech the previous January. While he forcefully articulated a North Pacific perimeter that the United States would defend against communist aggression (a line running along the Aleutian Islands southward to Japan to Okinawa to the Philippines), he had omitted South Korea. Although General MacArthur, in a March 1949 speech, also put Korea outside the American line of defense, Republicans would later charge that Acheson's omission was an invitation to aggression.[4]

Partisan rhetoric aside, many leading Republicans shared Acheson's and MacArthur's opinions about Korea. Heavily influenced by the isolationists who had once strongly opposed direct U.S. involvement in Europe prior to World War II, and who had offered mild support for fighting communism in Asia, many Republican leaders were instinctively opposed to sending troops into Asia. Thus in the early days of the conflict, while much of the nation rallied to Truman's support, most Republicans who spoke offered grudging support. Robert Taft, a leading Republican senator from Ohio, argued the president should have first sought the approval of Congress before committing ground troops to Korea. He added, however, "When you are in, you've got to go all out."[5] More than a week later, however, Taft went on the attack. He still supported Truman's action, but blamed the president for creating the crisis. "From the past philosophy and declarations of our leaders," Taft observed, "it was not unreasonable for the North Koreans to suppose that they could get away with it [the invasion] and that we would do nothing about it."[6]

Many of the Republicans who would later blame Truman for having ignored the communist threat in Korea until it was too late had opposed American intervention. For example, Republican Senator William Jenner of Indiana had once complained that it was "just downright idiotic" for the State Department to place so much emphasis on Korea. Senator Eugene Milliken of Colorado summarized the Republican view of the Korean situation when he said that Republican lawmakers were "unanimous" in believing the communist invasion "should not be used as a provocation for war." The nation, he said, had no obligation to fight with South Korean soldiers.[7]

In July 1950, however, the public largely supported the war. In one survey, 77 percent said they supported Truman's decision to send American troops. Republicans, too, now supported Truman. "The general principle of the policy is right," Taft admitted. Congress promptly ended its debate over whether to allow Truman to reinstate the draft. A united House and Senate not only gave the president that authority, but also the power to call up the National Guard and reservists. Both houses also authorized a $1.2 billion military aid program with provisions allowing Truman to spend up to $460 million to assist South Korea. The Senate unanimously approved both measures.[8]

As Congress rushed to endorse Truman's policies, one lonely House member opposed the U.S. military effort. New York Congressman Vito Marcantonio, of the American Labor Party, rose in the House chamber on June 27 to denounce American involvement in Korea as a misguided intervention in a civil war. "Oh, yes, you can indulge in attacks on communism," Marcantonio told the House. "You can keep on making impassioned pleas for the destruction of communism, but I tell you that the issue in China, in Asia, in Korea and in Viet Nam is the right of these peoples to self-determination, to a government of their own, to independence and national unity."[9] Just as Marcantonio was isolated and scorned in the House so were his allies outside Congress. The various peace activists, pacifist organizations, and liberal political parties opposed to the war found little public support. Others who might have raised questions about contesting Truman's policy feared being labeled procommunist—not a far-fetched notion in the early days of America's "Red Scare."[10]

Some dissidents, however, did speak out. Antiwar activist A. J. Muste argued that Korea "is war and may be the spark that sets off World War III." The American Friends Service Committee (AFSC), in a statement titled "War is Contrary to the Will of God," took exception to Truman's term "police action" to describe the mission of U.S. troops. The term, the AFSC said, was a "false analogy" that neglected to explain fully the nation's objectives in Korea. Unlike police officers, the Friends' argued, the solider "is required to destroy innocent and guilty alike . . . and to impose the will of the strong." While not rejecting its national organization's argument, the Washington, DC, branch of the AFSC took a different approach—demanding the immediate withdrawal of all U.S. troops from Korea. Far more radical was the statement by pacifist Robert Ludlow in the January 1961 edition of the *Catholic Worker*. Ludlow said that he was not opposed to the Korean War on religious grounds, rather "I am opposed to American armies in Korea or anywhere else in the world because I am opposed to that political and economic system called 'the American way.'"[11]

Groups opposing the war offered many reasons, which may explain why no broad, cohesive, and well-organized antiwar movement ever formed in the United States. For example, the Communist Party, the American Labor Party, and the left wing of the Progressive Party saw the war as an extension of American imperialism, while the right wing of the Progressive Party and the Socialist Party blamed the Soviet Union. Meanwhile, the Independent Socialist League, the Socialist Workers Party, and the Socialist Labor Party blamed the Soviet Union and the United States for waging a proxy war in Korea.[12]

Organized labor generally supported Truman's Korean policies. There were, however, exceptions. The San Francisco branch of the National Union of Marine Cooks and Stewards demanded the withdrawal of U.S. forces. In response, the Congress of Industrial Organizations put the union on probation. Also in San Francisco, the International Longshoremen's and Warehousemen's Union opposed the war. In July 1950, after the union's president, Harry Bridges, reportedly urged his members not to load ships carrying arms and supplies to Korea, U.S. Justice Department officials persuaded a federal judge to imprison the union leader. At the time, Bridges—a native of Australia—was free on bail following his April 1950 perjury conviction for denying membership in the Communist Party during his citizenship hearing. The Justice Department claimed that Bridges's opposition to the war made him "inimical to the security of the United States." Sentencing Bridges to five years in prison, the judge ruled that Bridges's "conduct since the beginning of the Korean crisis . . . [is] of such a nature to justify this court in concluding that his loyalty and allegiance are and must be with the Communists."[13] After twenty days in prison, an appeals court freed Bridges, ruling that "in the eyes of large numbers of well meaning and loyal people . . . he will appear a victim of judicial tyranny; and authentic material for propaganda is supplied for the use of the vociferous critics and implacable foes of our democratic way of life."[14]

There were other official efforts to repress antiwar speech. In New York, a state judge jailed four citizens for painting peace slogans—"Peace" and "No H-Bomb"— on sidewalks and monument pillars around Brooklyn's Prospect Park. "The flower of our youth is dying in Korea," the judge said as he sentenced the defendants to six years in the county prison, "and the least we can do is refrain from stabbing them in the back."[15] Also in New York, in July 1950, the city's police department refused a request by the New York Labor Conference for Peace to hold an antiwar rally in Union Square, arguing that a "meeting of this type would cause serious public disorder." When the mayor rejected its appeal, the group unsuccessfully petitioned the state's supreme court. The group went ahead with its rally, attracting a large crowd— possibly as many as ten thousand—and more than one thousand police officers. Police officers arrested fourteen demonstrators and, according to the *New York Times*, badly clubbed several others.[16]

Meanwhile, the fighting in Korea continued. Throughout the summer of 1950, MacArthur's United Nations (UN) troops fought communist forces in the mountains and hills of South Korea—and the struggle was not going well for the American forces. Media reports brought daily news of setbacks or stalemates. UN forces were greatly outnumbered, by as much as four to one. Slowly the troops were losing ground as communist forces pushed them toward the sea. By early September, communist forces controlled 90 percent of the Korean peninsula as South Korean and American forces retreated into an area near the southeast Korean town of Pusan.[17] These developments sparked a political war in Washington and across the country. By August, with the fall congressional elections just months away, Republicans intensified their attacks on Truman and the administration's "bungling" that they argued led to the Korean conflict.

Four leading Republican members of the Senate Foreign Relations Committee issued a statement asserting that Truman had given the Soviet Union a "green light to grab whatever it could in China, Korea and Formosa." Senator Kenneth Wherry was more strident, charging that "the blood of our boys in Korea" was on Acheson's hands. In Illinois, Republican Senate candidate Everett Dirksen, who would defeat Majority Leader Scott Lucas in November, castigated the "blunderers and stupid policy makers [who] sowed the seeds of war in Washington." As *Newsweek* observed, "Out of the confusion, the GOP's campaign strategy was emerging. Unpreparedness, false defense economy, bad weapons, and a feeble foreign policy would be the main targets."[18]

While it was acceptable for congressional opponents of Truman to attack his Korean War policies, the same standard clearly did not apply to labor leaders and other citizens. In February 1951, a federal grand jury indicted the leaders of the Peace Information Center (PIC), ostensibly for failing to register with the U.S. Justice Department under provisions of the Foreign Agents Registration Act, because U.S. officials maintained that the organization was an arm of a foreign government. What seemed to enrage U.S. officials, particularly Acheson, was the PIC's advocacy of the Stockholm Peace Appeal, which called for total worldwide nuclear disarmament.

Among those indicted was the organization's chairman, the noted civil rights leader W. E. B. DuBois, a vocal war critic.[19] An admirer of Soviet leader Josef Stalin, DuBois was already suspect by virtue of his attendance in 1949 at the all-Soviet Peace Conference in Moscow, where, as the only American, he delivered what one biographer called a "long and unimpeachably Marxist analysis of the United States' role in current world affairs." When DuBois and his fellow defendants faced trial in November 1951, the government's lawyers were no match for DuBois's legal team, led by now-former New York Congressman Vito Marcantonio. Five days into the trial, the judge dismissed the charges.[20]

The Justice Department had indicted DuBois when the popularity of the Korean War was waning. As Chinese and North Korean troops steadily pushed U.S. forces toward the south of the Korean peninsula, more Americans began to question the war. By December 1950, a poll revealed that only 39 percent of Americans surveyed believed that U.S. troops in Korea was a good idea. Half now said they believed the decision to fight in Korea had been a mistake.[21]

MacArthur tried to reverse his military misfortunes and, with them, domestic public opinion. On September 15, he launched a counterstrike that changed the course of the war and finally put communist forces on the defensive. After a massive bombing and resupply effort, American forces staged a daring and successful amphibious landing at the Yellow Sea port of Inchon, thirty miles from the South Korean capital of Seoul. By September 26, Seoul was liberated. By month's end, the North Korean army retreated to the thirty-eighth parallel and MacArthur began lobbying the administration for permission to cross into North Korea and vanquish communist forces.[22]

September also brought controversy over congressional passage of the Internal Security Act, a sweeping measure that, among other things, restricted the free-speech rights of aliens who taught or advocated any political or economic doctrines associated with communism or totalitarianism. The bill had languished in Congress since 1948, but events in China and Korea, as well as Joseph McCarthy's sensational allegations about communist subversives in the federal government, gave the legislation new life. The bill quickly became a prime vehicle for Republicans to link the turmoil in Asia to McCarthy's allegations about communist influence in the U.S. State Department.[23]

Truman vetoed the bill, unconcerned about the unpopularity of his position.[24] "In a free country we punish men for the crimes they commit but never for the opinions they have," Truman said in his veto message. "We can and we will prevent espionage, sabotage, or other actions endangering our national security. But we would betray our finest traditions if we attempted . . . to curb the simple expression of opinion."[25] Congress overwhelmingly overrode his veto. Truman's hands were not entirely clean on the question of internal security. In 1947 he had created a Loyalty Review Board in the federal government's Civil Service Commission. Its mission was to investigate the loyalty of every new federal employee. The program was a mess—poorly conceived and administered. Truman later said the program, which he argued had been forced upon him, amounted to "a secret police proposition."[26]

As the fall congressional campaigns of 1950 went into full swing, so did the war in Korea. U.S. forces fared so well that MacArthur gained Truman's permission to rout communist forces. In October he took the battle into North Korea, hoping to reunify the two countries under the South Korean government. The mission was a disaster. In November, as American troops approached the Chinese border at the Yalu River, three hundred thousand Chinese troops struck back and forced a humiliating U.S. retreat. By January, communist troops pushed MacArthur's beleaguered forces below the thirty-eighth parallel and once more controlled Seoul. Only months earlier, MacArthur had boldly predicted the war would end by Christmas. Now it was clear that the conflict was far from over. Weeks earlier a UN victory seemed assured. Even that was now in doubt.[27]

The Chinese attack caught Truman and his advisors by surprise. Responding quickly, the administration declared a national emergency, increased draft calls, imposed wage and price controls, and asked Congress to quadruple defense spending. Yet the last thing Truman had wanted was a direct conflict with communist China. He hoped to end the war—quickly—and was willing to abandon the forcible reunification of the two Koreas. Reluctantly the United States prepared to accept the prewar status quo of a divided Korean peninsula that was half communist.[28]

MacArthur, however, saw the Chinese intervention as an opportunity to take the battle directly to China and end the conflict, not by negotiation—as Truman wanted—but with a decisive military victory. The general urged Truman to bomb and blockade mainland China and proposed equipping Chiang Kai-shek's Chinese nationalist army to lead a ground offensive against the communist forces. Just as troubling were MacArthur's reports that his army suffered from fatigue and low morale—an assessment later proved erroneous. In fact, MacArthur's troops were still a potent force. Led by Lieutenant General Matthew Ridgway, the new commander of the Eighth Army, they reversed their retreat and regained the initiative. By late January, U.S. forces were again on the offensive.[29]

Despite having almost forfeited the American position in Korea with his recklessness, MacArthur pushed an even more aggressive strategy on Truman. Embarrassed that his promise to have U.S. troops home by Christmas 1950 had collapsed under the weight of the strong and unexpected Chinese offensive, MacArthur publicly tried to shift the blame to Truman. In December of 1950 he had first argued that his army's inability to resist the Chinese was the result, not of his own military missteps, but of limitations—"without precedent"—imposed on him by Washington. He complained that U.S. officials would not allow him to bomb Chinese bases in Manchuria and pursue enemy planes across the Chinese border.

Fearing that a direct confrontation with China might bring the Soviet Union into the conflict and precipitate another world war, Truman would not allow MacArthur to take the country into direct conflict with China.[30] Not averse to conflicting advice from advisors, Truman nonetheless regarded MacArthur as reckless.[31] On December 6 Truman ordered that no military official publicly discuss anything but the most routine foreign policy matters without first consulting his superior. MacArthur ignored

Truman's order. On March 15 he escalated his dispute with the president by inform-
ing a reporter that he opposed the administration's decision to stop the Eighth Army's
advance at the thirty-eighth parallel. The general ventured further into forbidden
territory by erroneously stating that his mission was "the unification of Korea"—a
matter of policy and one that Truman had expressly rejected.[32]

Nine days later, MacArthur did it again.[33] While U.S. officials composed a cease-
fire proposal, MacArthur unilaterally issued an ultimatum to the Chinese, threatening
to widen the war. In the United States, MacArthur's Republican supporters enthusiastically echoed the general's statement. Senator Robert Taft complained that Truman
had "refused to fight that war with all the means" at his command. MacArthur's hostile and threatening declaration, however, had torpedoed Truman's carefully crafted
cease-fire initiative. Furious at the flagrant disregard for his December 6 order, Truman again resisted the urge to fire the general and instead issued a stern warning.[34]

The end came in early April when House Republican Leader Joseph Martin
released a March 20 letter from MacArthur in which the general endorsed Martin's
view that the Nationalist Chinese forces should be enlisted. MacArthur declared that
"we must win. There is no substitute for victory."[35] Acheson saw the letter as "an open
declaration of war on the administration's policy." As Truman later said, "The time
had come to draw the line. MacArthur's letter to Congressman Martin showed that
the general was not only in disagreement with the policy of the government but was
challenging this policy in open insubordination to his Commander in Chief."[36] Truman fired MacArthur on April 11, 1951.[37]

Truman's decision sparked public fury. Angry citizens inundated the White House
with more than 250,000 telegrams of protest.[38] A Gallup poll revealed that almost 70
percent of voters supported MacArthur. Across the country, flags flew upside down
or at half-mast. In some places, citizens burned Truman and Acheson in effigy. On
Capitol Hill, Republicans were privately gleeful and publicly outraged because Truman, they believed, had once again fumbled the ball in Asia. Publicly they were more
than ready to milk the public's wrath. "Impeach him," rolled off the tongues of many
Republicans. In a Senate speech the morning of MacArthur's dismissal, Republican
William Jenner of Indiana even suggested that Truman was a Soviet agent. "I charge
that this country today is in the hands of a secret inner coterie, which is directed by
agents of the Soviet Union," Jenner said in April 1951.[39]

In most cases, however, Republicans assailed Truman not so much for firing
MacArthur, but for his unwillingness to follow MacArthur's advice to take the United
States into direct military conflict with communist China. Typical was the critique
of Republican Senator Richard Nixon of California, "I believe that rather than follow the advice of those who would appease the Communists what we should do
is . . . bring the war to a successful military conclusion by taking the necessary steps
in implementation of the resolution passed by the United Nations, to the effect that
Communist China was an aggressor."[40] Nixon and others were essentially urging Truman to launch a full-scale assault on China in the calculated belief that the Soviet
Union would not enter the fight.

As the nationwide vilification of Truman continued, MacArthur returned home to
a hero's welcome. On April 19, eight days after his dismissal, the defiant general stood
at the podium in the chamber of the House of Representatives. In perhaps one of the

more bizarre public events in U.S. history, the elected representatives of the American people cheered an insubordinate general who had challenged the constitutional principle of civilian control of the foreign and military policies of the United States.

Standing before a joint meeting of Congress, MacArthur defiantly articulated his own foreign policy. Decrying the Truman administration's refusal to fight the Chinese, MacArthur indirectly accused his critics of appeasement. "Like blackmail," said MacArthur, such an attitude "lays the basis for new and successively greater demands until, as in blackmail, violence becomes the only other alternative. Why, my soldiers asked of me, surrender military advantages to an enemy in the field? I could not answer."[41]

As MacArthur staged his triumphant return, Republicans praised the general and his policies. "The choice between MacArthur and Acheson is the only issue," Robert Taft said, adding that it was a choice between "a more aggressive war against China or an appeasement peace." This praise for MacArthur was predicated more on an appreciation of the general as a political club with which to pound Harry Truman than as a valuable foreign policy advisor. Despite the Republicans' professed agreement with MacArthur's desire to take the battle to the Chinese, no one offered a congressional resolution that embodied his proposed policy. During joint hearings of the Senate's Armed Services and Foreign Relations committees, a different image of MacArthur emerged. He was strangely uninformed or uninterested in world affairs and expressed confused and contradictory opinions about the nature and objective of Soviet communism. Worst, the Joint Chiefs of Staff and Defense Secretary George C. Marshall contradicted MacArthur's claims that they had supported his military strategy for Korea.[42] MacArthur's fading fortunes provided no great political boost for Truman. The crisis arrived on the heels of an embarrassing showing by Democrats in the 1950 congressional elections—Republicans gained five Senate and twenty-eight House seats—and an election year that had seriously and deeply weakened Truman's standing with the American public. Piled on top of other perceived mistakes in China and the damaging attacks on the loyalty and competence of Truman's State Department, the MacArthur episode made the weight of negative public opinion almost unbearable. By early 1952, Americans were weary of the Korean War (a conflict, in stalemate, that would continue until the summer of 1953). They also harbored serious and lasting doubts about Democratic foreign policies—doubts only confirmed by MacArthur's dismissal.

General Dwight Eisenhower, who had initially supported Truman's actions in Korean in 1950, expressed a different view about the war in 1952 after he became the Republican Party's nominee for president. The man who had been Truman's NATO commander in Europe now vigorously campaigned against his former commander's Korea policies with credibility and stature that few men of his time could claim. Only two weeks before the election, Eisenhower effectively sealed his election over Democratic nominee Adlai Stevenson when he told a crowd in Detroit that, if elected, "I shall go to Korea."[43] Despite talk about "liberation" for the "captive peoples," Eisenhower eventually settled for a Korean truce—instead of unifying the nation under a democratic system of government—that restored the prewar status quo.[44]

Soon the war was largely forgotten. By the time diplomats gathered in Geneva in June 1954 to discuss the future of Korea, there was another conflict brewing in Asia.

This one, in Indochina, would dominate their talks and eventually draw the United States into its longest and most divisive war.

VITO MARCANTONIO (1902–1954)

A congressman from East Harlem in New York City, Vito Marcantonio was the most prominent opponent of American participation in the Korean War. First elected to Congress in 1934 as a Republican, he was among the most avid supporters of President Franklin Roosevelt's New Deal programs. Despite his strong support for the Democratic president, Marcantonio lost reelection in the Democratic landslide of 1936. Two years later he was back, this time as a member of the newly organized American Labor Party. Marcantonio earned a reputation as a fierce advocate of the poor. "He is willing to live in their slums, rub elbows with the best and the worst of them, work himself to the thin edge of a frazzle for them," a Saturday Evening Post *reporter observed in 1947. In 1950, after President Harry Truman ordered U.S. forces into Korea, Marcantonio was the only House member to vote against the action. Widely considered the most liberal member of Congress during his tenure, he was finally defeated for reelection in 1950 after leaders of the Republican, Democratic, and Liberal parties joined forces against him. He died of a heart attack in 1954 while campaigning for his former congressional seat. The following speech to the House was delivered two days after the North Korean invasion and on the day of President Truman's decision to send U.S. forces to Korea to repel the invasion.[45]*

SPEECH TO U.S. HOUSE OF REPRESENTATIVES
June 27, 1950

The argument is advanced here that this action can be justified as a result of the United Nations Charter. That has been the tenor of the argument. I disagree with any such contention. However, I say that when we agreed to the United Nations Charter we never agreed to supplant our Constitution with the United Nations Charter. The power to declare and make war is vested in the representatives of the people, in the Congress of the United States. That power has today been usurped from us with the reading of this short statement by the President to the people of the world. We here in Congress are asked to supinely accept this usurpation of our right as representatives of the American people. We have abdicated it for I have heard no protest, I have heard not a single word against it. I have no other recourse but to stand up and point out exactly what this action is, how it violates our Constitution, our democratic traditions, and how it deprives the American people of the right to express themselves on the vital question of war and peace, a power and a right properly vested in the representatives of the American people, the Congress, by those who wisely wrote our Constitution. . . .

Here now we are sending American aviators to lay down their lives, sending American sailors to lay down their lives, and who knows how soon it will be before our infantry will be sent to lay down their lives to defend, aid and abet tyranny and perpetrate aggression against the Korean people who strive for a united and independent nation.

Now, you may want this action. I do not. I know that the American people will not want this action when they think it over, and I know that they will thrust through this terrible dark cloud of war that has been descending on them. Oh, yes, you can indulge in attacks on communism. You can keep on making impassioned pleas for the destruction of communism, but I tell you that the issue in China, in Asia, in Korea and in Viet Nam is the right of these peoples to self-determination, to a government of their own, to independence and national unity.

Remember one thing: A bomb was dropped on Hiroshima. It had terrible consequences, but it did not frighten the people of China and it did not frighten the people of Korea. For again, these people, despite the terror of the atom bomb, have refused to abandon their efforts for national liberation. They will no more abandon this objective than the American people did during our Revolution.

I also say, Mr. Chairman, that in the light of this background that before this action can be taken this question should be debated here and decided here. The vote must be taken here by us as representatives of the American people whether or not American aviators and American seamen shall be shot down, their blood spilled in defense of tyranny in a conflict similar to our own Civil War. That is a power which is vested in us by the Constitution. I shall do all that I can—alone perhaps, but living with my conscience—to oppose this course which is not in the defense of the best interests of the American people.

War is not inevitable; there are alternatives, but this declaration on the part of President Truman is an acceptance of the doctrine of the inevitability of war. I stand here and challenge that doctrine. I say that the ingenuity of Americans and people all over the world challenge this doctrine.[46]

KENNETH WHERRY (1892–1951)

The archconservative Kenneth Wherry from Nebraska was one of President Truman's harshest critics. Known to Washington reporters as the "Merry Mortician"—he was a licensed embalmer—Wherry entered the U.S. Senate in 1942 by defeating his mentor and former friend George Norris. An electrifying speaker, Wherry quickly rose to prominence. His Republican colleagues elected him whip after less than two years in the Senate. An isolationist who had opposed the Marshall Plan and other forms of foreign aid, Wherry launched a fierce attack on Truman after the president fired General Douglas MacArthur for insubordination in 1951. The MacArthur incident revived the partisan warfare over the war in Korea as Republicans exploited public outrage over the dismissal and launched a more forceful attack on Truman's military and foreign policies.[47]

SENATOR WHERRY DEFENDS GENERAL MACARTHUR
Nationwide radio broadcast, April 12, 1951

The American people are deeply disturbed over the dismissal of General MacArthur, our vacillating foreign policy, and our hit-or-miss national defense planning.

What the American people want is national security. They are asking for a sound program of national defense. They are demanding a thorough congressional ventilation of the Truman-MacArthur affair, and other phases of the administration's zigzag, inept foreign policies that have led our Nation to the brink of another world war.

Cries of "wolf, wolf" and charges that others are trying to maneuver the United States into another world war, will not enable those responsible for our present perilous situation to escape the wrath of the American people.

To charge General MacArthur with attempting to involve the United States in a gigantic war with Red China and precipitate unleashing of a third world war is resented by every thinking American familiar with the glorious record of this great statesman, soldier, patriot.

The pygmies cannot bring down this giant, this tower of strength and deserving idol of the American people.

Compare the monumental record of General MacArthur with that of his accusers, with their record of moral decay, greed, corruption, and confusion of these weaklings in the Truman administration.

The result of such a comparison can be only an alarm to the American people.

With all the force that is in me, fellow Americans, I ask you to remember the admonition that "eternal vigilance is the price of liberty." . . .

Yes, fellow Americans, it is high time to become vigilant and militant. Your freedoms are at stake, and there is danger that runaway inflation will consume the people's wealth and render our beloved country unable to stand as the bulwark of freedom against the communistic threat.

Pollyanna speeches by the President that he is against war and is trying to prevent a third world war are not enough. The American people do not question his sincerity or his patriotism. None of us wants another world war. But there is an old adage that the road to destruction is paved with good intentions.

Fellow Americans, Gen. Douglas MacArthur needs no defense. He will take care of that when he comes home. And this leader of our victorious forces in the Pacific in World War II, this wounded hero of World War I, will return to his beloved country in triumph armed with the sword of experience and a knowledge of economic, political, and military conditions in the Far East unsurpassed by any living American. . . .

General MacArthur has said that the United Nations forces are fighting with one arm behind their backs, meaning inability to bomb Communist supply bases across the Yalu River creates a great handicap. Everybody knows this is true. General MacArthur revealed no military secret in pointing that out.

And, fellow Americans, the constitutional power of the President—as Commander in Chief of the Armed Forces—gives him no authority to consign American troops to fight under conditions in which they cannot defend themselves.

Certainly the Constitution does not give the Commander in Chief the power to subject American boys to enemy fire without the right to fire back.

Certainly this is the position that the Commander in Chief has taken in Korea, and you can interpret it no other way.

Over and over, the President says, he is against a third world war growing out of the conflict in Korea. But our forces in Korea are now fighting Chinese Reds. They are there by many thousands and there are hundreds of thousands behind them in China. Indications now are that they are going to continue to pour into Korea, and the fighting against Red Chinese and perhaps other "volunteer" Communists, will continue on and on in Korea.

And, I ask you, what hope did President Truman offer to you, the American people, last night for a victorious conclusion of his mission to Korea? When will it ever end? Yes; and lest we forget, fellow Americans, it was his mission. He ordered the American forces into action without approval of the Congress. He usurped that power to make war. He did so without authority of the Congress; and, let me remind you, Congress never has surrendered its war-making power to the United Nations. It appears, from the President's radio address, that there is a new policy for our forces in Korea. They were sent there originally to liberate all of Korea, take the offensive, and punish the North Koreans and their helpers into submission.

But now it is evident we are to wage a holding action in Korea somewhere near the thirty-eighth parallel. Our forces are to stand there like the Rock of Gibraltar—beating down the onrushing hordes from across the Yalu River.

We now are to prove to the Communists by this firm stand that it is folly for them to continue the war and they should humbly appeal for peace, turn over all of Korea to the Koreans, and never make war again.

Fellow Americans, the President now has written off his original venture into Korea to defeat the North Koreans and restore freedom to the whole country. His new policy now is to show the North Koreans and Red China that they cannot drive us out.

That's the Korean policy of the administration.

Oh, Mr. President, there is not much comfort in this outlook. The new strategy means more and more tear-stained pillows throughout our land.

This is why the American people want to hear General MacArthur. They believe that from his vast knowledge and experience in the South Pacific, he can recommend a better way to accomplish vindication for the forces of freedom in Korea.[48]

CHAPTER 10

THE VIETNAM WAR

"YELLOW IN COLOR AND LACKING IN COURAGE"

THE DAY BEFORE HE KILLED HIMSELF TO PROTEST THE Vietnam War, Norman Morrison, a thirty-two-year-old pacifist and the executive secretary of a Baltimore-area Quaker meetinghouse, learned the sad news about forty-eight civilians in South Vietnam who had died after U.S. planes mistakenly bombed them. The next day, Monday, November 2, 1964, Morrison took his year-old daughter and drove to the Pentagon in Arlington, Virginia, and sat on the lawn under the office of Defense Secretary Robert McNamara. After placing his daughter safely away from the spot where he would die, Morrison doused his body with kerosene, struck a match, and set himself on fire.

Morrison had perished, the *New York Times* reported the next morning, in the same manner as the Buddhist monks in Vietnam who had begun taking their lives in 1963. In fact, on the day of Morrison's death, the paper reported the death of a monk from self-immolation in the South Vietnamese capital of Saigon. One week later, in New York, Roger LaPorte, a twenty-one-year-old member of the Catholic Worker movement, staged a similar protest at the United Nations building. Several days before, LaPorte had attended a draft card–burning ceremony at Union Square, where several hostile onlookers had shouted, "Burn yourselves, not your cards!" A melancholy LaPorte met that challenge, dousing himself with gasoline and setting himself on fire. Before he died, the young man explained, "I'm against war, all wars. I did this as a religious action."[1]

The war in Vietnam that Morrison and LaPorte protested with their lives had been fought since the early days of Harry Truman's administration. In that time, the United States had slowly escalated its involvement—at first, supporting the French, who, when expelled by the Japanese during World War II, unsuccessfully tried to reestablish their colonial presence. Under the guise of fighting communism, the French requested U.S. assistance. When the French failed and began leaving in 1954, the United States stepped in, helping support the new government of South Vietnam—and taking up the fight against the North Vietnamese leader, Ho Chi Minh. But Ho and his determined troops proved formidable. American guns, ammunition, equipment, and other material support alone could not win the war. By the early 1960s, it seemed clear that the South Vietnamese needed more U.S. assistance and military know-how. President John F. Kennedy gave them sixteen thousand U.S. military advisors, with many of them instructing the country's military in guerilla warfare. That failed, as the South Vietnamese army was lackluster and commanded by inept, but well-connected commanders.

When Kennedy died in November 1963, Lyndon Johnson inherited the war. Throughout 1964, Johnson kept Vietnam out of his presidential campaign. When he did speak of the issue, it was usually to reassure voters that he would seek "no wider war" and that "we don't want our American boys to do the fighting for Asian boys."[2] The North Vietnamese attacks on an American destroyer, the *Maddox*, in the Gulf of Tonkin in August 1964 drastically changed Johnson's policy. The incident first appeared to be unprovoked aggression in international waters (the Americans had actually provoked the incident by violating North Vietnam's territorial waters). Following what the Pentagon claimed was a second attack on an American ship in the gulf, Johnson asked Congress for expansive military authority and authorization to use the U.S. military in a broad fight against communist aggression in the region.

From the beginning, Democratic senators Wayne Morse of Oregon and Ernest Gruening of Alaska were skeptical of the Pentagon's story about the Tonkin Gulf incidents and, more importantly, were concerned that the congressional resolution was a blank check for war with no meaningful input from Congress. Morse believed the war was "illegal" and derided the conflict as the result of "sheer stupidity." Gruening said it was a "bloody and wanton stalemate," and insisted that "I consider the life of one American youth worth more than this putrid mess." About the Gulf of Tonkin Resolution, Morse predicted, "Senators who vote for it will live to regret it." Morse insisted the United States had provoked the North Vietnamese. Gruening agreed: "We have lost altogether too many American lives already." The two men were the only members of Congress to oppose the resolution.[3] Voters in their home states later turned both out of office, largely because of their outspoken opposition to the Vietnam War.

By 1965 the United States began to take over the fighting in Vietnam. In February 1965—after a Vietcong attack on a U.S. air base at Pleiku killed eight Americans and wounded another 126—Johnson steadily increased the U.S. role. That month, U.S. war planes began a three-year bombing campaign—named *Rolling Thunder*—over North Vietnam. In March 1965, the first wave of U.S. combat troops landed on the beaches at Da Nang. Before the year's end, eighty thousand American troops would be in Vietnam.

Back home, an antiwar movement was born. At first, it was peaceful. In March 1964, three thousand students and faculty members at a handful of universities turned out for a series of lectures and debates about the war known as "teach-ins." The idea quickly spread. Students and faculty members held teach-ins on thirty-five college campuses the following week. Before the summer break, more than 120 colleges across the nation had begun their own teach-in protests, including a six-hour event at the University of California at Berkeley in May, attended by more than twenty thousand people. Another teach-in that month, in Washington, DC, reached more than one hundred thousand people on 122 campuses via a closed-circuit radio network.[4]

Students and others were also hitting the streets in protest. In April, more than fifteen thousand protesters gathered in Washington, DC, many more than the organizers—Students for a Democratic Society (SDS)—had expected and the largest gathering of war protesters assembled in U.S. history. The protesters picketed the White House, three and four abreast, before adjourning to a theater near the Washington Monument to hear speeches by Senator Gruening, journalist I. F. Stone, civil rights leader Robert Moses, and Paul Potter, the twenty-two-year-old SDS president.[5]

In Congress and at the White House, some officials viewed the nascent protest movement with alarm. Democratic Senator Thomas Dodd of Connecticut said the mild protests were "tantamount to open insurrection," while Democratic Senator Richard Russell of Georgia labeled the protesters disloyal because their dissent "will cause the Communists to believe they can win if they hold on a little longer."[6]

The protests of students, and senators like Morse and Gruening, angered Johnson. He confessed confusion to his wife, "How can an American Senator or an American newspaperman or an American student tie the hands of our fellow military men? Are they duped; are they sucked in?"[7] Despite what Johnson and others believed about communist influence in the antiwar movement, students and other protest leaders were not getting their talking points from Hanoi or Beijing. The budding antiwar movement was already splitting into opposing camps—a traditional liberal group, which favored a negotiated settlement with the North Vietnamese followed by a gradual withdrawal of American troops, and a small group of radicals, including the SDS, which demanded immediate withdrawal of troops. The more radical group, which would eventually dominate the movement, saw the war in Vietnam as one symptom of the many ills that affected the United States in the mid-1960s, including racial strife, poverty, and economic and social injustice. (In this way, the latter group was reminiscent of the Progressives who opposed U.S. involvement in World War I for fear it would arrest the advance of progressive social reforms.)[8] "We feel passionately and angrily about things in America," an SDS spokesman said in April, "and we feel that a war in Asia will destroy what we're trying to do here."[9]

In October 1965, a more angry and vocal antiwar movement—sparked by the escalating violence in Vietnam—came to life in the form of draft card burning, explained by one protester as a "major symbolic act of renunciation of the war in Vietnam and U.S. militarism generally."[10] In mid-October, at an Army Induction Center in New York City, twenty-two-year-old David J. Miller became the first person to burn his draft card following passage of federal legislation making the act a felony. Miller burned his card for the benefit of television and newspaper photographers (as well as the mob that tried to attack him) and the result was a steady increase in the number of young men who protested the war by destroying their draft cards.[11] Between 1965 and 1975, federal officials charged more than twenty-two thousand Americans with various draft law violations, convicting 8,756. Most claimed their act was a political statement against the war and thus was protected by the First Amendment. In a 1968 decision, *United States v. O'Brien*, the Supreme Court rejected that argument, allowing the convictions to stand. Burning a draft card, the Court said, was not dissent, it was direct resistance to a federal law that prohibited the cards' willful destruction. In all, 4,001 Americans were jailed for draft violations.[12]

Protests across the nation grew more intense. Tens of thousands turned out for antiwar demonstrations and rallies in more than one hundred cities on October 16 and 17, 1965. General Maxwell Taylor, the former U.S. ambassador to Saigon, who still advised Johnson on Vietnam policy, worried aloud that the demonstrations would send the wrong signal to the communist leaders of North Vietnam that "there is a real division of strength in this country, and that may tempt them to prolong the war." Morse, however, applauded the marchers, "who will not be cowed into submission by the intolerant bigots who believe that because our country is on an illegal course we must support its illegality." Meanwhile, a State Department spokesman scoffed at what he called "noisy demonstrations," arguing that they reflected only an "infinitesimal fraction" of American public opinion.[13]

While the protesters clearly did not yet represent mainstream public opinion—that would not begin turning against the war until 1966—they represented a far greater percentage than the small fraction imagined by the State Department. In August 1965, 24 percent of those polled by the Gallup organization believed sending troops to Vietnam had been a mistake. (Sixty-one percent of those polled supported the administration's decisions in Vietnam.) While not insignificant, those favoring withdrawal were vastly outnumbered by the war's supporters.[14] During this early period—when popular support for the war ran high—dissent was a courageous act that opened up dissenters to charges of disloyalty, or worse. One charge was that the protestors were communists. In October 1965, the U.S. Senate's Internal Security subcommittee alleged "substantial Communist infiltration" in the teach-in movement. The report included the reckless statement by Senator Dodd that "control of the anti-Vietnam movement has clearly passed . . . into the hands of the Communists and extremists elements who are openly sympathetic to the Vietcong and openly hostile to the United States."[15]

The growing war protests sparked strong criticism from other Senate leaders, as well as the promise of an official investigation by the Johnson administration. Republican Senator Thomas Kuchel of California labeled anyone who argued against registering for the draft as "vile and venomous" whose protests "sow the seeds of treason." To Republican Senate leader Everett Dirksen, the draft protestors were "enough to make any person loyal to this country weep." Democrat Frank Lausche of Ohio said the demonstrators were "yellow in color and lacking in courage." At the White House, Johnson's press secretary, Bill Moyers, conveyed the president's feeling of disgust with the protestors and communicated the president's enthusiastic endorsement of a Justice Department investigation of possible communist infiltration of the movement.[16]

If the verbal assaults and threats of investigation were intended to dampen the protests, they failed. The following month, more than twenty-five thousand protestors converged on Washington for another large antiwar rally. Max Frankel, the *New York Times* reporter who covered the march, rebutted accusations that the protestors were radical traitors. Most of the protesters, he wrote, "would not have been out of place at the Army-Navy game." Frankel, however, also noted "small clusters of fired-up youth, some of whom carried the flags of the Vietcong."[17]

To many Americans, it was the unseemly image of protesters as pro-Vietcong, anti-American radicals that enabled Johnson and his prowar allies to portray the movement as dupes of the Vietcong and their communist propaganda. However, televised hearings in February 1966 by the Senate Foreign Relations Committee—chaired by Democratic Senator J. William Fulbright of Arkansas—gave the antiwar movement new credibility. Americans heard criticism of Johnson's war policies from respected military and foreign affairs experts, including retired Lieutenant General James Gavin and George F. Kennan. Gavin told senators that the Vietnam War had bogged down the nation in a "baited trap." Kennan asserted, "This is not only not our business, but I don't think we can do it successfully."[18]

Fulbright's hearings showed the nation a new face of dissent. It was not long-haired radicals pumping protest signs in the air; it was well-known, esteemed members of the military and diplomatic establishment who questioned the nation's policies in Vietnam. As one committee staff member later remarked, the witnesses "made dissent respectable." The results were unmistakable. Prior to the hearings, in January 1966, 63 percent of those surveyed by the Harris polling organization said they approved of Johnson's handling of the war. After the hearings, in late February, Johnson's approval rating on the same issue had dropped to 49 percent. The public, however, had not yet abandoned the war. Almost half of those polled wanted stronger military action to end the conflict. Only 9 percent favored immediate withdrawal.[19]

Throughout 1966, the protests continued—and escalated. Public doubts about the war continued to grow and Johnson continued to pour men and resources into Vietnam. In June, General William Westmoreland, the commander of U.S. troops in Vietnam, asked Johnson to increase the number of U.S. forces to 431,000 over the coming year (by year's end, 385,000 U.S. troops would be in Vietnam). As he awaited White House approval of his request, the general was already making plans to increase U.S. troops to 542,000 by December 1967. In all, 6,144 American soldiers would die in Vietnam in 1966, bringing the total of U.S. combat deaths since the war's beginning to 8,408.

While public support for the war remained relatively steady, media attention on the war and its conduct increased. American television audiences began seeing, for the first time, daily dramatic images of combat activities—including aerial bombing and the dropping of napalm. As the images of wounded soldiers began to appear, and the daily count of combat casualties began to invade American living rooms, a growing number of Americans began wondering where their president and his advisors were taking the country. By the summer of 1966, less than half of the public approved of Johnson's handling of the war. One in three now believed that U.S. involvement in Vietnam was a mistake.[20]

As the draft calls and battlefield deaths increased, so did outspoken domestic dissent. In May 1966, the Student Nonviolent Coordinating Committee (SNCC), a respected civil rights organization, broke with President Johnson. "We cannot be a party to attempts by the White House to use black Americans to recoup a loss of prestige internationally," the group said, announcing its refusal to attend a civil rights conference with Johnson.[21] At the heart of SNCC's dissent was growing concern that black Americans were being drafted, and were dying, in disproportionate numbers.

That concern prompted the nation's most respected and prominent civil rights leader, the Reverend Martin Luther King, to break with Johnson over the war in February 1967. King had previously expressed his concern over Vietnam. But his

more forceful dissent came after he saw photographs of a Vietnamese mother holding a baby killed by U.S. troops. In late February, King appeared in Los Angeles with
antiwar senators Gruening, Mark Hatfield of Oregon, Eugene McCarthy of Min-
nesota, and George McGovern of South Dakota. Bemoaning the nation's "declining
moral status in the world," King declared, "Our nation, which initiated so much of
the revolutionary spirit of the modern world, is now cast in the mold of being an arch
anti-revolutionary. We are engaged in a war that seeks to turn the clock of history
back and perpetuate white colonialism."[22]

In April, King outlined his dissent more fully in a speech to three thousand people
at the Riverside Church in New York. Calling the war "an enemy of the poor," King
alluded to his opposition to recent urban violence, "I knew that I could never again
raise my voice against the violence of the oppressed in the ghettos without having
first spoken clearly to the greatest purveyor of violence in the world today—my own
government."[23] The speech prompted some Johnson aides to speculate that King had
"thrown in with the commies."[24] Some civil rights leaders questioned his ability to
continue leading their movement. Even the New York Times criticized him in an editorial entitled "Dr. King's Error."[25]

King's protest fully blossomed in mid-April when he joined the massive Spring
Mobilization to End the War in Vietnam. Most of his advisors protested that his
dissent would only antagonize Johnson and harm the civil rights movement. King
persisted and joined several hundred thousand protestors in New York on April 15,
1967. As they marched from Central Park toward Fifth Avenue, some of protestors
chanted slogans that had become staples of the antiwar movement, "Hell no, we
won't go" and "Hey, Hey, L. B. J., how many kids did you kill today?" Most marched
quietly and peacefully. Some bystanders, however, pelted marchers with eggs and red
paint. Steel rods thrown from a construction site hit several marchers.[26]

King correctly sensed the growing level of discontent and anger brewing on college campuses. Prompted by the SDS and its desire to move "into a deeper and riskier
commitment" to action to end the war, draft resistance increased significantly in
1967. In March, an SDS group at Cornell University issued "A Call to Burn Draft
Cards," advising potential allies that "our action makes us liable to penalties of up
to five years in prison and $10,000 in fines." To some, civil disobedience seemed the
only way. "Murderers do not respond to reason," the group said. "Powerful resistance
is now demanded: radical, illegal, unpleasant, sustained." The group's first major protest occurred on the morning of the April 15 mobilization march in New York when
about 175 demonstrators tossed their burning draft cards into a coffee can. At least
one participant—Martin Jeezer, an editor of WIN magazine—compared his act to
prominent dissenters of earlier eras:

> To destroy one's draft card, to place one's conscience before the dictates of one's gov-
> ernment is in the highest tradition of human conduct. This country was not created
> by men subservient to law and government. It was created and made great by civil
> disobedients like Quakers who refused to compromise their religion to suit the Puri-
> tan theocracy; by Puritans who openly defied British authority; by provo-type Sons of
> Liberty who burned stamps to protest the Stamp Act and who dumped tea in Boston
> Harbor. . . . When people tell me that I have no respect for law and order and that I do

not love my country, I reply: "Thomas Jefferson, Tom Paine, Garrison, Thoreau, A. J. Muste, the Freedom Riders, these are my countrymen whom I love; with them I will take my stand.[27]

Draft resistance began to catch on. Supported by prominent writers like Arthur Miller and Norman Mailer, students at more than twenty-five universities organized draft resistance initiatives that would feature various acts of civil disobedience. In response, the Johnson administration announced that those who burned their draft cards would be among the first forced into the armed services and that those who violated other laws, such as blocking troop trains, would be prosecuted. In the coming years, federal officials would indict more than twenty-five thousand young people for draft resistance–related crimes and would send 3,250 of them to prison.[28] Johnson angrily told aides, "I'm not going to let the Communists take this government and they're doing it right now." On orders from Johnson (and in violation of federal law), the Central Intelligence Agency (CIA) began investigating leaders of the major antiwar groups and worked (unsuccessfully) to gather evidence that the organizations were controlled by communist organizations or foreign governments.[29]

By August 1967, McNamara acknowledged the futility of the bombing in testimony to a Senate committee. "We have no reason to believe," he said, "[that more bombing] would break the will of the North Vietnamese people or sway the purpose of their leaders."[30] Yet the bombing continued. Johnson kept sending more troops to Vietnam. As the fighting continued, antiwar protests throughout the country grew larger and more impassioned. A series of antiwar rallies around the country culminated in October 1967 with a huge protest at the Lincoln Memorial. More than one hundred thousand marchers demanded an end to the bombings, withdrawal of American forces from Vietnam, and immediate peace talks with the North Vietnamese.[31]

For Johnson, Vietnam was a quagmire threatening his political future. His approval ratings on the war dropped to 28 percent in October 1967. Many of his problems resulted from his deceptive ways with Congress and the American people. First, he and McNamara had lied about the Gulf of Tonkin incidents. Then, he concealed the costs of the war to maintain congressional support for his Great Society programs. Finally, he and his military advisors destroyed their credibility by continually depicting the flagging U.S. war effort in deceptively glowing terms. Despite the stalemate in Vietnam, most Americans believed that the U.S. Army had all but crippled the Vietcong fighters in South Vietnam. "We are making steady progress without any question," General Westmoreland declared in November 1967.[32]

The events of January and February 1968 proved how wrong Westmoreland was. In the early morning hours of January 30—during the traditional cease-fire period of Tet, the Vietnamese New Year—a squad of Vietcong commandos laid siege to the U.S. embassy in Saigon and killed a young U.S. Army guard. Before their assault was over six hours later, the commandos would kill five U.S. soldiers in fierce fighting that was amply covered by American network television crews. Elsewhere in the city, the Vietcong attacked Westmoreland's headquarters, as well as the South Vietnamese general staff offices. That evening in the United States, millions of shocked Americans watched the network news broadcasts and learned that, despite the presence of half a million American troops in South Vietnam, the Vietcong appeared strong and viable. By the time officials in Washington learned of the attacks, more than eighty-four thousand Vietcong and North Vietnamese troops were staging well-coordinated attacks on forty-four provincial capitals, sixty-four district capitals, and five of the six major cities in South Vietnam.

Vietcong attacks were soon quashed in almost every city and town, but the Tet offensive had a devastating impact on American public opinion. For months, Johnson and Westmoreland had promised that the U.S. military would soon begin turning over the fighting to the South Vietnamese. Many Americans, including those in Congress, now realized that Johnson had deceived them about the enemy's strength. In late February, CBS News anchor Walter Cronkite—the nation's most respected journalist—returned from Vietnam and delivered a devastating assessment of the war to his viewers, "To say that we are mired in stalemate seems the only realistic, yet unsatisfactory, conclusion."[33]

By early 1968, more than fifteen thousand American soldiers had died in Vietnam. Another 110,000 had been wounded. In Washington, the war claimed another casualty—Johnson. On March 31, he stunned the nation when, at the end of nationally televised speech declaring a partial bombing halt, he announced he would not seek reelection.

Johnson's retirement set off a furious campaign to replace him and set up a fierce struggle for the Democratic presidential nomination among Vice President Hubert Humphrey and senators Eugene McCarthy and Robert Kennedy. With Kennedy's assassination in Los Angeles in July, the way was clear for Humphrey to challenge the Republican nominee, former Vice President Richard Nixon. But Humphrey first had to get past his party's nominating convention where delegates—deeply divided over the war—gathered in Chicago during the last week of August 1968. Although Johnson and Humphrey both supported the war, 40 percent of the delegates favored a platform plank demanding immediate withdrawal of American troops from Vietnam.

Mayhem ruled outside the convention, as fifteen thousand antiwar demonstrators, some waving Vietcong flags, clashed violently with local police. When the protestors tried to march on the convention hall, five thousand police officers assaulted them with clubs, rifle butts, mace, and tear gas. Some demonstrators responded with a fusillade of rocks and bottles. In the violence, played out in prime time for a horrified national television audience, more than 1,000 protestors were injured and 662 arrested.[34]

The disaster at Chicago was a gift for Nixon, allowing him to appear as one who wanted to end the war with a negotiated settlement. "The war must be ended," Nixon said. "It must be ended honorably, consistent with America's limited aims and with the long-term requirements of peace in Asia." Nixon added for those worried about his resolve that the war "must be waged more effectively" in order to achieve a negotiated end.[35] In the end, Nixon's gambit worked. Humphrey tried to separate himself from Johnson's policies, but Nixon's rhetoric about ending the war honorably carried more weight. He beat Humphrey by fewer than half a million votes.

Johnson's retirement did not mean that, in the waning days of his term, he would not punish draft resisters and those who aided or encouraged them. In early January 1968, the Justice Department indicted the so-called Boston Five, a group of respected individuals who had urged young men to resist the draft. The five were famed pediatrician Dr. Benjamin Spock; Reverend William Sloan Coffin, chaplain of Yale

University; Mitchell Goodman, a New York writer; Marcus Raskin, codirector of the Institute for Policy Studies in Washington, DC; and Michael Ferber, a PhD student at Harvard University. The men barely knew each other prior to their indictments.

Their alleged crimes: in addition to attending antiwar press conferences and other gatherings at which young men turned over their draft cards to them, they had allegedly conspired to persuade draft evasion by signing a document—"A Call to Resist Illegitimate Authority"—written by Spock and Coffin the previous year. In the document they argued that the war "is unconstitutional and illegal." Therefore, they concluded, "every free man has a legal right and a moral duty to exert every effort to end this war, to avoid collusion with it, and to encourage others to do the same."[36] Twenty-three thousand people signed the "Call."[37] In June 1968, a federal jury convicted all but Raskin of conspiring to counsel draft evasion and the judge gave them two-year prison sentences. By the following summer, a federal appeals court overturned the convictions on technical grounds. The Justice Department dropped the cases.[38]

As much as Johnson resented and tried to punish the protest movement, his administration prosecuted only one Vietnam War–related conspiracy case—the Boston Five. Richard Nixon, who took office in 1969, was far more hostile to protest and dissent. Nixon's Justice Department extensively employed conspiracy law to jail and silence the radical antiwar protestors. The prosecutions always failed because of acquittals, government misconduct, or successful appeals.

Most prominent was the case against the so-called Chicago Eight, a loosely connected group of antiwar leaders charged by the Nixon Justice Department with conspiring to cross state lines to incite violence at the Chicago Democratic National Convention in August 1968. After a raucous, four-and-a-half-month trial in which the defendants openly and repeatedly expressed contempt for the presiding judge, the jury returned not-guilty verdicts on the conspiracy charges, but guilty verdicts for five defendants accused of inciting a riot. The judge rewarded the defendants' contempt by sentencing each to the maximum—five years—and then added 175 contempt sentences, increasing the defendants' (and their lawyers') sentences by two-and-a-half months to four years. An appeals court overturned the convictions and contempt sentences, noting the "deprecatory and often antagonistic attitude" of the judge. The Justice Department dropped the criminal charges and retried the defendants and their lawyers on the contempt charges alone. Despite securing guilty verdicts against three defendants, a new judge refused to impose a sentence, explaining that the defendants had been goaded by the previous judge's improper and "condemnatious conduct."[39]

In Southeast Asia, meanwhile, Nixon turned up the heat on North Vietnam and Cambodia while beginning the slow process of withdrawing American troops. Beginning in March 1969, Nixon ordered secret bombing raids over neighboring Cambodia to destroy enemy base camps. Over fourteen months the United States dropped one hundred thousand tons of bombs on Cambodia, killing as many as one hundred thousand civilians and driving another two million from their homes. The military impact on the war was negligible. As the antiwar movement planned its largest protest against the war—a series of nationwide moratorium rallies scheduled for October 15—Nixon hoped to deflate the protests by announcing the withdrawal of an additional sixty thousand troops by December 15 and canceling draft calls for November and December.

Critics attacked Nixon's policy of gradual withdrawal as just another tactic to prolong the conflict. Far from tamping down the antiwar movement, Nixon's actions gave it new life. The moratorium attracted enormous crowds—in Boston, 100,000, and more than 250,000 in New York City. Protestors also attended large rallies in Washington, Philadelphia, Chicago, Los Angeles, Minneapolis, and Baltimore.[40]

Nixon claimed to be unimpressed. "There is nothing new we can learn from the demonstrations," he said in a letter to a Georgetown University student, adding "under no circumstances will I be affected whatever" by the moratorium and campus protests.[41] In a nationally televised speech on November 3, Nixon attacked the antiwar movement, spelled out his gradual withdrawal plan—"Vietnamization"—and defended the nation's military commitment in Southeast Asia. Most notable was Nixon's appeal to "the great silent majority" and his insinuation that the protest movement was aiding the enemy. "North Vietnam cannot defeat or humiliate the United States," Nixon said. "Only Americans can do that."[42] Despite bragging that the protests would not influence him, the antiwar movement had, indeed, intimidated Nixon. He quietly abandoned plans for an escalation of the conflict and sped up troop withdrawals. His "silent majority" speech, while generating an outpouring of public support for his policies, did little to silence the protest movement, evidenced by the massive mobilization rally—the largest protest march ever in Washington, DC—on November 15.[43]

Further deepening outrage over the war was Nixon's decision in late April 1970 to send U.S. combat troops into Cambodia. Students at more than 440 U.S. colleges took to the streets in angry protest. At Kent State University in Ohio, the unrest turned deadly when National Guard troops shot and killed four protesting students. Four more students died in violence at Jackson State College in Mississippi. Nixon blamed the protestors. "When dissent turns to violence," he said, "it invites tragedy."[44] The Cambodian invasion spurred Congress to action. In June 1970 the Senate repealed the 1964 Gulf of Tonkin Resolution, the basis for Lyndon Johnson's initial escalation of the war. Later, Congress ended funding for the war in Cambodia.[45]

Prodded by Lyndon Johnson, throughout the 1960s the Federal Bureau of Investigation (FBI) and CIA had investigated, infiltrated, and harassed the antiwar movement, producing little evidence of communist or foreign influence. Toward the end of his presidency, Johnson demanded FBI investigations of citizens who sent him antiwar letters or telegrams. When Nixon took office, he directed the FBI to increase its surveillance of the antiwar movement, demanding information on the "income sources of revolutionary groups." FBI agents attended antiwar rallies, collected the names of speakers, and reported their findings to the White House and other federal agencies. Nixon also directed the CIA to intensify domestic spying activities (illegal under U.S. law), which included break-ins, phone wiretaps, and opening mail. Over time, the CIA gathered information on three hundred thousand citizens.

Nixon also used the Internal Revenue Service (IRS) to harass antiwar organizations. At his behest, the IRS created an Activist Organizations Committee to investigate antiwar organizations and their members. The agency later renamed the unit the Special Services Staff (SSS) in hopes of concealing its objective, which was to "deal a blow to dissident elements" by targeting them for tax audits and investigations. In five years, the SSS collected information on more than 8,500 members of antiwar organizations, much of which it turned over to the White House, FBI, Secret Service, and Army intelligence.[46] By one estimate, domestic dissent may have consumed as much as 40 percent of the FBI's field work by the fall of 1970.[47]

According to one survey, Americans now considered themselves against the war by a 55 to 31 percent margin. Four-fifths said they were "fed up and tired of the war" and believed the protesters were "raising real questions which ought to be discussed and answered." Americans were also conflicted about dissent. Despite the war's overwhelming unpopularity, a plurality opposed the protests' radical nature, including the October 1969 moratorium. Three-fourths objected to the November mobilization rally. Three-fifths agreed that the antiwar movement helped the enemy and inhibited Nixon's ability to make peace. Americans, historian Charles DeBenedetti observed, "wanted to quit the fighting more than ever, but not to surrender."[48]

The massive protests continued. In May 1971, more than two hundred thousand peaceful protestors marched on Washington, while in San Francisco an antiwar rally attracted 150,000 people. Nixon insisted on aggressive crowd control. Over several days, Washington police arrested more than 13,400 protestors—7,200 on the first day, the largest mass arrest in American history.[49]

Nixon's poll numbers continued to drop, but so did the number of American troops in Vietnam. By the spring of 1972, 139,000 remained in South Vietnam (down from a high of almost half a million). This fed the perception that Nixon was ending the war, a notion furthered by the president's decision in 1973 to end the draft. Contrary to public perception, however, the war was far from over. Nixon continued the bombing and American troops continued to die. As the war raged, an increasingly splintered antiwar movement began to ebb.[50] Nixon's Vietnamization strategy and his deft attacks on antiwar organizations were sapping the movement of its momentum.

The antiwar movement may also have been the victim of its own success. It was, after all, the participation of and protests from a broad cross section of the American public (not just radical college students) that had forced Lyndon Johnson from office and prompted Richard Nixon to campaign on a plan to end the war. Although Nixon prolonged and escalated the conflict, widespread public opposition to the nation's Vietnam policies forced him to begin withdrawing troops early in his administration. In January 1973, with Congress threatening to cut off war funding, the United States and North Vietnam finally struck a peace deal. By April, most U.S. troops had left Vietnam.

Debate over the causes of the U.S. defeat in Vietnam would continue for more than thirty-five years as historians, military leaders, and politicians blamed the dissenters. General William Westmoreland, commander of U.S. forces in Vietnam, voiced that sentiment when he charged that "a misguided minority opposition . . . masterfully manipulated by Hanoi and Moscow" helped bring down the U.S. military effort.[51] As recently as 2007, a senior U.S. Defense Department official blamed domestic dissent for the U.S. failure in Vietnam.[52]

Historians and political operatives will continue debating whether dissent emboldened the enemy to keep fighting in Vietnam, as well as whether some of the more extreme tactics of the antiwar movement (burning draft cards and waving Vietcong flags) were wise or even constitutionally permissible forms of free speech. Historians generally accept, however, that no war in American history provoked a larger out-pouring of dissent and protest.[53]

More than a generation after it ended, the reputations of Lyndon Johnson, Richard Nixon, and other government leaders who presided over the war remain in tatters. In addition to the soldiers who fought or were wounded or killed in Vietnam, the dissenters and antiwar movement leaders are often considered heroes for their courage, eloquence, and vision. Some, like the four students at Kent State, gave their lives for their cause. Thousands more endured jail terms for civil disobedience. Far from being disparaged for their dissent, they are now celebrated, much like the civil rights leaders of the 1950s and 1960s. Perhaps the enduring gift these men and women left for future generations is the way they fundamentally altered the public's view of wartime dissent—for it could be said that the Vietnam War made wartime dissent, if not popular, respectable.

WAYNE MORSE (1900–1974)

A law professor and former dean of the University of Oregon Law School, Wayne Morse entered the U.S. Senate from Oregon in 1945 as a Republican. He left the party in 1952 in disgust over presidential nominee Dwight Eisenhower's aggressive courtship of ultraconservative Republican leaders, including the selection of Richard Nixon as vice president. At first an independent, he became a Democrat in 1955. Always a maverick, Morse was one of two members of Congress to oppose the 1964 Gulf of Tonkin Resolution (the other was Ernest Greuning of Alaska). He remained a fierce opponent of the Vietnam War throughout the rest of his Senate career, which ended in 1968 when voters turned him out of office largely because of his opposition to the war. In the following speech, Morse states his opposition to the Gulf of Tonkin Resolution, arguing that the United States was not a hapless victim of aggression, but rather had provoked the incident.[54]

THE GULF OF TONKIN RESOLUTION
Speech to the U.S. Senate, August 5, 1964

For 10 years, the role of the United States in South Vietnam has been that of a pro-vocateur, every bit as much as North Vietnam has been a provocateur. For 10 years, the United States, in South Vietnam, has violated the Geneva agreement of 1954.[55] For 10 years, our military policies in South Vietnam have sought to impose a military solution upon a political and economic problem. For 10 years the Communist nations of that part of the world have also violated the Geneva accord of 1954.

Not only do two wrongs not make one right, but also I care not how many wrongs we add together, we still do not come out with a summation except a summation of wrong—never a right.

The American effort to impose by force of arms a government of our own choosing upon a segment of the old colony of Indochina has caught up with us.

Our violations of the Geneva accord have caught up with us. Our violations of the United Nations Charter have caught up with us.

Our failure to apply the provisions of the Southeast Asia Treaty have caught up with us. We have been making covert war in southeast Asia for some time, instead of seeking to keep the peace. It was inevitable and inexorable that sooner or later we would have to engage in overt acts of war in pursuance of that policy, and we are now doing so. . . .

In recent months, evidence has been mounting that both the Pentagon and the State Department were preparing to escalate the war into North Vietnam. Many of the policies they have initiated and the statements they have made in public have been highly provocative of military conflict beyond the borders of South Vietnam.

When the high emotionalism of the present crisis has passed, and historians of the future will disclose some of the provocative things that have occurred, I have no doubt that they will disclose that for quite some time past, there have been violations of the North Vietnamese border and the Cambodian border by South Vietnam, as well as vice versa.

I am also satisfied that they will disclose that the United States was not an innocent bystander. We will not receive a verdict of innocence from the jury box of history on several counts.

Our extensive military aid to South Vietnam was a violation of the Geneva accords in the first instance. Our sending troops into South Vietnam, even under the semantic camouflage of designation as military advisers, was a violation of the Geneva accords. In fact, both of those two counts were also a clear violation of the spirit and intent of the peaceful purposes of the United Nations Charter itself.

Any violations of the borders of Cambodia and North Vietnam by the South Vietnamese were not conducted in a vacuum so far as U.S. assistance was concerned.

We assisted not only with materiel, but we advised on war plans, and our military presence in South Vietnam served as an ever-present strong back-stop to the South Vietnamese. I doubt if their military leaders acted at any time without the tacit approval of their American advisers.

In a very recent incident which was the forerunner to the attacks on American destroyers in the Tonkin Bay, it is known that South Vietnamese naval vessels bombarded two North Vietnamese islands within three to five or six miles of the main coast of North Vietnam. Of course, the national waters of North Vietnam extend, according to our international claims, three miles seaward from the eastern extremity of those islands and 12 miles seaward under national water boundary claims of North Vietnam. While the South Vietnamese vessels were attacking the North Vietnamese islands, the newspapers tell us that U.S. vessels of war were patrolling Tonkin Bay, presumably some six to 11 miles off the shore of North Vietnam.

Was the U.S. Navy standing guard while vessels of South Vietnam shelled North Vietnam? That is the clear implication of the incident. . . .

The U.S. Government knew that the matter of national and international waters was a controversial issue in Tonkin Bay. The United States also knew that the South Vietnamese vessels planned to bomb, and did bomb, two North Vietnamese islands within three to six miles of the coast of North Vietnam. Yet, these war vessels of the United States were in the vicinity of that bombing, some miles removed.

Can anyone question that even their presence was a matter of great moral value to South Vietnam? Or the propaganda value to the military totalitarian tyrant and despot who rules South Vietnam as an American puppet—[South Vietnam President Nguyen Khanh], who is really, when all is said and done, the leader whom we have put in charge of an American protectorate called South Vietnam?

It should be unnecessary to point out either to the Senate or to the American people what the position of the United States and its people would be if the tables were reversed and Soviet warships or submarines were to patrol five to 11 miles at sea while Cuban naval vessels bombarded Key West. . . .

The United States has much to lose and little to gain by continuing our unilateral military action in southeast Asia, unsanctioned by the United Nations and unaccompanied by allies.

No nation in history has had such a great opportunity as this one now has to strike a blow for peace at an international conference table.

I shall not support any substitute which takes the form of a predated declaration of war. In my judgment, that is what the pending joint resolution is.

I shall not support any delegation of the duty of Congress—of Congress, not the President—to determine an issue of war or peace.

I shall not support any substitute which takes the form of military action to expand the war or that encourages our puppets in Saigon to expand the war.[56]

THE CHICAGO FIVE: BENJAMIN SPOCK, MARCUS RASKIN, MITCHELL GOODMAN, MICHAEL FERBER, AND WILLIAM SLOANE COFFIN

These individuals, known as the "Chicago Five," published their manifesto against the Vietnam War in 1967. Although twenty-three thousand people signed it, the U.S. Justice Department focused on its authors, indicting them for their authorship, which officials said amounted to conspiring to "counsel, aid and abet" resistance to the draft. The jury convicted all but Raskin. Eventually all convictions were overturned on appeal.

A CALL TO RESIST ILLEGITIMATE AUTHORITY
Statement, 1967

To the young men of America, to the whole of the American people, and to all men of goodwill everywhere:

1. An ever growing number of young American men are finding that the American war in Vietnam so outrages their deepest moral and religious sense that they cannot contribute to it in any way. We share their moral outrage.
2. We further believe that the war is unconstitutional and illegal. Congress has not declared a war as required by the Constitution. Moreover, under the Constitution, treaties signed by the President and ratified by the Senate have the same force as the Constitution itself. The Charter of the United Nations is such a treaty. The Charter specifically obligates the United States to refrain from

force or the threat of force in international relations. It requires member states to exhaust every peaceful means of settling disputes and to submit disputes which cannot be settled peacefully to the Security Council. The United States has systematically violated all of these Charter provisions for thirteen years.

3. Moreover, this war violates international agreements, treaties and principles of law which the United States Government has solemnly endorsed. The combat role of the United States troops in Vietnam violates the Geneva Accords of 1954 which our government pledged to support but has since subverted. The destruction of rice, crops and livestock; the burning and bulldozing of entire villages consisting exclusively of civilian structures; the interning of civilian non-combatants in concentration camps; the summary executions of civilians in captured villages who could not produce satisfactory evidence of their loyalties or did not wish to be removed to concentration camps; the slaughter of peasants who dared to stand up in their fields and shake their fists at American helicopters—these are all actions of the kind which the United States and the other victorious powers of World War II declared to be crimes against humanity. . . .

4. We also believe it is an unconstitutional denial of religious liberty and equal protection of the laws to withhold draft exemption from men whose religious or profound philosophical beliefs are opposed to what in the Western religious tradition have been long known as unjust wars.

5. Therefore, we believe on all these grounds that every free man has a legal right and a moral duty to exert every effort to end this war, to avoid collusion with it, and to encourage others to do the same. Young men in the armed forces or threatened with the draft face the most excruciating choices. For them various forms of resistance risk separation from their families and their country, destruction of their careers, loss of their freedom and loss of their lives. Each must choose the course of resistance dictated by his conscience and circumstances. Among those already in the armed forces, some are refusing to obey specific illegal and immoral orders, some are attempting to educate their fellow servicemen on the murderous and barbarous nature of the war some are absenting themselves without official leave. Among those not in the armed forces, some are applying for status as conscientious objectors to American aggression in Vietnam, some are refusing to be inducted. Among both groups, some are resisting openly and paying a heavy penalty, some are organizing more resistance within the United States and some have sought sanctuary in other countries.

6. We believe that each of these forms of resistance against illegitimate authority is courageous and justified. Many of us believe that open resistance to the war and the draft is the course of action most likely to strengthen the moral resolve with which all of us can oppose the war and most likely to bring an end to the war.

7. We will continue to lend our support to those who undertake resistance to this war. We will raise funds to organize draft resistance unions, to supply legal defense and bail, to support families and otherwise aid resistance to the war in whatever ways may seem appropriate.

8. We firmly believe that our statement is the sort of speech that under the First Amendment must be free, and that the actions we will undertake are as legal as is the war resistance of the young men themselves. . . .

9. We call upon all men of good will to join us in this confrontation with immoral authority. Especially we call upon the universities to fulfill their mission of enlightenment and religious organizations to honor their heritage of brotherhood. Now is the time to resist.[57]

GEORGE MCGOVERN (1922–)

George McGovern was an early skeptic of the Vietnam War who declared it "a failure" in a U.S. Senate speech in September 1963. The next year, the Democratic senator from South Dakota supported the Gulf of Tonkin Resolution, which he later regretted. By the late 1960s, McGovern was a leading congressional opponent of the war and, in 1970, joined Republican Senator Mark Hatfield of Oregon, to sponsor "End the War" legislation to end combat funding after December 1970. The amendment failed. In the following Senate speech in support of his amendment, McGovern tried to shock his colleagues with strong language that indicted them for the deaths of American soldiers in Vietnam. As the Democratic presidential nominee in 1972, McGovern challenged Richard Nixon's reelection, but lost in a landslide.[58]

THIS CHAMBER REEKS OF BLOOD
Speech to the U.S. Senate, September 1, 1970

All my life, I have heard Republicans and conservative Democrats complaining about the growth of centralized power in the Federal executive.

Vietnam and Cambodia have convinced me that the conservatives were right. Do they really believe their own rhetoric? We have permitted the war power which the authors of the Constitution wisely gave to us as the people's representatives to slip out of our hands until it now resides behind closed doors at the State Department, the CIA, the Pentagon, and the basement of the White House. We have foolishly assumed that war was too complicated to be trusted to the people's forum—the Congress of the United States. The result has been the cruelest, the most barbaric, and the most stupid war in our national history.

Every Senator in this Chamber is partly responsible for sending 50,000 young Americans to an early grave. This Chamber reeks of blood.

Every Senator here is partly responsible for that human wreckage at Walter Reed and Bethesda Naval and all across our land—young men without legs, or arms, or genitals, or faces, or hopes.

There are not very many of those blasted and broken boys who think this war is a glorious venture.

Do not talk to them about bugging out, or national honor, or courage.

It does not take any courage at all for a Congressman or a Senator or a President to wrap himself in the flag and say we are staying in Vietnam, because it is not our blood that is being shed.

But we are responsible for those young men and their lives and their hopes.

And if we do not end this damnable war, those young men will some day curse us for our pitiful willingness to let the Executive carry the burden that the Constitution places on us.

So before we vote, let us ponder the admonition of Edmund Burke, the great parliamentarian of an earlier day: A conscientious man would be cautious how he dealt in blood.[59]

JOHN KERRY (1943–)

A young Navy lieutenant and future U.S. senator from Massachusetts, John Kerry returned from Vietnam in 1970 and joined the Vietnam Veterans Against the War. In green fatigues, and wearing his service ribbons, Kerry testified against the war before the U.S. Senate Foreign Relations Committee in April 1971. Kerry's actions would haunt him for years. When he became the Democratic Party's presidential nominee in 2004, veterans and others still angered by his testimony attacked his dissent and questioned the veracity of reports about his combat record and his injuries. Kerry's statement highlighted one reason—atrocities committed by U.S. soldiers—that support for the war declined in the early 1970s. Kerry also addressed the growing sense of confusion and disillusionment about the war's objectives.

STATEMENT TO THE COMMITTEE ON FOREIGN RELATIONS
U.S. Senate, April 22, 1971

I would like to say for the record, and also for the men behind me who are also wearing the uniforms and their medals, that my sitting here is really symbolic. I am not here as John Kerry. I am here as one member of the group of one thousand, which is a small representation of a very much larger group of veterans in this country, and were it possible for all of them to sit at this table they would be here and have the same kind of testimony. . . .

I would like to talk, representing all those veterans, and say that several months ago in Detroit, we had an investigation at which over 150 honorably discharged and many very highly decorated veterans testified to war crimes committed in Southeast Asia, not isolated incidents but crimes committed on a day-to-day basis with the full awareness of officers at all levels of command. . . .

They told the stories at times they had personally raped, cut off ears, cut off heads, taped wires from portable telephones to human genitals and turned up the power, cut off limbs, blown up bodies, randomly shot at civilians, razed villages in fashion reminiscent of Genghis Khan, shot cattle and dogs for fun, poisoned food stocks, and generally ravaged the country side of South Vietnam in addition to the normal ravage of war, and the normal and very particular ravaging which is done by the applied bombing power of this country.

We call this investigation the "Winter Soldier Investigation." The term "Winter Soldier" is a play on words of Thomas Paine in 1776 when he spoke of the Sunshine

Patriot and summertime soldiers who deserted at Valley Forge because the going was rough.

We who have come here to Washington have come here because we feel we have to be winter soldiers now. We could come back to this country; we could be quiet; we could hold our silence; we could not tell what went on in Vietnam, but we feel because of what threatens this country, the fact that the crimes threaten it, no reds, and not redcoats but the crimes which we are committing that threaten it, that we have to speak out. . . .

In our opinion, and from our experience, there is nothing in South Vietnam, nothing which could happen that realistically threatens the United States of America. And to attempt to justify the loss of one American life in Vietnam, Cambodia or Laos by linking such loss to the preservation of freedom, which those misfits supposedly abuse, is to use the height of criminal hypocrisy, and it is that kind of hypocrisy which we feel has torn this country apart. . . .

We found that not only was it a civil war, an effort by a people who had for years been seeking their liberation from any colonial influence whatsoever, but also we found that the Vietnamese whom we had enthusiastically molded after our own image were hard put to take up the fight against the threat we were supposedly saving them from.

We found most people didn't even know the difference between communism and democracy. They only wanted to work in rice paddies without helicopters strafing them and bombs with napalm burning their villages and tearing their country apart. They wanted everything to do with the war, particularly with this foreign presence of the United States of America, to leave them alone in peace, and they practiced the art of survival by siding with whichever military force was present at a particular time, be it Vietcong, North Vietnamese, or American.

We found also that all too often American men were dying in those rice paddies for want of support from their allies. We saw firsthand how money from American taxes was used for a corrupt dictatorial regime. We saw that many people in this country had a one-sided idea of who was kept free by our flag, as blacks provided the highest percentage of casualties. We saw Vietnam ravaged equally by American bombs as well as by search and destroy missions, as well as by Vietcong terrorism, and yet we listened while this country tried to blame all of the havoc on the Vietcong.

We rationalized destroying villages in order to save them. We saw America lose her sense of morality as she accepted very coolly a My Lai and refused to give up the image of American soldiers who hand out chocolate bars and chewing gum.

We learned the meaning of free fire zones, shooting anything that moves, and we watched while America placed a cheapness on the lives of Orientals.

We watched the U.S. falsification of body counts, in fact the glorification of body counts. We listened while month after month we were told the back of the enemy was about to break. We fought using weapons against "oriental human beings," with quotation marks around that. We fought using weapons against those people which I do not believe this country would dream of using were we fighting in the European theater or let us say a non-third-world people theater, and so we watched while men charged up hills because a general said that hill has to be taken, and after losing one platoon or two platoons they marched away to leave the high for the reoccupation by the North Vietnamese because we watched pride allow the most unimportant of battles to be blown into extravaganzas, because we couldn't lose, and we couldn't retreat, and because it didn't matter how many American bodies were lost to prove that point. And so there were Hamburger Hills and Khe Sanhs and Hill 881's and Fire Base 6's and so many others.

Now we are told that the men who fought there must watch quietly while American lives are lost so that we can exercise the incredible arrogance of Vietnamizing the Vietnamese. . . . Each day to facilitate the process by which the United States washes her hands of Vietnam someone has to give up his life so that the United States doesn't have to admit something that the entire world already knows, so that we can't say that we have made a mistake. Someone has to dies so that President Nixon won't be, and these are his words, "the first President to lose a war."

We are asking Americans to think about that because how do you ask a man to be the last man to dies in Vietnam? How do ask a man to be the last man to die for a mistake? But we are trying to do that, and we are doing it with thousands of rationalizations, and if you read carefully the President's last speech to the people of this country, you can see that he says, and says clearly: "But the issue, gentlemen, the issue is communism, and the question is whether or not we will leave that country to the communists or whether or not we will try to give it hope to be a free people." But the point is they are not a free people now under us. They are not a free people, and we cannot fight communism all over the world, and I think we should have learned that lesson by now. . . .

Finally, this administration has done us the ultimate dishonor. They have attempted to disown us and the sacrifice we made for this country. In their blindness and fear they have tried to deny that we are veterans or that we served in Nam. We do not need their testimony. Our own scars and stumps of limbs are witnesses enough for others and for ourselves.[60]

CHAPTER 11

THE PERSIAN GULF WAR

"A HEADLONG COURSE TOWARD WAR"

THE GHOSTS OF THE VIETNAM WAR HOVERED OVER WASHINGTON in August 1990, fifteen years after that conflict had ended. The "Vietnam syndrome," the nation's self-conscious lack of confidence about its ability to use military force, would not end until the United States proved it could again effectively project military power overseas.[1] On August 2, 1990, Iraqi leader Saddam Hussein gave President George H. W. Bush an opportunity to exorcise the demons of Vietnam.

A year earlier, Hussein picked a fight with Kuwait, his tiny, oil-rich neighbor to the south. The issue was oil and Kuwait's practice of subverting the production quotas established by the Organization of Petroleum Exporting Countries (OPEC), which drove down oil prices and reduced Iraq's oil revenues. Hoping to drive up oil prices and rake in another $60 billion a year, Hussein charged that Kuwait was stealing oil along the Iraqi border by slanting wells into neighboring territories. Furthermore, the Iraqi leader complained that Kuwait had illegally extended its border forty-five miles north into Iraq during the recent Iraq-Iran War.

Despite massive Iraqi troop movements toward Kuwait in July, U.S. officials in Washington and Iraq were complacent, until August 2, when the vanguard of Hussein's one hundred thousand troops in southern Iraq smashed across the border. Within two days the ineffective Kuwaiti forces fell and Iraq had its prize. Kuwait was suddenly the southernmost province of Iraq and Hussein's troops began plundering the country and kidnapping and murdering many of its leading citizens.[2]

If Hussein calculated that the U.S. government and his Middle East neighbors would acquiesce in what he considered a border dispute, he was wrong. The United Nations (UN) Security Council promptly, and unanimously, condemned the invasion. The Council of the Arab League also deplored the Iraqi action, as did other prominent Arab states, including Algeria, Egypt, and Syria. Joining the United States in its condemnation were Russia, Canada, Japan, Britain, France, and most other European nations.[3]

Bush initially worried about the fate of the 2,500 Americans in Kuwait, as well as another 600 in the Iraqi capital of Baghdad. He feared the kind of hostage situation that had occurred in Iran more than a decade earlier and had doomed Jimmy

Carter's presidency.[4] Heightening Bush's concern were fears that, if left unchallenged, Hussein would plunge his military into the heart of oil-rich Saudi Arabia. General Colin Powell, chairman of the Joint Chiefs of Staff, urged Bush to "draw a line in the sand" by sending enough troops to the region so that Hussein would know "that if he attacks Saudi Arabia, he attacks the United States."[5] To reporters during an August 5 briefing, he signaled his resolve. Of Kuwait, he said, "They are staunch friends and allies, and we will be working with them all for collective action. This will not stand, this aggression against Kuwait."[6]

Bush adopted a two-pronged strategy, ordering 125,000 U.S. troops to the Persian Gulf and endorsing strong, UN-backed economic sanctions. Supported by a U.S. military blockade, the sanctions—aimed at breaking Hussein's will—cost Iraq $80 million a day in lost oil revenue, while stopping all shipments into the country of consumer goods and food supplies like flour, sugar, tea, and cooking oil.[7]

In support of the U.S. forces that began pouring into the region—most were stationed at temporary bases in Saudi Arabia—Britain, France, Saudi Arabia, and Egypt provided forces. By late September, as troops headed to the Persian Gulf, the American people generally supported Bush's goal of driving Iraq out of Kuwait with a combination of diplomacy and economic sanctions, backed up by the threat of military action. However, while the public supported Bush's efforts, it overwhelming opposed war with Iraq. In a poll by a bipartisan consortium of public opinion firms in late September, 87 percent instead supported economic sanctions. Twenty percent opposed a war under all circumstances.[8]

Bush, however, knew that war was probable, if not certain. In late November he announced he would seek a UN resolution authorizing the use of force, if necessary, to expel Iraqi troops from Kuwait.[9] He made that decision with little or no congressional input. In addition, Bush unilaterally decided to send an additional two hundred thousand troops to the region—a move that would increase the total to more than four hundred thousand. He waited, however, until after the November congressional elections to tell Congress and the American people about his decision. "The public thought it meant war was inevitable," one Bush aide told *Newsweek* in 1991. "We saw it as part of the Big Bluff." Bluff or not, the results of public opinion surveys suggest why Bush wanted to keep his decision secret until after the elections—the public still strongly favored economic sanctions to "peacefully" end the conflict. Only about a quarter of Americans polled in November said they favored a war to liberate Kuwait.[10]

The reaction to Bush's troop escalation, especially among Democrats in Congress, was less than encouraging for the White House. Senate Armed Services Committee Chairman Sam Nunn of Georgia was particularly angry that administration officials did not brief him or other congressional leaders before making a decision that many regarded as a decisive step toward war. A public opinion poll after Bush's announcement revealed that only 41 percent of those surveyed believed Bush had adequately explained the need for the additional troops, compared to 60 percent who said Bush had properly explained the original deployment in the summer of 1990.[11] Public approval of Bush's handling of the crisis fell to just above 50 percent in November, compared to 80 percent in August.[12]

In response to Bush's troop escalation announcement, Nunn convened his committee and held a series of public hearings that sparked a vigorous national debate.

Nunn made it clear he was not unilaterally opposed to military action. "The question," he said, "is whether military action is wise at this time." The question that Nunn raised, and that many administration critics in and out of Congress began asking, was whether Bush was willing to allow the sanctions to work, or if they were merely a formality along an inexorable path to war. "The issue is not whether an embargo will work, but whether we have the patience to let it work," Admiral William J. Crowe Jr., former chairman of the Joint Chiefs of Staff, told the committee. Crowe added that, given time, the international blockade would likely undermine Hussein's regime. Former defense secretary and CIA director James Schlesinger agreed, telling the committee that sanctions might take twelve to eighteen months to work, at which time the administration could reassess its options.[13]

With Congress adjourned for the year, some leading Democrats, and even some Republicans, demanded a special session to debate and vote on Bush's Iraq policies. "Silence by Congress now is an abdication of our constitutional responsibility and an acquiescence in war," Democratic Senator Edward Kennedy of Massachusetts said in mid-November, deriding a "headlong course toward war." Although he was reluctant to call the Senate back into session—not wanting congressional action to be seen as undermining Bush's diplomatic efforts—Majority Leader George Mitchell of Maine joined Kennedy in asserting that Bush "has no legal authority, none whatever" to start a war over Kuwait. "The Constitution clearly invests that great responsibility in the Congress and the Congress alone."[14]

With Mitchell and other Democratic leaders hesitant to convene Congress, congressional opponents of war appeared ineffective, unwilling to assert their constitutional power to decide the issue while allowing Bush to dominate the debate by effectively comparing Hussein to Adolf Hitler. "A half century ago, our nation and the world paid dearly for appeasing an aggressor who should, and could, have been stopped," Bush said in mid-August. "We are not going to make the same mistake again."[15] While Bush and his spokesmen sometimes had difficulty maintaining a clear and consistent message about the reasons for U.S. troops and a looming war—among the rationales cited were a dependable oil supply and protecting U.S. jobs—Bush appeared genuinely appalled by what he considered Iraqi barbarity in Kuwait. He returned often to the theme of repelling "aggression." In late October, in a speech in Vermont, Bush labeled Iraqi army actions in Kuwait as "crimes against humanity."[16] In early November, Bush called Hussein "the brutal dictator" and suggested he was worse than Hitler for using hostages as "human shields" in locations possibly targeted for military strikes.[17]

One consequence of the administration's increasingly belligerent rhetoric about Iraqi atrocities was that it became increasingly difficult to sustain the sanctions as an alternative to war. Bush's national security advisor, Brent Scowcroft, charged in late September that Iraq had "ransacked and pillaged a once-peaceful and secure country, its population assaulted, incarcerated, intimidated and even murdered."[18] The supercharged rhetoric about barbarity made sanctions a less-than-satisfactory weapon against a regime that Bush now compared to Nazi Germany.

Meanwhile, outspoken opposition to the impending war was spreading beyond Congress. Early in the crisis, a wide range of groups—nine large labor unions, women's groups, and major student organizations—warned against a rush to war. In early

August, a group of antiwar activists formed the Coalition to Stop U.S. Intervention in the Middle East, chaired by former Attorney General Ramsey Clark. The following month, a group of peace organizations formed the National Campaign for Peace in the Middle East. Of the two, the Coalition took the more radical stance, refusing to condemn the Iraqi invasion while arguing that economic sanctions were an act of aggression against Iraq.[19]

Religious groups also mobilized against the looming war. In early September the president of the National Baptist Convention—with 7.8 million members, it was the largest association of black Americans—denounced Bush's policy. The National Council of Churches, representing major religious denominations, spoke out in a resolution adopted in mid-November, "As Christians in the U.S., we must witness against weak resignation to the illogical logic of militarism and war."[20] The same month, the National Conference of Catholic Bishops overwhelmingly declared war in Iraq morally wrong.[21]

News media organizations mostly ignored these and other opponents, focusing instead on a more compelling narrative—the impending confrontation between Bush and his congressional critics. With a UN resolution establishing a deadline of January 15, 1991, for Iraq to withdraw from Kuwait or face military action, Congress scrambled to weigh in. Some members feared that allowing Bush to invade Iraq without congressional approval would render their branch of government largely irrelevant in military affairs. While he argued that his role as commander in chief of the U.S. military meant that he did not need congressional approval for an invasion, Bush and his advisors also recognized the domestic and international peril of waging war without the support of the people's elected representatives. "It would be a hell of a thing to have half a million Americans fighting the war in the Gulf to get Saddam Hussein out of Kuwait," Congressman Stephen Solarz of New York argued, "while a serious effort was being made in Washington to get George Bush out of the White House."[22]

That in mind, Bush's congressional allies reluctantly returned to Washington after their Christmas break and launched a vigorous debate on a use of force resolution.[23] Bush made it clear, speaking to reporters on January 2, that overwhelming congressional opposition would not deter him if he decided on war. If need be, he would defy Congress. "If I have to go, it's not going to matter to me if there isn't one congressman who supports this, or what happens to public opinion. If it's right, it's gotta be done."[24] By early January, public opinion appeared to favor war. Bush's approval rating on the crisis in one major poll had risen to 67 percent and public willingness to go to war increased from 55 percent in December to 63 percent.[25]

Further adding to the public and congressional support was the failure of negotiations between Secretary of State James Baker and the Iraqi foreign minister, which ended the day before the congressional debate began. Baker's reputation as a consummate dealmaker who did not relish the prospect of a war over Kuwait lent credibility to the notion that the Bush administration—bellicose rhetoric and the abbreviated sanctions period notwithstanding—was making every effort to solve the conflict peacefully.[26]

On January 10, five days before the UN deadline, the House and Senate began their debates. In the House and Senate, Republicans almost uniformly supported giving Bush authority to launch a war   only two Republican senators and three House members were opposed. Democrats, meanwhile, were more divided. From the first days of the conflict, Senate Majority Leader Mitchell, House Speaker Thomas Foley, House Majority Leader Richard Gephardt, and Senator Nunn opposed what they considered a premature use of military force. On the other side, senators Al Gore of Tennessee and Joseph Lieberman of Connecticut were the most prominent freshman senators who supported Bush; they were joined in the House by Foreign Affairs Committee Chairman Dante Fascell and Armed Services Chairman Les Aspin.[27]

"No one proposes to rule out the use of force," Mitchell told the Senate on January 10. "The question is: Should war be truly a last resort when all other means fail, or should we start with war before other means have been fully and fairly exhausted?" Kennedy urged the Senate to "vote for peace, not war. . . . War is not the only option left to us in the Persian Gulf." Acknowledging that the sanctions policy "is not perfect," Nunn argued that it must "be weighed against the alternatives. . . . What guarantees do we have that war will be brief? American casualties will be light? No one can say whether war will last five days, five weeks, or five months."

It was Dole, the Republican Senate leader, who may have best summarized the majority opinion in Congress when he observed that the time for Congress to effectively guide the nation's military policy had long passed. "The Congress of the United States certainly has a role to play," Dole said. "I said last November and December that we ought to have been here debating then, when the policy was being formulated, instead of coming in at the eleventh hour after having been AWOL for three or four months and trying to change the direction of the policy President Bush has so patiently and successfully put together."[28]

After three days of solemn debate, the Senate and House authorized war against Iraq. House members approved the resolution 250 to 183 (with 164 Republicans and 86 Democrats in support and 179 Democrats, 3 Republicans, and 1 independent opposed). The Senate vote was much narrower, 52 to 47 (42 Republicans and 10 Democrats supported the resolution). The Senate had not been so divided over authorizing a war since its 19 to 12 vote in favor of the War of 1812.[29]

Five days after the congressional vote, early on January 17, Bush launched the air war against Iraq with devastating attacks against the country's command-and-control structure, including targets in and around Baghdad. By January 24, UN forces established command of the skies over Iraq and focused attacks on Iraqi ground forces in Kuwait and Iraq. On February 24, after a month of relentless bombing, the UN commander in the Persian Gulf, General Norman Schwarzkopf, launched ground troops into Kuwait. After only two days of fighting, UN troops reached Kuwait City and the southern Iraqi town of Nasiriya. Later that day, Iraq announced its withdrawal from Kuwait. The next day, Bush announced that the military offensive would cease on February 28, meaning that the United States would adhere to the UN mandate to liberate Kuwait—and not depose Saddam Hussein, as some proponents of the war publicly desired. On April 6, Iraqi officials signed the official cease-fire document in which they agreed to observe all UN resolutions regarding their conduct in the region. The Persian Gulf War was over, but Saddam Hussein was still in power, firmly in control of his country, the remnants of his military, and a still-sizable stock of chemical weapons. He would remain an irritant—and perceived threat—for U.S. policymakers for next decade. Bush's decision not to send ground troops to Baghdad in pursuit of

Hussein would prove the most controversial decision of the war—defended at the time by some officials who would later advocate a preemptive war against Iraq after the terrorist attacks of September 11, 2001.

Domestically the Persian Gulf War generated limited dissent because of its brevity—including the build-up to the war, the conflict lasted only seven months—and the widespread belief that it fit the criteria for a "just war." Another important factor that limited dissent was the overwhelmingly favorable media coverage of the conflict, partly a consequence of the strict controls and censorship imposed upon media organizations by the U.S. Defense Department. Unlike media coverage of the Vietnam War, reporters were not free to roam the battlefield and were, instead, forced to cover the conflict in small "pools," escorted to the front lines and strictly supervised by military officials. (The escorts were particularly effective in deterring military officials from sharing criticism of U.S. military policy or tactics with reporters.) The Pentagon required reporters to submit their pool stories and news footage to officials for "security review" before release to the larger press corps stationed in Saudi Arabia. One consequence of this strict censorship was that Americans were rarely subjected to images of death and destruction which might have undermined public support for the war.[30]

The result of this strict media control was a bonanza of favorable media coverage. According to one study, 95 percent of the more than three hundred sources featured in network television news stories about the military's effectiveness were positive.[31] Despite the bombardment of favorable news coverage, dissidents raised their voices. Immediately after the air war began, Congress passed a resolution to "support the commander-in-chief and the troops." Only twelve representatives—ten of them Congressional Black Caucus members—voted no. During the first two weekends of the war, large crowds of protesters turned out in Washington, DC, San Francisco, and Los Angeles. In Washington, over two successive weekends, more than three hundred thousand marchers protested the war. Protests also sprung up on college campuses across the country, finally prompting Bush to send a letter to five hundred college newspapers urging support for the conflict.

Bush dismissed the protests and insisted "this country is united" in support of the troops. In fact, the slogan that supporters parroted and placed on bumper stickers and yellow ribbons—"Support Our Troops"—was a clever and effective way to secure popular support for the war by suggesting that one could not oppose the war *and* support the troops. In response, antiwar demonstrators adopted the theme, chanted at antiwar rallies, "Support our troops, bring them home."[32]

Dissent against the Persian Gulf War rarely made news and barely registered in the national consciousness, its meager momentum destroyed by the war's quick and successful end. Unlike the Vietnam War, the lingering popular image of the Persian Gulf War was the successful deployment of U.S. military forces in pursuit of a just cause. Some of those who opposed the war, particularly Democrats in Congress with presidential ambitions, would later regret their votes, believing their opposition left them on the wrong side of history. For Bush, the successful execution of the war and his Pentagon's masterful management of media coverage of the conflict, allowed him to claim victory not only over Saddam Hussein, but also over the ghosts of Vietnam. "By God," Bush told reporters in early March 1991, "we've kicked the Vietnam syndrome once and for all."[33]

PATRICK BUCHANAN (1938–)

A combative conservative columnist, television commentator, and political activist, Patrick Buchanan began his professional career as a reporter and editorial writer for the St. Louis Globe-Democrat *in 1964. Two years later he went to work for Richard Nixon, writing speeches and newspaper columns for the former vice president, who was preparing another presidential campaign. After Nixon won in 1968, Buchanan became his special assistant and worked for him until August 1974 and, a few months after Nixon's resignation, for President Gerald Ford.*

For the next ten years, Buchanan was a prominent syndicated newspaper columnist and lecturer. He returned to the White House in 1985 to serve as President Ronald Reagan's communications director, but left that post after two years to resume his newspaper column. Buchanan ran for president twice—in 1992 against President George H. W. Bush in the Republican Party's presidential primaries and in 2000 as a third-party candidate against Republican George W. Bush and Democrat Albert Gore.

IS STOPPING SADDAM'S BOMB A U.S. PROBLEM?
Newspaper Column, November 28, 1990

For the first century of the republic, it was a first principle of U.S. foreign policy that our president kept his country out of foreign wars.

How times have changed. Now, Secretary of State James A. Baker III conducts a global arm-twisting operation to win support for our going to war to restore the independence of an Arab country not one in 10 Americans could have located on a map four months ago. And, President Bush is working on his fifth argument why we have to fight: i.e., if we don't fight now, we will face a nuclear-armed Iraq tomorrow:

"No one knows precisely when this dictator may acquire atomic weapons or exactly who they may be aimed at down the road. But, we do know this: He has never possessed a weapon he did not use."

Is it coincidence that Bush raised the nuclear specter the same week polls showed this was the only argument that might persuade Americans to support a pre-emptive strike?

First, our aim was to "restore the legitimate government of Kuwait," put the emir back on his throne. When that dog didn't hunt, we were there to protect the West's oil. When it was clear we were doing fine without a teaspoon of Iraqi-Kuwaiti crude, the casus belli was hostages. When Saddam said he would begin releasing them all at Christmas, Baker said the issue was now "jobs." When that was hooted off stage, there arrived the new one: nukes.

But, let us inspect this ultimata ratio, this last argument of the warhawks, who will not rest until the FB-111s are over Baghdad and the B-52 Arc Light strikes are slicing-and-dicing the pathetic conscripts of Saddam Hussein along the Saudi-Kuwaiti line.

When, exactly, did Iraq's work on atomic weapons become a cause for war? After all, Saddam's scientists were working patiently on nuclear weapons all those years during which we provided him $5 billion in loans to buy our grain and goods.

Where is the evidence Saddam is about to test a bomb? He has, after all, invited inspection of the weapons-grade uranium the French gave him; it has not been converted into a bomb. If he is about to build a weapon, would not the Israelis, whose intelligence is better than ours, have paid him a visit?

If Stalin's building of atomic weapons, and Mao's building of atomic weapons, did not call for U.S. first strikes—when both regimes were waging hot and Cold War against the United States—why does the R&D program of Saddam?

During the Cold War, we pursued a policy of containment of communism and deterrence of nuclear war. If Moscow or Beijing used an atomic bomb against us, we warned, "massive retaliation"' would ensue. Containment and the balance of terror did not define an ideal world, but, they succeeded. Magnificently.

If we could "contain" both the largest nation on earth, and the most populous nation on earth, can we not contain Iraq?

With 17 million people in a small, land-locked country halfway around the world, is Iraq a greater threat to the United States or its vital interests than was Stalin's Evil Empire, or Mao's "billion Chinese"?

This is not to suggest an atomic bomb in the hands of Saddam is a swell idea. It isn't. But, it is not, first and foremost, a U.S. problem. It is a problem of the Middle East, of the Arab world, of the United Nations.

Even, if Iraq, five or 10 years hence, acquired a small atomic arsenal, with a crude missile to deliver a warhead halfway around the world, why would Saddam, who is now desperate to avoid war with the U.S. Marine Corps, risk war with the U.S. Strategic Air Command?

Of all the nations who have something to fear from Saddam, the United States is the least threatened. Why, then, are we seeking the world's permission to have our soldiers, sailors, airmen and Marines go and die fighting him?

Certainly, an Iraqi bomb would concentrate minds wonderfully in Tehran and Damascus. But these regimes are not our friends. And, if they are preoccupied with Saddam, they may not have time to blow up our airliners. As for Israel, it not only has the atomic weapons to deter Iraq, but the requisite disposition, as it exhibited in the 1981 attack on Baghdad's Osirak reactor.

What is it about these establishmentarian presidents—Woodrow Wilson, Franklin Delano Roosevelt, George Herbert Walker Bush—that they think America's destiny is to police the planet?[34]

WILLIAM J. CROWE JR. (1925–2007)

A U.S. Navy admiral, William Crowe Jr. was chairman of the Joint Chiefs of Staff from 1985 to 1989 under presidents Ronald Reagan and George H. W. Bush. Upon his death in 2007, the Washington Post *described him as "a nonconformist whose background combined political skills with military experience."[35] Respected as an intellectual and diplomat (he earned a PhD in political science from Princeton University), Crowe served as U.S. ambassador to the United Kingdom during President Bill Clinton's administration.*

GIVE SANCTIONS A CHANCE

Testimony before the Armed Services Committee, U.S. Senate, November 28, 1990

War is always a grave decision and one which deserves both deep thought and wide public discussion. . . .

If Saddam Hussein initiates an attack on Saudi Arabia or U.S. forces, we have no choice but to react vigorously and to use force to bring Iraq to heel. It is imperative once we engage that we bring it to a successful conclusion no matter what it requires. It would be disastrous to do otherwise. I believe such a response would be defensible and acceptable to all constituencies, domestic and international.

For that reason alone, it is unlikely that Saddam Hussein will initiate further military action. Certainly everything we see to date suggests he is hunkering down for the long haul. If that prediction proves correct, President Bush will be confronted with some very painful choices.

If deposing Saddam Hussein would sort out the Middle East and permit the United States to turn its attention elsewhere and to concentrate on our very pressing domestic problems, the case for initiating offensive action immediately would be considerably strengthened. The Middle East, however, is not that simple. I witnessed it firsthand. I lived in the Middle East for a year.

Put bluntly, Saddam's departure or any other single act I am afraid will not make everything wonderful. In fact, a close look at the Middle East is rather depressing. While we may wish it otherwise, the fact is that the region has been, is, and will be for the foreseeable future plagued with a host of problems, tensions, enmities, and disagreements.

For instance, the Arab-Israeli dispute is alive and well. To say the least, the Palestinians have been irrevocably alienated by the Israeli government's policies. There will never be true stability in the area until this dispute is sorted out ultimately. . . .

Income differences on both national and individual levels are a constant source of tensions and envy throughout the region, and I witnessed this friction at close hand when I lived in Bahrain.

Muslim fundamentalism is spreading, and the process highlights the cultural, religious, and ethnic differences that abound in the area as well as the widespread distrust of the West. . . .

Put another way, today's problem is a great deal more complex than merely defeating Saddam Hussein. In my view, the critical foreign policy questions we must ask are not whether Saddam Hussein is a brutal, deceitful, or as Barbara Bush would put it, a dreadful man—he is all of those things. Whether initiating conflict against Iraq will moderate the larger difficulties in the Gulf region and will put Washington in a better position to work with the Arab world in the future, is in my estimation, the more important question. . . .

In working through the problems myself, I am persuaded that the U.S. initiating hostilities could well exacerbate many of the tensions I have cited and perhaps further polarize the Arab world. Certainly, many Arabs would deeply resent a campaign which would necessarily kill large numbers of their Muslim brothers and force them to choose sides between Arab nations and the West. . . .

I firmly believe that Saddam Hussein must be pushed out of Kuwait. He must leave Kuwait. At the same time, given the larger context, I judge it highly desirable to achieve this goal in a peaceful fashion, if that is possible. In other words, I would argue that we should give sanctions a fair chance before we discard them. I personally believe they will bring him to his knees ultimately, but I would be the first to admit that is a speculative judgment.

If, in fact, the sanctions will work in twelve to eighteen months instead of six months, a trade-off of avoiding war, with its attendant sacrifices and uncertainties, would in my estimation be more than worth it. . . .

It would be a sad commentary if Saddam Hussein, a two-bit tyrant who sits on seventeen million people and possesses a gross national product of $40 billion, proved to be more patient than the United States, the world's most affluent and powerful nation.[36]

PATRICK LEAHY (1940–)

A former prosecutor, in 1974 Patrick Leahy became the first Democrat elected to the U.S. Senate from Vermont. In the early 1990s, Leahy led the successful effort to pass legislation against the manufacture, use, and export of land mines, helped create a fund to help victims of land mines, and worked to enact an international treaty banning their use. Leahy is best known as the senior Democrat and later chair of the Senate Judiciary Committee during the presidency of George W. Bush, from which position he championed civil liberties and opposed Bush administration antiterrorism initiatives that he deemed unconstitutional. In the following speech, Leahy advances a familiar argument of congressional dissenters dating back to the Mexican War—that the president does not possess unilateral authority to start a war.

SPEECH TO THE U.S. SENATE
January 10, 1991

We are united on the goal that Iraq must leave Kuwait.

But I would hope that every single Senator, Republican and Democrat, and every member of the other body, would be united on one other overriding point: that the Constitution is extremely clear that the Congress and only the Congress can declare war, that the votes we cast today must ultimately lead to the decision, are we declaring war or not. If we ignore the Constitution in this regard, at a time nearly half a million American troops are poised, heavily armed, in Saudi Arabia, then we set a precedent which says that in the most powerful Nation known in history, one person, whoever is President, has the sole power to unleash that enormous power in a war that can engulf any part of the world. One person and one person alone, could commit the lifeblood of our Nation to war solely on his decision. The Constitution does not say that.

For 200 years, it said the Congress would declare war. The President will then carry out such a war. That is really what we are deciding today. I cannot imagine any democracy long surviving that did not adhere to such a principle. The Founding Fathers said at the time of the constitutional convention that to do otherwise would put all the power in one person, and would in effect have an elected monarch and nobody—Republican, Democrat—in the Congress or in the administration or anywhere in our country should want that conclusion. The Constitution stands above all else.

Today . . . the Senate is engaged in a historic debate on one of the most fundamental decisions that can come before the U.S. Government. Shall this Nation commit its Armed Forces to war against another country? As I have already stated, as the majority leader stated, as the distinguished senior Senator from Georgia [Sam Nunn] stated, there is no disagreement between the President and the Congress that Iraq's aggression against Kuwait must not be allowed to stand. Certainly, nobody in Iraq, from Saddam Hussein down, could ever discern disagreement on that. The Government stands united both in the legislative branch and in the executive branch that Iraq's aggression against Kuwait must not be allowed to stand.

But this agreement between the President and Congress is not about restoring the Emir of Kuwait to his throne or returning democracy to Kuwait. Kuwait was not a democratic nation before the invasion and restoration of the Sabah family to its palaces and pleasures is not worth one American life nor is the agreement about preserving low oil prices to maintain the prosperity of the industrialized Nations. If anything, continued American and Western dependence on Persian Gulf oil is an indictment of the lack of serious energy policy over the last decade. Neither Congress nor the American people should support a war just for cheap oil, especially when the cheap oil would go primarily to those countries that are doing precious little to help.

No, Mr. President. The agreement is about stopping the use of brutal force by the strong against the weak. Saddam Hussein is striving for regional hegemony with the use of force. If collected security under the United Nations is to replace the law of the jungle in international relations, if we are to emerge from the cold war with a better and more stable international community, what Saddam Hussein has done cannot be left unchallenged.

President Bush displayed brilliant diplomacy in uniting the world community against Saddam Hussein in marshaling a strong coalition force in Saudi Arabia, and in obtaining United States approval of the most comprehensive embargo against a nation in history.

President Bush's leadership in securing a United Nations authorization of the use of force if necessary to compel Iraq to leave Kuwait is a triumph for the role and authority of the United Nations in establishing collective security as a basis for international relations. Up until his decision announced on November 8 to alter the whole character of United States policy in the Desert Shield Operation, the President had enjoyed broad bipartisan support in Congress and among the American people for his actions to deter further Iraqi aggression and to bring together the multinational coalition against Saddam Hussein.

But since then a gap between the President and many in Congress has appeared. We have to ask what has happened to produce this unfortunate division between our President and a large part of the Congress?

Mr. President, we know this divergence has come about. But let nobody think that the divergence is the consequence of disagreement on goals. All agree that the United States and the world community must stand against the destruction of a sovereign nation, in this case a fellow member of the United Nations. Failure to act decisively against the seizure of Kuwait would destroy the chance for a fundamental change in the norms of international behavior. In my judgment, the disagreement that we see is the result of a far different perception of the right course of action to attain what really are shared goals in the Persian Gulf. . . .

Mr. President, President Bush is right not to base U.S. policy on public opinion polls. There is far too much willingness in both the executive and legislative branches of Government these days to shift course according to which way the polls go that day.

Sometimes it is necessary, if you want to carry out the responsibilities that are conferred upon us, that we are all sworn to uphold, to make decisions ostensibly at odds with public opinion polls.

At the same time, we are a democracy; a government is supposed to express the will of the people. Nowhere is this principle more evident and more compelling than in a decision to commit this Nation to war. That is why the Constitution makes it very clear that the democratic process must be used in a declaration of war.

War is borne by the people. It is the sons and daughters of the American people, our constituents, who have to do the fighting and the dying. We have an obligation to attempt to reflect the will of the people in this most fundamental decision.

Politically, morally, and even militarily, we must not go to war if it is not fully supported by the American people. Vietnam proved that truth, after great moral, human, financial, and diplomatic costs to the United States. . . .

Sanctions have not been given an adequate amount of time to undermine Iraqi armed forces or the Saddam Hussein regime. Five months is not long enough to degrade the Iraqi war machine or weaken the economy such that Saddam Hussein might think the cost too great to remain in Kuwait.[37]

CHAPTER 12

THE GLOBAL WAR
ON TERRORISM

"THE PATRIOT GAMES,
THE LYING GAMES"

THE RUBBLE ON GROUND ZERO IN NEW YORK CITY—SITE of the September 11, 2001, terrorist attacks—was still smoldering as Congresswoman Barbara Lee strolled down a hallway in the Cannon House Office Building in Washington, DC. Nearby was a Capitol Police officer, in Lee's presence because of death threats against the California Democrat after she opposed a resolution authorizing President George W. Bush to wage war against the perpetrators of the September 11 attacks. Several days before, the Senate had voted 98 to 0, and the House 420 to 1, for war. Lee's was the only dissenting vote. "We need to step back and think about this so that it doesn't spiral out of control," she told a reporter several days after the vote. While courageous and principled, Lee's vote was not particularly perilous to her career. Her Oakland district was one of the most liberal in the nation. Still, not all her constituents, even Democrats, found her argument persuasive. Said one Democratic state senator in her district, "This is a time for a united front in America, particularly in Congress."[1]

Whatever the degree of political risk, Lee's dissent was unusual in the early days of what Bush, his supporters, and the news media began calling a "war on terror." Around the country, citizens flew American flags in solidarity with the over three thousand people killed in the terrorist attacks on New York's World Trade Center towers and, in Virginia, on the Pentagon. The flags also expressed a newfound patriotic fervor in a nation that was, according to its president, at war. "Our nation stands united," proclaimed a banner hanging from a fraternity house at George Washington University. The banner expressed the profound sentiment of many Americans in times of national crisis or emergency throughout history: dissent or debate is a threat to a perceived guarantor of national security, unanimity of thought and purpose. A college freshman in Washington, DC, expressed that sentiment succinctly, "I guess I'll put my faith in [the government] because there's nothing else."[2]

It was fear of dissent that prompted outrage in late September 2001 when comedian Bill Maher, the host of a late-night talk show on ABC television, *Politically Incorrect*, returned to the air for the first time after the September 11 attacks. Contrasting the alleged "cowardice" of the suicide hijackers with U.S. military tactics of waging war with air power, Maher said, "We have been the cowards, lobbing cruise missiles from 2,000 miles away. That's cowardly. Staying in the airplane when it hits the building—say what you want about it, it's not cowardly."

Maher's remarks were not particularly outrageous or even original. Commenting on former President Bill Clinton's policy of using air attacks against terrorist targets, President Bush had reportedly told aides he was opposed to "firing two-million-dollar cruise missiles into a ten-dollar empty tent and hit a camel in the butt."[3] However, the response to Maher's dissent—post-September 11—was furious and costly. Within days, several advertisers pulled commercials from the show and seven ABC affiliates stopped airing the broadcast. Although Maher apologized, it was not enough to save his show. Several months later, ABC cancelled the program.[4]

It was the White House response, however, that some found more disturbing. "There are reminders to all Americans that they need to watch what they say, watch what they do, and this is not a time for remarks like that; there never is," White House press secretary Ari Fleischer said.[5] It was not clear the extent to which Bush agreed with Fleischer's attempt to suppress domestic dissent in the days after September 11, but the U.S.-led invasion of Afghanistan in October 2001 served the same purpose. Public and congressional support for the American and British bombing campaign against the Taliban and al-Qaeda forces, thought to provide sanctuary for terrorist leader Osama bin Laden, was high. Ninety percent of those polled by the *Washington Post* in late September 2001 favored the attacks on Afghanistan and 80 percent supported sending "a significant number of U.S. ground forces" to kill or capture bin Laden.[6]

By mid-November, the bombing campaign, supported by indigenous Northern Alliance forces, had routed the Taliban leaders in the nation's capital, Kabul, and degraded the al-Qaeda leadership, sending bin Laden and his allies into the sanctuary of the mountainous Tora Bora region on the Afghanistan-Pakistan border. Early December saw the surrender of Taliban forces in their last remaining stronghold—the city of Kandahar.

Bin Laden, however, was still at large, the consequence of a half-hearted American effort to track him down in Tora Bora. Instead of committing significant military personnel to the manhunt, U.S. forces provided support to tribal forces, many on horseback and on foot, who were searching for the terrorist leader. While the tribal militia killed as many as two hundred al-Qaeda fighters, some experts asserted that bin Laden slipped into Pakistan, where he took refuge in the Waziristan region, a no-man's land given nominal protection from U.S. attack by the Pakistan government.[7]

As Bush celebrated the Taliban's defeat and focused on Iraq—the next target in his war on terrorism—the war in Afghanistan was far from over. By early 2002, al-Qaeda forces regrouped in Afghanistan's Shahi-Kot mountains. Nearby Taliban forces also reassembled the remnants of their fighting forces in Pakita province. U.S. forces responded to this renewed enemy activity with another military operation, dubbed *Operation Anaconda*, which achieved only limited success. While American forces attacked and degraded the Taliban and al-Qaeda troops, several hundred enemy fighters reportedly escaped across the Pakistan border and established sanctuaries from which to reconstitute and stage cross-border attacks on U.S. forces. Despite the stubbornness of these enemy forces, U.S. officials increasingly focused on planning a war against Iraq and Pentagon officials began diverting attention and resources from Afghanistan. "Afghanistan is just the beginning," Bush said in November 2001, warning Americans that a worldwide struggle against terrorism could last for years.[8]

As the military effort in Afghanistan flagged, dissent emerged. In late February 2002, U.S. Senate Majority Leader Tom Daschle critiqued what Bush called "the war against terrorism," observing that it lacked focus, was too open-ended, and would only succeed if bin Laden were captured. "We're not safe until we have broken the back of al-Qaeda, and we haven't done that yet," the South Dakota Democrat said. Although Daschle's comments would eventually prove to be rather mild criticism of Bush—in light of the widely acknowledged failure and mismanagement of the subsequent war in Iraq—any early critique of Bush sent Republican leaders into a rage. "How dare Senator Daschle criticize President Bush while we are fighting our war on terrorism, especially when we have troops in the field," Senate Republican leader Trent Lott of Mississippi fumed. "He should not be trying to divide our country while we are united." House Majority Whip Tom DeLay, a Texas Republican, issued a one-word response, "Disgusting." Possibly the strongest criticism of Daschle came from Republican Congressman Tom Davis of Virginia, who seemed to suggest the Senate leader had committed treason. Daschle's comments, Davis said, "have the effect of giving aid and comfort to our enemies by allowing them to exploit divisions in our country."[9]

Despite the furious counterassault, criticism by Democrats began to spread as it became clear that U.S. troops would be in Afghanistan for many years and that Bush was looking to expand the war against terrorism beyond that country. "Some of us, maybe foolishly, gave this president the authority to go after the terrorists," Democratic Congresswoman Maxine Waters of California said in mid-February 2002. "We didn't know that he, too, was going to go crazy with it." Some Democrats were also having second thoughts about passage of the USA Patriot Act (United and Strengthening America by Providing Appropriate Tools Required to Intercept and Obstruct Terrorism Act of 2001), which Democratic Congressman Dennis Kucinich of Ohio said had allowed Bush to proceed with "canceling, in effect, the First, Fourth, Fifth, Sixth and Eighth Amendments" to the Constitution. Kucinich attacked what he called "the patriot games, the lying games, the war games of an unelected president."[10]

It was the Patriot Act's passage that set the stage for a drawn-out struggle between civil libertarians and some Democrats over how much Americans were willing to restrict constitutional rights in order to combat terrorism. Six weeks after September 11, Congress hastily enacted the USA Patriot Act under heavy pressure from Bush administration officials, particularly Attorney General John Ashcroft. The House rushed the bill through without testimony from one critic, while the Senate did not submit the bill to the formality of a committee hearing. After it passed the Senate by a 98 to 1 vote on October 11, it was clear that most of its supporters had never read the 342-page bill and did not understand its provisions.

Among its many provisions, the bill tightened border security, especially at Canadian entry points; strengthened money laundering laws; allowed federal law enforcement agencies and intelligence agencies to share information more readily; eased some restrictions on foreign intelligence operations within the United States; created several new federal crimes for terrorist attacks; and increased penalties for other acts of terrorism.[11]

Civil libertarians harshly criticized the bill for giving the government vast, unchecked investigative powers, including authority for secret searches in cases not related to terrorism, and expanded authority for criminal searches and wiretaps without the requirement to demonstrate probable cause of criminal activity. The law allowed federal immigration officials to deny an alien entry into the United States based on a speech or statement of opinion. The only mitigating factor was a provision repealing the law at the end of 2005 if Congress failed to renew it. In 2005, however, Congress would add some civil liberty safeguards to a renewed bill (including increased congressional oversight of some the government's new and expanded investigative powers) while making permanent fourteen of law's sixteen expiring provisions.

Responding to criticism of the Patriot Act and other administration antiterrorism proposals, Attorney General Ashcroft told the Senate Judiciary Committee in December 2001, "To those who scare peace-loving people with phantoms of lost liberty, my message is this: your tactics aid terrorists." Criticism of the administration, he argued, "gives ammunition to America's enemies and pause to America's friends."[12] Ashcroft's contempt for dissent alarmed his critics. Congressional oversight and criticism of the administration's proposals, Senator Patrick Leahy of Vermont noted, was not meant "as some have mistakenly described it, to protect terrorists. It is to protect ourselves as Americans and protect our American freedoms."[13] Among the media critics of the attorney general was the *St. Petersburg Times*, which called Ashcroft's attitude "stunning for its arrogance and its contempt for the democratic process."[14]

Just as troubling was the Bush administration's attitude toward the indefinite detention of thousands of noncitizens lawfully in the country on September 11. Not charged with any crime, many of these individuals were secretly jailed for months or years and denied lawyers. According to one study, federal authorities arrested more than five thousand individuals under provisions of the post-September 11 antiterrorism laws. Of that number, only three were charged with having committed or plotted an act of terrorism. Of those three, only one was convicted—and that person, the study noted, was not convicted of "actually engaging in terrorist activity or even planning terrorist activity, but of conspiring to support some unidentified terrorist act in the unidentified future."[15] The arrests suggested a troubling encore of the treatment of resident aliens during World War I.[16]

Cowed by Bush, Ashcroft, and an angry public into repealing basic civil liberties in the name of national security, Congress had some limits. Besides imposing the five-year sunset provision on the Patriot Act, it rejected Ashcroft's proposal to recruit citizens to spy on friends and neighbors as part of a proposed Terrorism Information and Prevention System (TIPS). Congress also rejected a proposed Total Information Awareness program that would have created a vast domestic intelligence system that one leading Republican senator complained was "chilling in its threat to civil liberties."[17]

The fear of another terrorist attack was vivid enough in most Americans' minds that they expressed little concern about the antiterrorism measures and their impact on civil liberties. Indeed, a significant percentage of public opinion sided with Bush and Ashcroft—many of them willing to support measures more extreme than anything seriously contemplated by the White House and the Justice Department. Fifty-seven percent of Americans polled in 2002 by the Media and Society Research Group at Cornell University said law enforcement officials should be able to detain indefinitely suspected terrorists. Forty percent agreed with the statement, "We need to outlaw some un-American actions, even if they're constitutionally protected." At the same time, however, a larger percentage polled—62 percent—agreed that in times of war or crisis, individuals should be allowed to publicly criticize the government.[18]

This was, of course, not the first time Americans and their leaders had reacted to a national crisis by restricting civil liberties. For Bush and his advisors, the national outrage over the September 11 attacks appeared to have the added benefit of providing public support for a military objective the administration had nursed since its earliest days—deposing, by force if necessary, Iraqi dictator Saddam Hussein. "Terrorism is a problem, weapons of mass destruction is a problem, the potential link between the two is a real problem," Bush's national security advisor, Condoleezza Rice, told a reporter in September 2002. "What September 11 did was to vivify what happened if evil people decide that they're going to go after you, and that it doesn't take much."[19] As another senior Bush advisor said at the time, "Without September 11, we never would have been able to put Iraq at the top of our agenda."[20]

Indeed, there were some Bush advisers— particularly Vice President Dick Cheney and Secretary of Defense Donald Rumsfeld—who wanted an attack on Iraq along with Afghanistan, contending that Iraq had been involved in the September 11 attacks. Bush and then-Secretary of State Colin Powell focused first on Afghanistan. Bush, however, clearly had his sights on Iraq from the beginning. "We're putting Iraq off," he reportedly told Rice. "But eventually we'll have to return to that question." In late November 2002, Bush secretly ordered the Pentagon to start planning for such a war.[21]

Many observers of the 2003 war against Iraq have concluded that Bush and his supporters persuaded the public and Congress to support their military plans by falsely implicating Iraq in the September 11 attacks and by manufacturing evidence that Hussein's regime possessed significant stockpiles of weapons of mass destruction (WMDs) and was actively pursuing development of nuclear weapons. While it is true that the administration took the nation to war on false pretenses, it may be wrong to conclude that the American people were skeptical of war until Bush began his public relations effort. As Richard Haass, then-director of policy planning for the State Department told the *New Yorker* in early 2002, "I don't think the American public needs a lot of persuading about the evil that is Saddam Hussein."[22] Even as Bush lumped Iraq with the rogue regimes of North Korea and Iran in his January 2002 State of the Union address—referring to Iraq as part of the "axis of evil"—the public appeared primed to believe the worst about Hussein and his government.

A Quinnipiac University poll in mid-February 2002 revealed that 67 percent of Americans surveyed favored U.S. military action "to force Saddam Hussein from power," while only 24 percent were opposed. Despite this strong support for war, Americans believed Bush needed congressional and UN approval before launching an attack. Seventy-five percent of those interviewed in August for an ABC News and *Washington Post* poll said UN support was necessary, while in a Gallup-CNN and *USA Today* poll, a slightly smaller majority held that view.[23]

Bush pretended to encourage debate over the question, but he signaled that the decision for war was up to him and that it had likely been made. To British journalists in April, Bush said, "I made up my mind that Saddam needs to go. That's about all I'm willing to share with you."[24] In August, Bush said that "it's a healthy debate for people to express their opinion. People should be allowed to express their opinion. But America needs to know, I'll be making up my mind based on the latest intelligence and how best to protect our own country plus our friends and allies."[25]

What most Americans did not know was that the intelligence that Bush relied upon—suggesting proof of stockpiles of Iraqi WMDs, including an active nuclear weapons program—was almost completely erroneous. There were no WMDs in Iraq, despite the fearful cries of administration officials, including Bush and Cheney, who said there was "no doubt" Iraq possessed WMDs and that "time is not on our side."[26] Rice perhaps put the matter in its most chilling terms, "Facing clear evidence of peril, we cannot wait for the final proof, the smoking gun, that could come in the form of a mushroom cloud."[27]

While there was still significant opposition in Congress to war with Iraq, Bush helped silence much of that dissent in a speech to the United Nations (UN) on September 12, 2002—the day after the first anniversary of the September 11 terrorist attacks. Bush cast his policy toward Iraq as moderate and patient, stressing his hope for peacefully disarming Iraq. "We will work with the UN Security Council for the necessary resolutions," Bush said. The speech was a feint, designed to portray Bush as a man of peace, pursuing every diplomatic angle before being forced into a preemptive war to protect America from a devastating nuclear or biological attack. As the *New York Times* reported the next day, Bush's speech "drew wide support from Congress" and "criticism of the administration was tamped down." Democratic leaders in Congress, the paper reported, "praised the president while staying noncommittal about a quick vote on Iraq." Daschle credited Bush with "a strong speech" and told reporters he was "encouraged by his express desire to go to the international community."[28]

Not every member of Congress was so beguiled. House Minority Whip Nancy Pelosi said she did not believe Bush had provided persuasive evidence of the need for war against Iraq. "We are clearly not there yet," she said. Democratic Senator John Kerry of Massachusetts argued for giving the UN ample time to enforce the Security Council resolutions against Iraq. "We don't want to see this initiative turned into a charade, where it is merely a pro forma step on a road to an already determined decision," Kerry said.[29] Kerry's fears of pro forma diplomacy were soon justified. While he demanded action from the UN, Bush also demanded from Congress a resolution authorizing military force to disarm Iraq, even before the UN acted. With midterm congressional elections looming, Democratic leaders were eager to put the Iraq issue behind them—some fearful of being cast as weak on national security. Daschle admitted, "The bottom line is, we want to move on [to other issues]. We've got to support this effort. We've got to do it in an enthusiastic way."[30] With Democrats largely absent from the debate, and the American people amply terrified and already largely supportive, Congress overwhelmingly endorsed Bush's war—296 to 133 in the House and 77 to 33 in the Senate.[31]

As it became clear that war was inevitable, protests in the United States and around the world erupted. On the weekend of January 18 and 19, 2003, tens of thousands marched on Washington to register their dissent, waving banners that said, "No War With Iraq." Authorities said it was the largest protest rally in Washington since the Vietnam War. Protesters marched in opposition to war in other cities. Bush was unmoved. He knew a majority of the public was with him. What concerned him about the protests was the signal he believed they might send to Hussein about the country's resolve. In response, his administration launched a major public relations offensive to persuade Americans and potential allies that Iraq was a dangerous regime with a murderous intent.[32]

On January 23, Condoleezza Rice published an op-ed column in the *New York Times* titled, "Why We Know Iraq Is Lying," and alleged that Hussein had been trying to purchase uranium on the world market. Several days later, talking with European reporters, Secretary of State Powell claimed there was evidence of a post-September 11 link between Iraq and al-Qaeda. In his January 28 State of the Union address, Bush told Congress (falsely, it was later revealed) that Iraq had "recently sought significant quantities of uranium from Africa" and had tried to buy "high-strength aluminum tubes suitable for nuclear weapons production."[33]

Next, Bush and his advisors turned to the task of selling the UN on a war resolution. Powell staked his reputation on the question by presenting faulty intelligence to the UN Security Council on February 5, 2003. The Council, however, refused to approve the war after Russia and France threatened to veto the resolution. Powell's presentation seemed to serve the secondary purpose of shoring up support for the war in the United States. Following the speeches by Bush and Powell, 66 percent of those surveyed in mid-March for a CNN/*USA Today*/Gallup poll approved of the administration's decision to invade Iraq. As *New York Times* columnist Frank Rich later observed, "It was all over except for the shouting, and there was not to be much shouting."[34]

As the date for launching the invasion approached, and millions around the world took to the streets to protest the coming war, Bush was serenely dismissive—or at best tolerant—of the dissent. "Democracy is a beautiful thing," he said in mid-February when asked about the protests. "I welcome people's right to say what they believe." Bush made it clear he would disregard the protests. "The role of a leader is to decide policy based upon the security—in this case, the security of the people. Evidently some in the world don't view Saddam Hussein as a risk to peace. I respectfully disagree."[35]

Bush's patience with diplomacy quickly expired. On March 20, U.S. and British forces began the invasion and quickly deposed Hussein and his regime. On March 20—standing on the aircraft carrier USS *Abraham Lincoln* before a large banner declaring "Mission Accomplished"—Bush announced the end of "major combat operations" in Iraq. The U.S.-led forces had achieved functional dominance of the country, including Baghdad, had deposed or captured most of the country's leaders, and had disbanded the Iraqi army and much of the nation's civilian bureaucracy led by members of Hussein's Baath Party. In December 2003, U.S. forces captured Hussein. In December 2006, after they convicted him of crimes against humanity, Iraqi officials executed the former Iraqi dictator.

While the initial invasion of Iraq was widely deemed a success, the U.S.-directed occupation stumbled. Pentagon and U.S. State Department officials were ill prepared for the postwar reconstruction, as lawlessness and violence swept the country. Insurgents loyal to Hussein—many of them former members of the now-defunct Iraqi army—began staging deadly attacks on U.S. and British forces. Despite assurances from Cheney and other administration officials that U.S. troops would be greeted as liberators, American forces often found themselves at war with the very people they had liberated. By 2006, with 130,000 U.S. troops mired in the country and with the reconstruction a dismal failure, sectarian violence escalated to the point that most nonadministration observers agreed the country had dissolved into a civil war between the two major Muslim groups in Iraq, Sunni and Shia.

Dissent and opposition to the war escalated rapidly when it became clear in the summer of 2003 that the Iraqi regime had no weapons of mass destruction, nor a nuclear weapons program. One study indicated that support for the Iraq war dropped more quickly than for the Korean and Vietnam wars.[36] According to the Pew Research Center, public support for the war—which Bush launched with an approval rating of 71 percent in March 2003—had slumped to 55 percent by March 2004 and to 47 percent in February 2005 (the declining public support for the war in November 2004 was just high enough to help Bush win a second term).[37]

By November 2006, public disillusionment over Iraq and Bush's perceived mishandling of the postwar reconstruction had escalated to dangerous levels for Bush and his Republican supporters in Congress. In the 2006 congressional elections, Republicans lost control of the House and the Senate.[38] A public that had, in March 2003, supported Bush by 68 percent—and his war by 71 percent—now judged him a failure.[39] By 2007—with more than 3,700 American soldiers killed in Iraq and tens of thousands more wounded—Bush's overall approval rating hovered in the low 30s, while Americans assessed him just as harshly on Iraq. In September 2007, the Pew Research Center reported that 47 percent of those surveyed believed the United States "will probably or definitely fail to achieve its goals in Iraq" and 54 percent "believe U.S. forces should be brought home as soon as possible."[40] Even after Bush sent a so-called surge of additional U.S. troops into Iraq in 2007—which appeared to quell some of the worst violence in and around Baghdad—public opinion surveys continued to measure strong opposition to the war.[41]

While public dissatisfaction over Iraq forced Bush to fire Defense Secretary Donald Rumsfeld in November 2006, Bush generally disregarded public opposition to the war—clinging to his stated belief that the war was justified and was making Americans safer. Critics, however, believed the war had been a costly and deadly diversion from what they regarded as the real war against terrorism—the battle in Afghanistan, the languid hunt for Osama bin Laden, and the growing influence of al-Qaeda in neighboring Pakistan. "America has never had enough troops in Afghanistan, not in 2001, when Osama bin Laden was on the run in the caves of Tora Bora, and not today, when much of the country is still without effective authority," the *New York Times* said in an editorial in August 2007. "Washington's mistakes have made Iraq a new staging area for international terrorism."[42]

The war was so unpopular in 2007, and dissent so widely accepted by the public, that a vigorous statement of dissent by seven infantrymen and noncommissioned officers with the 82nd Airborne Division published in the *New York Times* in August created a minor sensation, but no cries of outrage from the war's supporters. "Counterinsurgency is, by definition, a competition between insurgents and counterinsurgents for the control and support of a population," the soldiers wrote. "To believe that Americans, with an occupying force that long ago outlived its reluctant welcome, can win over a recalcitrant local population and win this counterinsurgency is far-fetched."[43] Such was the war's disrepute, and the public's tolerance—if, perhaps, only temporary—for dissent.

By 2008, Bush's job approval ratings remained stuck in the low thirties, one indication of how poorly Americans regarded his stewardship of the war. The 2008 presidential election between Democrat Barack Obama and Republican John McCain featured a spirited debate over the war in Iraq, as well as the nation's strategy for fighting terrorism. McCain promised to keep U.S. troops in the country long enough to establish a working democracy, while Obama promised a withdrawal of combat troops within sixteen months of his election.

It was Obama's dissent over the war in 2002, however, which made the most difference with many Americans. Alone among the major presidential candidates of either party, Obama could truthfully say that he had opposed the war from the beginning. "I don't oppose all wars," he had told a Chicago antiwar rally in October 2002. "What I am opposed to is a dumb war."[44]

Not long into Obama's first year in office, the United States marked the sixth anniversary of its invasion of Iraq. Now the president who led the country's armed forces was a prominent dissenter who quickly announced a plan to withdraw combat troops by August 2010, while leaving residual troops until December 2011. Obama also signaled that the country's most important war was in Afghanistan. Shortly after taking office, he ordered twenty-one thousand additional troops to supplement the seventy thousand NATO troops already in the country—and suggested he might order another ten thousand. Obama's decision to increase the U.S. presence in Afghanistan initially sparked only scattered opposition in Congress and elsewhere.

By the summer of 2009, as fighting with the Taliban escalated and U.S. troop deaths spiked, discontent surfaced. "The war is going badly," Andrew J. Bacevich, Boston University historian, wrote in the *Los Angeles Times*. "The Taliban is gaining in strength. Seven-plus years of allied efforts in Afghanistan have accomplished very little."[45] By the fall of 2009, Obama considered recommendations by military leaders to reinforce the U.S. military presence in Afghanistan with as many as forty thousand additional troops. After months of contemplation, in December, Obama said he would send thirty thousand additional troops to Afghanistan (augmented with another five to seven thousand NATO troops), increasing the total number of American personnel to one hundred thousand, with a goal of beginning withdrawals in July 2011.

Some, including conservative *Washington Post* columnist George Will, argued that the job of counterinsurgency in Afghanistan was far larger and more costly than the determination of Americans to sustain it. "Counterinsurgency theory concerning the time and the ratio of forces required to protect the population indicates that, nationwide, Afghanistan would need hundreds of thousands of coalition troops, perhaps for a decade or more," Will wrote in September 2009. "That is inconceivable."[46]

In the liberal magazine *The Nation*, editor Katrina vanden Heuvel worried in December that Obama will now be "held hostage" to "the continuing grip of the National Security State" as "a war bequeathed to him by a reckless and destructive administration becomes his own war." Vanden Heuvel also observed a disturbing absence of vigorous dissent over Obama's decision, "This retro thinking and failure to explore real alternatives to military escalation reveal a deeper structural problem—the fact that there are too few countervailing voices or centers of power and authority to challenge the liberal hawks and interventionists, and very few if any are allowed to enter the halls of power. The political establishment works from its narrow consensus; meanwhile, the media fails to offer a full range of views."[47]

If history is any guide, the dissent that vanden Heuvel desired will come, only too late to stop the troop escalation. Obama's war in Afghanistan will likely not grow in popularity. Before the end of his presidency, the president and his military policies may increasingly be the targets of attacks from Republicans *and* Democrats. No U.S. president who has led the nation in war has yet avoided the withering criticism of his countrymen.

BARBARA LEE (1946–)

Barbara Lee was the only member of either house of Congress to vote against the use-of-force resolution passed after the attacks of September 11, 2001. A Democrat who has represented Oakland, California, in the U.S. House since 1998, Lee became a hero of antiwar organizations. Since 2008 she has chaired the Congressional Black Caucus.

WAR AGAINST AFGHANISTAN
Speech to the U.S. House, September 14, 2001

Mr. Speaker, I rise today really with a very heavy heart, one that is filled with sorrow for the families and the loved ones who were killed and injured this week. Only the most foolish and the most callous would not understand the grief that has really gripped our people and millions across the world.

This unspeakable act on the United States has forced me, however, to rely on my moral compass, my conscience, and my God for direction. September 11 changed the world. Our deepest fears now haunt us. Yet I am convinced that military action will not prevent further acts of international terrorism against the United States. This is a very complex and complicated matter.

This [use of force] resolution will pass, although we all know that the President can wage a war even without it. However difficult this vote may be, some of us must urge the use of restraint. Our country is in a state of mourning. Some of us must say, let us step back for a moment. Let us just pause for a minute and think through the implications of our actions today so that this does not spiral out of control.

I have agonized over this vote, but I came to grips with it today and I came to grips with opposing this resolution during the very painful yet very beautiful memorial service. As a member of the clergy so eloquently said, "As we act, let us not become the evil that we deplore."[48]

SCOTT RITTER (1961–)

A former U.S. Marine, Scott Ritter served from 1991 to 1998 as a top weapons inspector for the United Nations Special Commission. In August 1998 he resigned in protest over the failure of the United States and to take action against Iraq for its failure to cooperate with weapons inspectors.

IS IRAQ A TRUE THREAT TO THE US?
Boston Globe *column, July 20, 2002*

Recent press reports indicate that planning for war against Iraq has advanced significantly. When combined with revelations about the granting of presidential authority to the CIA for covert operations aimed at eliminating Saddam Hussein, it appears that the United States is firmly committed to a path that will lead toward war with Iraq.

Prior to this occurring, we would do well to reflect on the words of President Abraham Lincoln who, in his Gettysburg Address, defined the essence of why democracies like ours go to war: so ". . . that government of the people, by the people, for the people, shall not perish from the earth."

Does Iraq truly threaten the existence of our nation? If one takes at face value the rhetoric emanating from the Bush administration, it would seem so. According to President Bush and his advisers, Iraq is known to possess weapons of mass destruction and is actively seeking to reconstitute the weapons production capabilities that had been eliminated by UN weapons inspectors from 1991 to 1998, while at the same time barring the resumption of such inspections.

I bear personal witness through seven years as a chief weapons inspector in Iraq for the United Nations to both the scope of Iraq's weapons of mass destruction programs and the effectiveness of the UN weapons inspectors in ultimately eliminating them.

While we were never able to provide 100 percent certainty regarding the disposition of Iraq's proscribed weaponry, we did ascertain a 90–95 percent level of verified disarmament. This figure takes into account the destruction or dismantling of every major factory associated with prohibited weapons manufacture, all significant items of production equipment, and the majority of the weapons and agent produced by Iraq.

With the exception of mustard agent, all chemical agent produced by Iraq prior to 1990 would have degraded within five years (the jury is still out regarding Iraq's VX nerve agent program—while inspectors have accounted for the laboratories, production equipment and most of the agent produced from 1990–91, major discrepancies in the Iraqi accounting preclude any final disposition at this time.)

The same holds true for biological agent, which would have been neutralized through natural processes within three years of manufacture. Effective monitoring inspections, fully implemented from 1994–1998 without any significant obstruction from Iraq, never once detected any evidence of retained proscribed activity or effort by Iraq to reconstitute that capability which had been eliminated through inspections.

In direct contrast to these findings, the Bush administration provides only speculation, failing to detail any factually based information to bolster its claims concerning Iraq's continued possession of or ongoing efforts to acquire weapons of mass destruction. To date no one has held the Bush administration accountable for its unwillingness—or inability—to provide such evidence.

Secretary of Defense [Donald] Rumsfeld notes that "the absence of evidence is not evidence of absence." This only reinforces the fact that the case for war against Iraq fails to meet the litmus test for the defense of our national existence so eloquently phrased by President Lincoln.

War should never be undertaken lightly. Our nation's founders recognized this when they penned our Constitution, giving the authority to declare war to Congress and not to the president. Yet on the issue of war with Iraq, Congress remains disturbingly mute. . . .

The apparent unwillingness of Congress to exercise its constitutional mandate of oversight, especially with regard to matters of war, represents a serious blow to American democracy. By allowing the Bush administration, in its rush toward conflict with Iraq, to circumvent the concepts of democratic accountability, Congress is failing those to whom they are ultimately responsible—the American people.[49]

ROBERT C. BYRD (1917–2010)

In July 2006, Robert Byrd became the longest-serving senator in U.S. history. First elected to the Senate from West Virginia in 1959, as of November 2006 his constituents had elected him nine times. Byrd served several terms as the Senate's president pro tempore (third in line of succession to the president) and as Senate majority leader. A fierce guardian of congressional prerogatives, Byrd was among the most vehement critics of the war in Iraq and the unwillingness of Congress to stop it. Byrd later said that of all the votes he cast as a senator, he was proudest of his vote against the Iraq War resolution. The following speech was delivered in the U.S. Senate on the eve of the war.

AMERICA'S IMAGE IN THE WORLD
Speech to the U.S. Senate, March 19, 2003

Today I weep for my country. I have watched the events of recent months with a heavy, heavy heart.

No more is the image of America one of strong, yet benevolent peacekeeper. The image of America has changed. Around the globe, our friends mistrust us, our word is disputed, our intentions are questioned.

Instead of reasoning with those with whom we disagree, we demand obedience or threaten recrimination. Instead of isolating Saddam Hussein, we seem to have succeeded in isolating ourselves. We proclaim a new doctrine of preemption which is understood by few but feared by many. We say that the United States has the right to turn its firepower on any corner of the globe which might be suspect in the war on terrorism. We assert that right without the sanction of any international body. As a result, the world has become a much more dangerous place.

We flaunt our superpower status with arrogance. We treat U.N. Security Council members like ingrates who offend our princely dignity by lifting their heads from the carpet. Valuable alliances are split. After war has ended, the United States will have to rebuild much more than the country of Iraq. We will have to rebuild America's image around the globe.

The case this administration tries to make to justify its fixation with war is tainted by charges of falsified documents and circumstantial evidence. We cannot convince the world of the necessity of this war for one simple reason: This is not a war of necessity, but a war of choice.

There is no credible information to connect Saddam Hussein to 9/11, at least up to this point. The Twin Towers fell because a world-wide terrorist group, al Qaida, with cells in over 60 nations, struck at our wealth and our influence by turning our own planes into missiles, one of which would likely have slammed into the dome of this beautiful Capitol except for the brave sacrifice of some of the passengers who were on board that plane.

The brutality seen on September 11th and in other terrorist attacks we have witnessed around the globe are the violent and desperate efforts by extremists to stop the daily encroachment of Western values upon their cultures. That is what we fight. It is a force not confined to territorial borders. It is a shadowy entity with many faces, many names, and many addresses.

But, this administration has directed all of the anger, fear, and grief which emerged from the ashes of the Twin Towers and the twisted metal of the Pentagon towards a tangible villain, one we can see and hate and attack. And villain he is. But he is the wrong villain. And this is the wrong war. If we attack Saddam Hussein, we will probably drive him from power. But the zeal of our friends to assist our global war on terrorism may have already taken flight. . . .

What is happening to this country—my country, your country, our country? When did we become a nation which ignores and berates our friends and calls them irrelevant? When did we decide to risk undermining international order by adopting a radical and doctrinaire approach to using our awesome military might?

How can we abandon diplomatic efforts when the turmoil in the world cries out for diplomacy?

Why can this President not seem to see that America's true power lies not in its will to intimidate, but in its ability to inspire? . . .[50]

BARACK OBAMA (1961–)

The future forty-fourth U.S. president, then the junior senator from Illinois, had long opposed the U.S. war in Iraq, delivering a speech in October 2002 opposing the loom-ing war. "I don't oppose all wars," Barack Obama said at rally in Chicago. "What I am opposed to is a dumb war." In 2006, after the U.S. Supreme Court declared as unconstitu-tional the Bush administration's system of military commissions at Guantanamo Bay—the system for trying "unlawful enemy combatants" suspected of terrorism—Congress drafted legislation to ratify the practice of trying detainees outside of U.S. federal courts. Among other things, the law prevented detainees from filing suit in federal court to enforce any rights under the Geneva Conventions. In his speech to the Senate, Obama attacked the legislation as a "betrayal of American values." As president, in 2000, Obama revived the military tribunals that he had once decried as a "failure," although he imposed new rules on evidence and detainee rights.

MILITARY COMMISSIONS ACT OF 2006
U.S. Senate Speech, September 28, 2006

All of us, Democrats and Republicans, want to do whatever it takes to track down terrorists and bring them to justice as swiftly as possible. All of us want to give our President every tool necessary to do this, and all of us were willing to do that in this bill. Anyone who says otherwise is lying to the American people.

In the five years the President's system of military tribunals has existed, the fact is not one terrorist has been tried, not one has been convicted, and in the end, the Supreme Court of the United States found the whole thing unconstitutional because we were rushing through a process and not overseeing it with sufficient care. Which is why we are here today.

We could have fixed all this several years ago in a way that allows us to detain and interrogate and try suspected terrorists while still protecting the accidentally accused from spending their lives locked away in Guantanamo Bay. Easily. This was not an either or question. We could do that still. . . .

Instead of allowing this President—or any President—to decide what does and does not constitute torture, we could have left the definition up to our own laws and to the Geneva Conventions, as we would have if we passed the bill that the Armed Services Committee originally offered.

Instead of detainees arriving at Guantanamo and facing a Combatant Status Review Tribunal that allows them no real chance to prove their innocence with evi-dence or a lawyer, we could have developed a real military system of justice that would sort out the suspected terrorists from the accidentally accused.

And instead of not just suspending, but eliminating, the right of habeas corpus—the seven-century-old right of individuals to challenge the terms of their own detention, we could have given the accused one chance—one single chance—to ask the Government why they are being held and what they are being charged with.

But politics won today. Politics won. The administration got its vote, and now it will have its victory lap, and now they will be able to go out on the campaign trail and tell the American people that they were the ones who were tough on the terrorists.

And yet, we have a bill that gives the terrorist mastermind of 9/11 his day in court, but not the innocent people we may have accidentally rounded up and mistaken for terrorists—people who may stay in prison for the rest of their lives.

And yet, we have a report authored by sixteen of our own Government's intelligence agencies, a previous draft of which described, and I quote, ". . . actions by the United States government that were determined to have stoked the jihad movement, like the indefinite detention of prisoners at Guantanamo Bay." . . .

And yet, we have al-Qaida and the Taliban regrouping in Afghanistan while we look the other way. We have a war in Iraq that our own Government's intelligence says is serving as al-Qaida's best recruitment tool. And we have recommendations from the bipartisan 9/11 commission that we still refuse to implement 5 years after the fact.

The problem with this bill is not that it is too tough on terrorists. The problem with this bill is that it is sloppy. And the reason it is sloppy is because we rushed it to serve political purposes instead of taking the time to do the job right.

I have heard, for example, the argument that it should be military courts, and not Federal judges, who should make decisions on these detainees. I actually agree with that.

The problem is that the structure of the military proceedings has been poorly thought through. Indeed, the regulations that are supposed to be governing administrative hearings for these detainees, which should have been issued months ago, still haven't been issued. Instead, we have rushed through a bill that stands a good chance of being challenged once again in the Supreme Court.

This is not how a serious administration would approach the problem of terrorism. I know the President came here today and was insisting that this is supposed to be our primary concern. He is absolutely right it should be our primary concern—which is why we should be approaching this with a somberness and seriousness that this administration has not displayed with this legislation.

Now let me make clear—for those who plot terror against the United States, I hope God has mercy on their soul, because I certainly do not.

For those who our Government suspects of terror, I support whatever tools are necessary to try them and uncover their plot.

We also know that some have been detained who have no connection to terror whatsoever. We have already had reports from the CIA and various generals over the last few years saying that many of the detainees at Guantanamo shouldn't have been there—as one U.S. commander of Guantanamo told the Wall Street Journal, "Sometimes, we just didn't get the right folks." And we all know about the recent case of the Canadian man who was suspected of terrorist connections, detained in New York, sent to Syria, and tortured, only to find out later that it was all a case of mistaken identity and poor information. In the future, people like this may never have a chance to prove their innocence. They may remain locked away forever.

The sad part about all of this is that this betrayal of American values is unnecessary.

We could have drafted a bipartisan, well-structured bill that provided adequate due process through the military courts, had an effective review process that would've prevented frivolous lawsuits being filed and kept lawyers from clogging our courts, but upheld the basic ideals that have made this country great. . . .

That is not how we should be doing business in the U.S. Senate, and that is not how we should be prosecuting this war on terrorism. When we are sloppy and cut corners, we are undermining those very virtues of America that will lead us to success in winning this war.[51]

RON PAUL (1935–)

A Texas Republican who has served off and on in the U.S. House since 1976, Ron Paul is a longtime critic of U.S. foreign and monetary policies. An obstetrician, Paul has twice run for president—in 1988 as nominee of the Libertarian Party and in 2008 for the Republican presidential nomination. In 2001 he introduced legislation to repeal the 1973 War Powers Act, arguing that Congress should return to considering formal war declarations. That same year, however, Paul supported the use-of-force resolution requested by President George W. Bush following the September 11, 2001, terrorist attacks. Paul opposed the February 2003 Iraq War resolution.

WHAT IF?
Speech to the U.S. House, February 12, 2009

Madam Speaker, I have a few questions for my colleagues.

What if our foreign policy of the past century is deeply flawed and has not served our national security interests?

What if we wake up one day and realize that the terrorist threat is a predictable consequence of our meddling in the affairs of others and has nothing to do with us being free and prosperous?

What if propping up repressive regimes in the Middle East endangers both the United States and Israel?

What if occupying countries like Iraq and Afghanistan—and bombing Pakistan— is directly related to the hatred directed towards us?

What if some day it dawns on us that losing over 5,000 American military personnel in the Middle East since 9/11 is not a fair trade-off for the loss of nearly 3,000 American citizens—no matter how many Iraqi, Pakistani, and Afghan people are killed or displaced?

What if we finally decide that torture—even if called "enhanced interrogation techniques"—is self-destructive and produces no useful information and that contracting it out to a third world nation is just as evil?

What if it is finally realized that war and military spending is always destructive to the economy?

What if all wartime spending is paid for through the deceitful and evil process of inflating and borrowing?

What if we finally see that wartime conditions always undermine personal liberty? . . .

What if the American people woke up and understood the official reasons for going to war are almost always based on lies and promoted by war propaganda in order to serve special interests?

What if we, as a Nation, came to realize that the quest for empire eventually destroys all great nations?

What if Obama has no intention of leaving Iraq? . . .

What if President Obama is completely wrong about Afghanistan and it turns out worse than Iraq and Vietnam put together? . . .

What happens if my concerns are completely unfounded? Nothing.

But what happens if my concerns are justified and ignored? Nothing good.[52]

MATTHEW P. HOH

At the time of his dissent in September 2009, Matthew Hoh was the senior U.S. civilian official in Afghanistan's violent Zabul province. A former Marine Corps captain, who served honorably in Iraq's Anbar province in 2006, Hoh turned heads with his strongly worded resignation letter in which he challenged the wisdom of U.S. military policy in Afghanistan. "The dead return only in bodily form to be received by families who must be reassured their dead have sacrificed for a purpose worthy of futures lost, love vanished and promised dreams unkept," Hoh wrote. "I have lost confidence such assurances can anymore be made."

After receiving Hoh's letter, published widely on the Internet, U.S. State Department officials tried to dissuade Hoh from resigning. Richard Holbrooke, the Obama administration's special representative for Afghanistan and Pakistan, offered him a position on his Washington staff. Hoh initially accepted, but rejected the offer a week later.[53]

LETTER TO DIRECTOR GENERAL OF THE FOREIGN SERVICE
September 10, 2009

In the course of my five months of service in Afghanistan, in both Regional Commands East and South, I have lost understanding of and confidence in the strategic purposes of the United States' presence in Afghanistan. I have doubts and reservations about our current strategy and planned future strategy, but my resignation is based not upon how we are pursuing this war, but why and to what end. To put simply: I fail to see the value or the worth in continued U.S. casualties or expenditures of resources in support of the Afghan government in what is, truly, a 35-year-old civil war.

This fall will mark the eighth year of U.S. combat, governance and development operations within Afghanistan. Next fall, the United States' occupation will equal in length the Soviet Union's own physical involvement in Afghanistan. Like the Soviets, we continue to secure and bolster a failing state, while encouraging an ideology and system of government unknown and unwanted by its people.

If the history of Afghanistan is one great stage play, the United States is no more than a supporting actor, among several previously, in a tragedy that not only pits tribes, valleys, clans, villages and families against one another, but, from at least the end of King Zahir Shah's reign, has violently and savagely pitted the urban, secular, educated and modern of Afghanistan against the rural, religious, illiterate and traditional. It is this latter group that composes and supports the Pashtun insurgency. The Pashtun insurgency, which is composed of multiple, seemingly infinite, local groups, is fed by what is perceived by the Pashtun people as a continued and sustained assault, going back centuries, on Pashtun land, culture, traditions and religion by internal and external enemies. The U.S. and NATO presence and operations in Pashtun valleys and villages, as well as Afghan army and police units that are led and composed of non-Pashtun soldiers and police, provide an occupation force against which the insurgency is justified. In both RC [Regional Commands] East and South, observed that the bulk of the insurgency fights not for the white banner of the Taliban, but rather against the presence of foreign soldiers and taxes imposed by an unrepresentative government in Kabul.

The United States military presence in Afghanistan greatly contributes to the legitimacy and strategic message of the Pashtun insurgency. In a like manner our backing of the Afghan government in its current form continues to distance the government from the people. The Afghan government's failings, particularly when weighed against the sacrifice of American lives and dollars, appear legion and metastatic:

- Glaring corruption and unabashed graft;
- President whose confidants and chief advisers comprise drug lords and war crimes villains, who mock our own rule of law and counternarcotics efforts;
- A system of provincial and district leaders constituted of local power brokers, opportunists and strongmen allied to the United States solely for, and limited by, the value of our USAID and CERP contracts and whose own political and economic interests stand nothing to gain from any positive or genuine attempts at reconciliation; and
- The recent election process dominated by fraud and discredited by low voter turnout, which has created an enormous victory for our enemy who now claims a popular boycott and will call into question worldwide our government's military, economic and diplomatic support for an invalid and illegitimate Afghan government.

Our support for this kind of government, coupled with a misunderstanding of the insurgency's true nature, reminds me horribly of our involvement with South Vietnam; an unpopular and corrupt government we backed at the expense of our Nation's own internal peace, against an insurgency whose nationalism we arrogantly and ignorantly mistook as a rival to our own Cold War ideology.

I find specious the reasons we ask for bloodshed and sacrifice from our young men and women in Afghanistan. If honest, our stated strategy of securing Afghanistan to prevent al-Qaeda resurgence or regrouping would require us to additionally invade and occupy western Pakistan, Somalia, Sudan, Yemen, etc. Our presence in Afghanistan has only increased destabilization and insurgency in Pakistan where we rightly fear a toppled or weakened Pakistani government may lose control of its nuclear weapons. However, again, to follow the logic of our stated goals we should garrison Pakistan, not Afghanistan. More so, the September 11th attacks, as well as the Madrid and London bombings, were primarily planned and organized in Western Europe; a point that highlights the threat is not one tied to traditional geographic or political boundaries. Finally, if our concern is for a failed state crippled by corruption and poverty and under assault from criminal and drug lords, then if we bear our military and financial contributions to Afghanistan, we must reevaluate and increase our commitment to and involvement in Mexico. . . .

I realize the emotion and tone of my letter and ask you excuse any ill temper. I trust you understand the nature of this war and the sacrifices made by so many thousands of families who have been separated from loved ones deployed in defense of our Nation and whose homes bear the fractures, upheavals and scars of multiple and compounded deployments. Thousands of our men and women have returned home with physical and mental wounds, some that will never heal or will only worsen with time. The dead return only in bodily form to be received by families who must be reassured their dead have sacrificed for a purpose worthy of futures lost, love vanished, and promised dreams unkept. I have lost confidence such assurances can anymore be made. As such, I submit my resignation.[54]

CONCLUSION

IN HIS 1957 CHRONICLE OF BRITISH WARTIME DISSENT, HISTORIAN A. J. P. Taylor scoffed at the notion of history as a guide to the future. "The present," he argued, "enables us to understand the past, not the other way around."1 Indeed, as Taylor's analysis suggests, the fear—or terror—Americans are experiencing since the attacks of September 11, 2001, does help us understand the repression of civil liberties enacted out of fear during World War I.

It is also true that subsequent studies about the suspension of civil liberties in 1917 to 1919 (historians are publishing new studies of this subject every year) have, to some degree, prevented a repeat of that terrible era. Taylor's warning, however, was sound. It is wise to be cautious when looking to history to predict the future. "The life of the law has not been logic," Justice Oliver Wendell Holmes observed, "it has been experience."2

History can, however, serve as a lantern to light our future path. That is the intent of this book—by learning from our mistakes we might prevent future ones. If we value dissent, how should we protect it? If John Stuart Mill was correct when he wrote that all dissenters have something worth hearing, how can we ensure that the lessons from the painful mistakes of the past are internalized? How do we prevent future abuses of civil liberties?

I offer here some suggestions with the understanding that the examination of each could (and has) consume numerous books:

The news media must do a better job of adding a more diverse mix of voices to any debate, but especially those about war. Too often the media narrow the range of "acceptable" dissent, which eliminates most so-called radical voices. As studies have shown, opposition to war often fails to make news until prominent, official voices speak out in protest. Editors and reporters would do well to heed Taylor's astute observation, "Today's realism will appear tomorrow as shortsighted blundering. Today's idealism is the realism of the future."3

The Internet and its vast potential for facilitating political activism and organization may be a partial antidote to the news media's tendency to exclude radical dissent in favor of official voices. The Internet's vast potential as an antiwar organizing and communications tool has not been put to any real test. The 2003 invasion of Iraq occurred before the advent of YouTube, Facebook, MySpace, Twitter, and other social networking sites which are now being used so effectively by political and social activists. We must be vigilant, however, to stop any attempts by the government to exert greater control over the Internet. As events in China, Iran, and elsewhere have proved, nescient political movements can be severely hamstrung by government intrusion into cyberspace.

Our government's leaders—and its citizens—must resist appeals to primal instincts during times of national or international crisis. The terrorists succeed only when their attacks terrorize Americans and prompt us to destroy that which makes us distinct from much of the world—our commitment to civil liberties. America "needs to stop cowering in fear," journalist Fareed Zakaria has written. "It is fear that has created a climate of paranoia and panic in the United States and fear that has enabled our strategic missteps."[4] We need leaders who will remain coolly focused on the fundamental liberties guaranteed by the Constitution and who refuse to pander to Americans' fears but, instead, appeal to our "better angels."

Basic governmental reforms can foster greater tolerance for dissent. Almost fifty years ago, President Dwight D. Eisenhower left office with a warning about the dangers of the "military-industrial complex." War has always been profitable for those who manufacture its weapons and machinery, and those interests remain very influential in Washington because of their sway over the media (including access to power, advertising dollars, and public relations budgets) and their ability to purchase influence in Congress with campaign contributions. Reforming the nation's campaign finance system to limit the influence of defense contractors and their lobbyists will not solve the problem, but it would be a good start.

Congress should also reassert its constitutional role as the dominant power in decisions about war and peace. In recent generations, Congress has so thoroughly abdicated its responsibilities in this area that it is now almost a rubber stamp for the president's military policy. One way that Congress could easily begin to assert its prerogatives in this area is to insist on comprehensive debates on reasoned, formal declarations of war. As Brien Hallett persuasively argues in his book *The Lost Art of Declaring War*, "war is a matter of policy" and, as such, that policy should be clearly articulated and debated by Congress in open session. "The primary military functions of a fully reasoned declaration," Hallett argues, "are to justify cogently the resort to war and to establish the meaning of peace and victory—the war aims."[5] Extended debates over reasoned war declarations would create an environment in which dissent is more likely to be heard and one in which the dissenters might, short of stopping the war, at least have the opportunity to influence the war's aims.

Congress should also demand reforms of the public affairs and public relations operations of the Pentagon. During wartime, these amply funded offices (some estimates put the Pentagon's annual public affairs budget at more than $1 billion) are little more than highly effective propaganda units aimed at building and maintaining public support for war and drowning out and eliminating dissent.

Average citizens bear a great deal of responsibility for creating a climate in which dissent is heard and encouraged. We must aggressively guard against suppression of opinions, especially those with which we disagree. Furthermore, we must seek out, read, and listen to opinions widely divergent from our own, especially the more "radical" voices that the mainstream media do not include in their reporting.

Parents should encourage their children's teachers and school leaders to consider bringing into the classroom discordant voices on a variety of issues, as well as teaching students to recognize and guard against propaganda. Regarding dissent, schools should teach not simply its toleration (which carries with it a negative connotation), but rather its great value to democracy.

More than two hundred years ago, during our nation's birth, the founders spent much time fretting about, in James Madison's words, "the violence of faction." Writing in *Federalist 10*, Madison expounded, "The friend of popular governments never finds himself so much alarmed for their character and fate, as when he contemplates their propensity to this dangerous vice." In the minds of Madison and others, factions meant, among other things, political parties. What we now know is that political parties quickly developed and strengthened American democracy by institutionalizing dissent. Brief attempts to crush such factions and their dissent (the Federalists' attacks on the Democrat-Republicans in 1798 that resulted in the Sedition Act) largely failed and only strengthened the aggrieved party. While the inherent role of the dissenting minority party has not made dissent any more pleasant to the majority, it had made it much more difficult to crush and punish dissidents (especially those in Congress who enjoy immunity from prosecution if their words are spoken in the House and Senate chambers). Madison, of course, did not envision much good coming from the dissent of factions. "It may clog the administration, it may convulse the society," he warned, "but it will be unable to execute and mask its violence under the forms of the Constitution."[6]

This leads to my final suggestion, perhaps highly impractical, but which would further institutionalize dissent in the halls of our government.

In 1708 Pope Clement XI established the role of Promoter of the Faith, a position within the Sacred Congregation of Rites, which dealt with the process of beautification and canonization. Of the role of the position, also known as *Advocatus Diaboli*, or Devil's Advocate, *The Catholic Encyclopedia* observes, "No important act in the process of beautification or canonization is valid unless performed in the presence of the Promoter of the Faith. . . . His duty is to protest against the omission of forms laid down, and to insist upon the consideration of any objection."[7] Because the call to war so often comes to us in religious or righteous tones, an official devil's advocate may be doubly necessary in these unique moments. (In a perfect world, the news media would be expected to play this role, but as history demonstrates, the press is rarely willing or able to effectively challenge the prevailing view in times of national crisis.) Therefore Congress might consider creating a committee or commission whose sole responsibility would be to investigate and argue (with, perhaps, a formal report) against any war declaration or use-of-force resolution. The creation of a devil's advocate committee would not necessarily be to prevent war and so must not be populated with the most extreme antiwar advocates. Rather, members would simply resolve to put any decision about war to the most rigorous test and to ensure that their colleagues and constituents are fully informed about any decision regarding war. In addition, the committee's chairman should be given time to make a formal presentation of the committee's investigation. Such an arrangement does not mean that a devil's advocate committee will be the only or even the most prominent dissenter, but it will ensure that Congress will not go to war without hearing a sober presentation of the reasons for delaying or preventing war.[8]

The British author Samuel Butler delighted in playing the role of devil's advocate. Using matters of faith as his example, Butler wrote, "It must be remembered that we have heard only one side of the case. God has written all the books." The devil, Butler believed, should be allowed to present his side.[9] Butler apparently presumed that God was secure enough to tolerate the scrutiny. The purpose of this book, therefore, is not so much to argue against war as to argue in favor of a democracy strong and confident enough during times of national and international crisis to tolerate scrutiny and dissent.

NOTES

INTRODUCTION

1. Plato, *The Last Days of Socrates*, trans. Hugh Tredennick (New York: Penguin, 1954), 52, 62–63, 73.
2. A. J. P. Taylor, *The Trouble Makers: Dissent over Foreign Policy, 1792–1939* (London: Panther Books, 1969), 14, 17.
3. John Stuart Mill, *On Liberty* (Indianapolis: Bobbs-Merrill, 1956), 56, 58, 63.
4. Luther Gulick, *Administrative Reflections from World War II* (Birmingham: University of Alabama Press, 1948), 126–27.
5. Mill, *On Liberty*, 59.
6. John F. Kennedy, *Profiles in Courage,* memorial edition (New York: Harper & Row, 1964), 264.
7. J. William Fulbright, *The Arrogance of Power* (New York: Vintage Books, 1966), 27.
8. John Quincy Adams, *Addresses of John Quincy Adams to His Constituents of the 12th Congressional District at Braintree* (Boston: J. H. Eastburn, 1842), 54.
9. Clemens P. Work, *Darkest before Dawn: Sedition and Free Speech in the American West* (Albuquerque: University of New Mexico Press, 2005), 4.
10. William A. Dorman, "Press Theory and Journalistic Practice: The Case of the Gulf War," in *Do the Media Govern? Politicians, Voters, and Reporters in America*, ed. Shanto Iyengar and Richard Reeves (Thousand Oaks, CA: Sage Publications, 1997), 124.
11. William L. Lunch and Peter W. Sperlich, "American Public Opinion and the Vietnam War," *Political Research Quarterly* 32, no. 1 (1979): 21–44.
12. W. Lance Bennett, Regina G. Lawrence, and Steven Livingston, *When the Press Fails: Political Power and the News Media from Iraq to Katrina* (Chicago: University of Chicago Press, 2007), 3–4.
13. W. Lance Bennett, "Cracking the News Code: Some Rules That Journalists Live By," and William A. Dorman, "Press Theory and Journalistic Practice: The Case of the Gulf War," in *Do the Media Govern? Politicians, Voters, and Reporters in America, ed.* Shanto Iyengar and Richard Reeves (Thousand Oaks, CA: Sage Publications, 1997), 103–40.
14. Jonathan Mermin, *Debating War and Peace: Media Coverage of U.S. Intervention in the Post-Vietnam Era* (Princeton, NJ: Princeton University Press, 1999), 27.
15. Center for Media and Public Affairs and Fairness and Accuracy in Reporting surveys, cited in Robert M. Entman, *Projections of Power: Framing News, Public Opinion and U.S. Foreign Policy* (Chicago: University of Chicago Press, 2004), 111, 150.
16. Entman, *Projections of Power*, 151.

17. David Cole, "The New McCarthyism: Repeating History in the War on Terrorism," in *Dissent in Dangerous Times, ed.* Austin Sarat (Ann Arbor: University of Michigan Press, 2005), 111–45.

18. Nancy Chang, *Silencing Political Dissent* (New York: Seven Stories Press, 2002), 103, 113.

19. Cass R. Sunstein, *Why Societies Need Dissent* (Cambridge, MA: Harvard University Press, 2003), 3.

20. Mill, *On Liberty*, 7.

21. Fulbright, *Arrogance of Power*, 25.

22. John W. Spainer, *The Truman-MacArthur Controversy and the Korean War* (New York: W. W. Norton, 1965), 43.

23. Robert A. Taft, *The Papers of Robert A. Taft: 1939–1944* (Kent, OH: Kent State University Press, 2001), 303.

24. *The Writings of George Washington*, vol. 10, *1782–1785*, ed. Worthington Chauncey Ford (New York: G. P. Putnam's Sons, 1891), 172.

CHAPTER 1

1. Frank W. C. Hersey, "Tar and Feathers: The Adventures of Captain John Malcolm" (Boston: The Colonial Society of Massachusetts, April 1941), 427–73; Wallace Brown, *The Good Americans: The Loyalists in the American Revolution* (New York: William Morrow, 1969), 134–36; R. S. Longley, "Mob Activities in Revolutionary Massachusetts," *The New England Quarterly* 6, no. 1. (March 1933): 98–130.

2. Robert McCluer Calhoon, *The Loyalists in Revolutionary America 1760–1781* (New York: Harcourt Brace Jovanovich, 1973), 191–93.

3. Brown, *The Good Americans*, 136.

4. Henry J. Young, "Treason and its Punishment in Revolutionary Pennsylvania," *Pennsylvania Magazine of History and Biography 90* (July 1966): 287–91.

5. Ibid.

6. Bradley Chapin, "Colonial and Revolutionary Origins of the American Law of Treason," *The William and Mary Quarterly*, 3rd ser., 17, no. 1. (January 1960): 3–21.

7. Arthur Meier Schlesinger, "Political Mobs and the American Revolution, 1765–1776," *Proceedings of the American Philosophical Society* 99, no. 4 (August 30, 1955): 244–50. See also Gordon S. Wood, "A Note on Mobs in the American Revolution," *The William and Mary Quarterly*, 3rd ser., 23, no. 4 (October 1966): 635–42.

8. Levy, Leonard W. *Freedom of Speech and Press in Early American History: Legacy of Suppression* (New York: Harper Torchbook, 1963), 176. (Originally published by Harper in 1960 as *Legacy of Suppression*.)

9. *Journals of the Continental Congress, 1774–1789*, ed. Worthington C. Ford et al. (Washington, DC, 1904–37), 1:108.

10. Levy, *Legacy of Suppression*, 177; Arthur M. Schlesinger, *Prelude to Independence: The Newspaper War on Britain 1764–1776* (New York: Knopf, 1958), 222.

11. Schlesinger, *Prelude to Independence*, 226, 240.

12. Levy, *Legacy of Suppression*, 191.

13. Claude Halstead Van Tyne, *The Loyalists in the American Revolution* (New York: Peter Smith, 1929), 199.

14. Levy, *Legacy of Suppression*, 183.

15. Brown, *The Good Americans*, 21.

16. Thomas Jefferson, "Notes on the State of Virginia, 1743–1826," 247, http://etext
    .virginia.edu/toc/modeng/public/JefVirg.html.
17. David McCullough, *1776* (New York: Simon and Schuster, 2005), 11–13.
18. Thomas Paine, *Common Sense, Rights of Man, and Other Essential Writings of Thomas
    Paine* (New York: Signet Classics, 2003), 3–68.
19. Eric Foner, *Tom Paine and Revolutionary America* (New York: Oxford, 1976), 74.
20. Scott Liell, *46 Pages: Thomas Paine, Common Sense, and the Turning Point to Indepen-
    dence* (Philadelphia: Running Press, 2003), 95, 117; Foner, *Tom Paine and Revolutionary
    America*, xvii.
21. Liell, *46 Pages*, 17.
22. Brown, *The Good Americans*, 227; Jack P. Greene and J. R. Pole, ed., *A Companion to the
    American Revolution* (Malden, MA: Blackwell Publishers, 2000), 235.
23. Willard Hurt, "Treason in the United States," *Harvard Law Review* 58, no. 2 (December
    1944): 266.
24. M. Christopher New, *Maryland Loyalists in the American Revolution* (Centreville, MD:
    Tidewater Publishers, 1996), 18–34.
25. Thomas Paine, *Common Sense, ed.* Edward Larkin (Peterborough, ON: Broadview Press,
    2004), 158–70.
26. Lorenzo Sabine, *Biographical Sketches of Loyalists of the American Revolution* (Boston:
    Little Brown, 1864), 562–63.
27. "Charles Inglis," *Dictionary of Canadian Biography Online,* http://www.biographi.ca/EN/
    ShowBio.asp?BioId=36595; "Charles Inglis," *Encyclopedia Britannica Online,* http://www
    .wip.britannica.com/ebc/article-9042417.
28. John J. Patrick, *Founding the Republic: A Documentary History* (Westport, CT: Green-
    wood, 1995), 19–23.
29. Donald Barr Chidsey, *The Loyalists: The Story of Those Americans Who Fought Against
    Independence* (New York: Crown, 1973), 93–96; Catherine Snell Crary, "The Tory and
    the Spy: The Double Life of James Rivington," *The William and Mary Quarterly*, 3rd
    ser., 16, no. 1. (January 1959): 66–67.
30. Crary, "The Tory and the Spy," 61–71.
31. "William Smith," *Dictionary of Canadian Biography Online,* http://www.biographi.ca/
    EN/ShowBio.asp?BioId=36293.
32. William Smith, *The Candid Retrospect; or the American War Examined by Whig Principles*
    (Charleston: Robert Wells & Son, 1780).

CHAPTER 2

1. David Mayers, *Dissenting Voices in America's Rise to Power* (New York: Cambridge University Press, 2007), 33.
2. James Madison, "War Message to Congress," June 1, 1812, Liberty Library of Constitutional Classics, http://www.constitution.org/jm/18120601_war.htm.
3. Donald R. Hickey, *The War of 1812: A Forgotten Conflict* (Urbana: University of Illinois
   Press, 1989), 30.
4. Ibid., 30–35; Richard Buel Jr., *America on the Brink: How the Political Struggle Over the
   War of 1812 Almost Destroyed the Young Republic* (New York: Palgrave Macmillan, 2005),
   128–29.
5. Mayers, *Dissenting Voices*, 35.
6. Buel, *America on the Brink*, 132.
7. Garry Wills, *James Madison* (New York: Times Books, 2002), 97.

8. Buel, *America on the Brink*, 129–30.
9. Randolph quoted in *Voices in Dissent: An Anthology of Individualist Thought in the United States*, ed. Arthur A. Ekirch Jr. (New York: Citadel Press, 1964), 41–47.
10. Roger H. Brown, *The Republic in Peril: 1812* (New York: Columbia University Press, 1964), 45; T. Harry Williams, *The History of American Wars: From 1745 to 1918* (Baton Rouge: LSU Press, 1981), 94; Walter R. Borneman, *1812: The War that Forged a Nation* (New York: HarperCollins, 2004), 50; Samuel Eliot Morison, "Dissent in the War of 1812," in *Dissent in Three American Wars, ed. Samuel Eliot Morison*, Frederick Merk, and Frank Freidel (Cambridge: Harvard University Press, 1970), 3; Mayers, *Dissenting Voices*, 36.
11. Borneman, *The War that Forged a Nation*, 50–51.
12. Henry Adams, *History of the United States of America During the Administrations of James Madison* (New York: Library of America, 1986), 439.
13. Borneman, *The War that Forged a Nation*, 58.
14. Buel, *America on the Brink*, 150–51.
15. Ibid., 156–58.
16. *Morison, "Dissent in the War of 1812,"* 5, 7.
17. Buel, *America on the Brink*, 162–63.
18. J. C. A. Stagg, "War of 1812," in *The Oxford Companion to American Military History*, ed. John Whiteclay Chambers (New York: Oxford University Press, 1999), 783–85; Borneman, *The War that Forged a Nation*, 127–32, 153–61.
19. Ibid., 96–107.
20. Ibid., 219; Morison, "Dissent in the War of 1812," 12–13.
21. Williams, *The History of American Wars*, 105.
22. Adams, *History of the United States of America During the Administrations of James Madison*, 887.
23. Morison, "Dissent in the War of 1812," 14.
24. Borneman, *The War that Forged a Nation*, 253–56; Hickey, *The War of 1812*, 273–78.
25. Buel, 229.
26. Hickey, *The War of 1812*, 307–9.
27. *Hugh A. Garland, Life of John Randolph* (Philadelphia: D. Appleton, 1850), 1:289.
28. "John Randolph," *Dictionary of American Biography*, http://galenet.galegroup.com/servlet/BioRC; John F. Kennedy, *Profiles in Courage*, Memorial Edition (New York: Harper & Row, 1964), 49.
29. "John Randolph," *Dictionary of American Biography,* http://galenet.galegroup.com/servlet/BioRC.
30. *Garland, Life of John Randolph*, 299–303.
31. "Josiah Quincy," *Dictionary of American Biography*, http://galenet.galegroup.com/servlet/BioRC.
32. Francis Walker, *The Making of a Nation, 1783–1817* (New York: Charles Scribner's Sons, 1895), 225–26.
33. *Annals of Congress*, 12th Cong., 1st sess., vol. 2, appendix, 2196–2221.
34. "John Lowell," *Dictionary of American Biography*, http://galenet.galegroup.com/servlet/BioRC; Ferris Greenslet, *The Lowells and Their Seven Worlds* (Cambridge, MA: Riverside Press, 1946), 131–53.
35. John Lowell, *Mr. Madison's War: A Dispassionate Inquiry into the Reasons Alleged by Mr. Madison for Declaring an Offensive and Ruinous War against Great Britain* (Boston: Russell & Cutler, 1812).

CHAPTER 3

1. T. Harry Williams, *The History of American Wars: From 1745 to 1918* (Baton Rouge: LSU Press, 1981), 149–50.

2. Michael A. Morrison, "New Territory versus No Territory": The Whig Party and the Politics of Western Expansion, 1846–1848," *The Western Historical Quarterly* 23, no. 1 (February 1992): 25–51.

3. John S. D. Eisenhower, *So Far From God: The U.S. War with Mexico, 1846–1848* (New York: Random House, 1989), 44–48.

4. Frederick Merk, "Dissent in the Mexican War," in *Dissent in Three American Wars, ed.* Samuel Eliot Morison, Frederick Merk, and Frank Freidel (Cambridge, MA: Harvard University Press, 1970), 37; Eisenhower, *So Far From God,* 49–64; Joseph G. Dawson III, "Mexican War," in *The Oxford Companion to American Military History,* ed. John Whiteclay Chambers (New York: Oxford University Press, 1999), 433.

5. Eisenhower, *So Far From God,* 66.

6. Russell D. Buhite, ed., *Calls to Arms: Presidential Speeches, Messages, and Declarations of War* (Wilmington, DE: Scholarly Resources, 2003), 35–41.

7. Merk, "Dissent in the Mexican War," 37–41.

8. David Mayers, *Dissenting Voices in America's Rise to Power* (New York: Cambridge University Press, 2007), 118; John H. Schroeder, *Mr. Polk's War: American Opposition and Dissent, 1846–1848* (Madison: University of Wisconsin Press, 1973), 6–7; Merk, "Dissent in the Mexican War," 42.

9. Morrison, "New Territory versus No Territory," 25–51.

10. *Congressional Globe,* 29th Cong., 1st sess., 1846, appendix, 644.

11. Schroeder, *Mr. Polk's War,* 23–24.

12. Merk, "Dissent in the Mexican War," 45.

13. *Congressional Globe,* 29th Cong., 1st sess., 1846, appendix, 949; Schroeder, *Mr. Polk's War,* 29.

14. James Arnold, *Presidents Under Fire* (New York: Random House, 1995), 101–4.

15. Schroeder, *Mr. Polk's War,* 34.

16. "James K. Polk, Second Annual Message, Dec. 8, 1846," John Woolley and Gerhard Peters, *The American Presidency Project,* http://www.presidency.ucsb.edu/ws/index.php ?pid=29487&st=James+K.+Polk&st1=.

17. "Dissent in the Mexican War," in Joseph G. Dawson III, *The Oxford Companion to American Military History* (New York: Oxford University Press, 1999), 435.

18. Arnold, *Presidents Under Fire,* 120.

19. *House Journal,* 30th Cong., 1st sess., January 3, 1848, 184–85.

20. Merk, "Dissent in the Mexican War," 63.

21. Morrison, "New Territory versus No Territory," 25–51.

22. "Charles Sumner," *Dictionary of American Biography,* http://galenet.galegroup.com/servlet/BioRC.

23. Arthur A. Ekirch, ed., *Voices in Dissent: An Anthology of Individualist Thought in the United States* (New York: Citadel Press, 1964), 87–95; Charles Sumner, *The True Grandeur of Nations* (Boston: Lee & Shepard), 1893.

24. "John Caldwell Calhoun," *Encyclopedia of World Biography,* http://galenet.galegroup .com/servlet/BioRC.

25. *Congressional Globe,* 30th Cong., 1st sess., January 4, 1848, 96–101.

26. David Herbert Donald, *Lincoln* (New York: Simon & Schuster, 1995), 119–25.

27. *Congressional Globe,* 30th Cong., 1st sess., January 12, 1848, appendix, 93–95.

CHAPTER 4

1. John H. Aughey, *Tupelo* (Lincoln, NE: State Journal Co., 1888), 21–76.
2. Carleton Beals, *War Within a War: The Confederacy Against Itself* (Philadelphia: Chilton Books, 1965), 1.
3. James M. McPherson, *Battle Cry of Freedom: The Civil War Era* (New York: Oxford University Press, 1988), 255.
4. Beals, *War Within a War*, 3, 4; James Alex Baggett, *The Scalawags: Southern Dissenters in the Civil War and Reconstruction* (Baton Rouge: Louisiana State University Press, 2003), 43.
5. Baggett, *The Scalawags*, 43, 47.
6. Georgia Lee Tatum, *Disloyalty in the Confederacy* (Chapel Hill: University of North Carolina Press, 1934), 5, 143.
7. Beals, *War Within a War*, 79.
8. Ibid., 79; Tatum, *Disloyalty in the Confederacy*, 6.
9. McPherson, *Battle Cry of Freedom*, 276–77.
10. Tatum, *Disloyalty in the Confederacy*, 9–10.
11. Beals, *War Within a War*, 66–67.
12. Tatum, *Disloyalty in the Confederacy*, 73–74.
13. Ibid., 57.
14. Ibid., 24–25, 37–38.
15. Ibid., 36–43.
16. Clement Eaton, "Censorship of the Southern Mails," *The American Historical Review* 48, no. 2 (January 1943): 255–80; William W. Freehling, *The Road to Disunion*, vol. 2, *Secessionists Triumphant, 1854–1861* (New York: Oxford, 2007), 22–23; Beals, *War Within a War*, 71.
17. McPherson, *Battle Cry of Freedom*, 285–89; Geoffrey R. Stone, *Perilous Times: Free Speech in Wartime* (New York: W. W. Norton, 2004), 122.
18. Stone, *Perilous Times*, 120; John G. Nicolay and John Hay, ed., *Complete Works of Abraham Lincoln* (Harrogate, TN: Lincoln Memorial University, 1894), 8:41–42.
19. Stone, *Perilous Times*, 124.
20. Ibid., 125.
21. Ibid., 17–21.
22. Ibid., 23.
23. Page Smith, *Trial By Fire: A People's History of the Civil War and Reconstruction* (New York: McGraw-Hill, 1982), 5:417–18.
24. Jennifer L. Weber, *Copperheads: The Rise and Fall of Lincoln's Opponents in the North* (New York: Oxford, 2006), 33, 65.
25. McPherson, *Battle Cry of Freedom*, 592–93; Weber, *Copperheads*, 80–81.
26. Frank Klement, *The Limits of Dissent: Clement L. Vallandigham and the Civil War* (New York: Fordham University Press, 1998), 111.
27. McPherson, *Battle Cry of Freedom*, 593; Klement, *The Limits of Dissent*, 125.
28. Ibid., 138–53.
29. Ibid., 100–101.
30. *Stone, Perilous Times,* 102, 106–7n109.
31. Ibid., 108–18.
32. Ibid., 118–19.
33. Weber, *Copperheads,* 135–38, 141.
34. David Herbert Donald, *Lincoln* (New York: Simon & Schuster, 1995), 530–32.
35. Weber, *Copperheads,* 202.

36. Kenneth Michael Stickney, "Silenced: The Abrupt Demise of Catahoula Parish's Unionist Newspaper" (master's thesis, University of Louisiana at Monroe, 2007); Wyona Gillmore Mills, "James Govan Taliaferro (1798–1876): Louisiana Unionist and Scalawag" (master's thesis, Louisiana State University, January 1968); John M. Sacher, *A Perfect War of Politics: Parties, Politicians, and Democracy in Louisiana, 1824–1861* (Baton Rouge: Louisiana State University Press, 2003), 298.

37. James Govan Taliaferro, "*Protest delivered at the Secession Convention, 1861*" (broadside on file at Louisiana and Lower Mississippi Valley Collections, Hill Memorial Library, Louisiana State University).

38. Richard K. Call, *Union.-Slavery.-Secession* (Philadelphia: C. Sherman & Son, 1861).

39. "Clement Laird Vallandigham," *Dictionary of American Biography,* http://galenet.galegroup .com/servlet/BioRC; "Clement Laird Vallandigham" *Encyclopedia of World Biography*, http://galenet.galegroup.com/servlet/BioRC.

40. Clement L. Vallandigham, *Speeches, Arguments, Addresses and Letters of Clement L. Vallandigham* (New York: J. Walter, 1864), 306–24.

41. "Benjamin Robbins Curtis." *Dictionary of American Biography,* http://galenet.galegroup .com/servlet/BioRC; "Benjamin Robbins Curtis," *Encyclopedia of World Biography*, http://galenet.galegroup.com/servlet/BioRC.

42. Arthur A. Ekirch Jr., ed., *Voices in Dissent: An Anthology of Individualist Thought in the United States* (New York: Citadel Press, 1964), 137–47.

CHAPTER 5

1. *Congressional Record*, 56th Cong., 1st sess., March 17, 1898, 2916–19.

2. Ivan Musicant, *Empire By Default: The Spanish-American War and the Dawn of the American Century* (New York: Henry Holt, 1998), 165; G. J. A. O'Toole, *The Spanish War: An American Epic, 1898* (New York: W. W. Norton, 1984), 147.

3. Musicant, *Empire By Default*, 166; John L. Offner, "McKinley and the Spanish-American War," *Presidential Studies Quarterly* 34, no. 1 (March 2004): 50–61.

4. Marcus M. Wilkerson, *Public Opinion and the Spanish-American War: A Study in War Propaganda* (Baton Rouge: Louisiana State University Press, 1932), 31, 43.

5. Quoted in Wilkerson, *Public Opinion and the Spanish-American War*, 33.

6. Ibid., 35.

7. Ibid., 45.

8. Warren Zimmerman, *First Great Triumph: How Five Americans Made Their Country a World Power* (New York: Farrar, Straus and Giroux, 2002), 356.

9. Lewis L. Gould, *The Spanish-American War and President McKinley* (Lawrence: University Press of Kansas, 1980), 41.

10. Peiro Gleijeses, "1898: The Opposition to the Spanish-American War," *Journal of Latin American Studies* 35, no. 4 (2003): 681–719.

11. Offner, "McKinley and the Spanish-American War," 50–61.

12. Ibid.

13. Gleijeses, "1898: The Opposition to the Spanish-American War," 684.

14. Ibid., 691.

15. Moorfield Storey, "Nothing to Excuse Our Intervention," in *Advocate of Peace* (Boston: American Peace Society, 1898), 112–14.

16. Charles Eliot Norton, "True Patriotism," in *Public Opinion: A Comprehensive Summary of the Press Throughout the World on All Important Current Topics*, vol. 24 (New York: Public Opinion Company, 1898), 775–76.

17. Musicant, *Empire By Default*, 168.
18. Ibid., 178.
19. Gleijeses, "1898: The Opposition to the Spanish-American War," 713.
20. "McKinley's War Message," *Documents of American History, vol. 2, Since 1898, 7th ed.*, ed. Henry Steele Commager (New York: Appleton-Century-Crofts, 1963), 1–4.
21. Musicant, *Empire By Default*, 184–87.
22. Frank Freidel, "Dissent in the Spanish-American War," in *Dissent in Three American Wars*, ed. Samuel Eliot Morison, Frederick Merk, and Frank Freidel (Cambridge, MA: Harvard University Press, 1970), 74.
23. James M. Drake, "Spanish American War," in *The Oxford Companion to American Military History*, ed. John Whiteclay Chambers II (New York: Oxford University Press, 1999), 667–69.
24. Freidel, "Dissent in the Spanish-American War," 77; Zimmerman, *First Great Triumph*, 311.
25. Quoted in G. J. A. O'Toole, *The Spanish War: An American Epic, 1898* (New York: Norton, 1984), 386.
26. Freidel, "Dissent in the Spanish-American War," 79.
27. *Congressional Record*, 56th Cong., 1st sess., January 9, 1900, 704–12.
28. William Jennings Bryan, "Speech at Indianapolis, January 8, 1900," in William Jennings Bryan, *Under Other Flags: Travels, Lectures, Speeches* (Lincoln, NE: Woodruff-Collins, 1904), 307–39.
29. Zimmerman, *First Great Triumph*, 324; Freidel, "Dissent in the Spanish-American War," 82.
30. Zimmerman, *First Great Triumph*, 323; Adams quoted by Freidel, "Dissent in the Spanish-American War," 83.
31. George S. Boutwell, *The Crisis of the Republic* (Boston: Dana Estes and Co., 1900), 196.
32. Freidel, "Dissent in the Spanish-American War," 83–85.
33. "Soldiers' Letters: Being Materials for the History of a War of Criminal Aggression" (Boston: Anti-Imperialist League, 1899).
34. O'Toole, *The Spanish War*, 390.
35. Bryan, "Speech at Indianapolis, January 8, 1900," 307–39.
36. Freidel, "Dissent in the Spanish-American War," 92.
37. John V. Denson, *The Costs of War: America's Pyrrhic Victories* (New Brunswick, NJ: Transaction, 1997), 188; Zimmerman, *First Great Triumph*, 405.
38. Denson, *The Costs of War*, 188.
39. Ibid., 405–10.
40. Ibid., 410–11.
41. Moorfield Storey and Julian Codman, *Secretary Root's Record: "Marked Severities" in Philippine Warfare* (Boston: Geo. H. Ellis, 1902).
42. Bolton Hall, "Why I am Opposed to Imperialism," *The Arena* 28 (July 1902), 4–7.
43. Ernest Crosby, "Why I am Opposed to Imperialism," *The Arena* 28 (July 1902), 10–11.
44. O'Toole, *The Spanish War*, 395–96.
45. Grover Cleveland, "Ex-President Grover Cleveland on the Philippine Problem" (Boston, New England Anti-Imperialist League, 1904).
46. Linda Dowling, *Charles Eliot Norton: The Art of Reform in Nineteenth-Century America* (Lebanon, NH: University Press of New England, 2007).
47. Lowell (1819–1891) was a prominent poet and satirist, outspoken in his opposition to slavery and the Mexican-American War.
48. Bright (1811–1889) was a veteran member of the British parliament who, in 1857, spoke out against Britain's role in the popular Crimean War.

49. Charles Eliot Norton, "True Patriotism."

50. Official Report of the Proceedings of the Democratic National Convention, Held in Kansas City, Missouri, July 4–6, 1900, pp. 205–27.

CHAPTER 6

1. David S. Jordan, "Is War Eternal?" *Rice Institute Pamphlet* 3, no. 3 (July 1916): 218–30.

2. David M. Kennedy, *Over Here: The First World War and American Society* (Oxford: Oxford University Press, 1980), 3.

3. "Three Fights Mark Big Peace Meeting," *New York Times*, March, 25, 1917.

4. "Dr. Jordan Hissed By Princeton Men," *New York Times*, March 27, 1917.

5. Ibid.; David Starr Jordan, *The Days of a Man*, vol. 2, *1900–1921* (Yonkers-on-Hudson, NY: World Book, 1922), 727.

6. Jordan, *The Days of a Man*, vol. 2, 726–29, 731–32.

7. Kennedy, *Over Here*, 11.

8. Ibid., 12, 33; Harry N. Scheiber, *The Wilson Administration and Civil Liberties, 1917– 1921* (Ithaca, NY: Cornell University Press, 1960), 9.

9. Paul L. Murphy, *World War I and the Origin of Civil Liberties in the United States* (New York: W. W. Norton, 1979), 54.

10. Harry N. Scheiber, *The Wilson Administration and Civil Liberties* (Ithaca: Cornell University Press, 1960), 6.

11. Murphy, *World War I and the Origin of Civil Liberties*, 52.

12. Geoffrey R. Stone, *Perilous Times: Free Speech in Wartime* (New York: W. W. Norton, 2004), 140; Ronald Schaffer, *America in the Great War: The Rise of the War Welfare State* (New York: Oxford University Press, 1991), 20; Thomas Fleming, *The Illusion of Victory: America in World War I* (New York: Basic Books, 2003), 60.

13. *Congressional Record*, 65th Cong., spec. sess., April 5, 1917, 326–28, 348.

14. Ibid., 349.

15. Kennedy, *Over Here*, 21.

16. Ibid., 23.

17. *Congressional Record*, 65th Cong., spec. sess., April 5, 1917, 311.

18. "It is War Now; We Must Fight Forward to Lasting Peace, is Dr. Jordan's Message," *San Francisco Bulletin*, April 10, 1917.

19. William Allen White, *The Autobiography of William Allen White* (New York: MacMillan, 1946), 534; "President Wilson's Message to Congress Requesting Declaration of War Against Germany, April 2, 1917," in *Call to Arms: Presidential Speeches, Messages, and Declarations of War*, ed. Russel D. Buhite (Wilmington, DE: Scholarly Resources, 2003), 147–58.

20. Woodrow Wilson, *President Wilson's State Papers and Addresses* (New York: George H. Dolan, 1918), 418.

21. Scheiber, *The Wilson Administration and Civil Liberties*, 14–15.

22. George Creel, *How We Advertised America* (New York: Harper & Brothers, 1920), 3.

23. Creel, *How We Advertised America*, 16.

24. Kennedy, *Over Here*, 61.

25. Scheiber, *The Wilson Administration and Civil Liberties*, 16.

26. Creel, *How We Advertised America*, 5, 85–87.

27. Scheiber, *The Wilson Administration and Civil Liberties*, 18.

28. *Congressional Record*, 65th Cong., April 18, 1917, 779.

29. Scheiber, *The Wilson Administration and Civil Liberties*, 18.

30. Ibid., 19, 46–47; "80 I.W.W. Members Must Serve Terms," *New York Times*, April 12, 1921.

31. Scheiber, *The Wilson Administration and Civil Liberties*, 17–29.

32. *Congressional Record*, 65th Cong., 1st sess., May 11, 1917, 2114.

33. Scheiber, *The Wilson Administration and Civil Liberties*, 20–21.

34. "The Espionage Act," Henry Steele Commager, ed., *Documents of American History, vol. 2, Since 1898, 7th ed.* (New York: Appleton-Century-Crofts, 1963), 145–46.

35. Theodore Roosevelt, "Citizens or Subjects?" April 6, 1918, in *Roosevelt in the Kansas City Star: War-Time Editorials* (Kansas City Star, 1921), 129–30.

36. Scheiber, *The Wilson Administration and Civil Liberties*, 26–27.

37. Zechariah Chafee, *Freedom of Speech* (New York: Harcourt, Brace), 74.

38. Schaffer, *America in the Great War*, 15; see also Clemens P. Work, *Darkest Before Dawn: Sedition and Free Speech in the American West* (Albuquerque: University of New Mexico Press, 2005).

39. Work, *Darkest Before Dawn*, 177–81.

40. "The Promoters of the War Mania," in *Anarchy! An Anthology of Emma Goldman's Mother Earth, ed.* Peter Glassgold (Washington: Counterpoint, 2001), 392–97.

41. Stone, *Perilous Times*, 143–44.

42. Ibid., 196–97.

43. Ibid., 196–98; Murphy, *World War I and the Origin of Civil Liberties*, 228; *Eugene V. Deb's Canton Speech* (Chicago: Socialist Party of the United States, 1921).

44. Murphy, *World War I and the Origin of Civil Liberties*, 89–90; Michael Linfield, *Freedom Under Fire: U.S. Civil Liberties in Times of War* (Boston: South End Press, 1999), 38; Schaffer, *America in the Great War*, 17.

45. Albert F. Gunns, *Civil Liberties in Crisis: The Pacific Northwest, 1917–1940* (New York: Garland, 1983), 14.

46. Schaffer, *America in the Great War*, 18–19.

47. Kennedy, *Over Here*, 78.

48. Schaffer, *America in the Great War*, 21–22; Kennedy, *Over Here*, 54.

49. Kennedy, *Over Here*, 88.

50. Woodrow Wilson, *The Politics of Woodrow Wilson: Selections from His Speeches and Writings* (New York: Harper, 1956), 326; John Morton Blum, *Woodrow Wilson and the Politics of Morality* (Boston: Little, Brown, 1956), 159.

51. Ibid., 89.

52. Michael Wreszin, *Oswald Garrison Villard: Pacifist at War* (Bloomington: Indiana University Press, 1965), 101.

53. George Creel, *The War, the World and Wilson* (New York: Harper & Brothers, 1920), 145–46.

54. Stone, *Perilous Times*, 221.

55. Robert K. Murray, *Red Scare: A Study of National Hysteria, 1919–1920* (New York: McGraw-Hill, 1964), 83.

56. Ibid., 210–19; Stone, *Perilous Times*, 223–24.

57. Stone, *Perilous Times*, 226.

58. "Emma Goldman," *Encyclopedia of World Biography*, http://galenet.galegroup.com/servlet/BioRC; "Emma Goldman," *American Decades*, http://galenet.galegroup.com/servlet/BioRC; John Chalberg, *Emma Goldman, American Individualist*, ed. Oscar Handlin (New York: HarperCollins, 1991).

59. *Anarchy! An Anthology of Emma Goldman's Mother Earth*, ed. Peter Glassgold (Washington, DC: Counterpoint, 2001), 392–97.

60. Kennedy, *Over Here*, 74.

61. H. C. Peterson and Gilbert C. Fite, *Opponents of War, 1917–1918* (Madison: University of Wisconsin Press, 1957), 6–7.

62. Nancy Unger, *Fighting Bob La Follette: The Righteous Reformer* (Chapel Hill: University of North Carolina Press, 2000), 249, 254.

63. The Entente Allies were the wartime alliance of the United Kingdom, France, and Russia.

64. *Congressional Record, 65th Cong., 1st sess.*, April 4, 1917, 223–34.

65. Nick Salvator, *Eugene V. Debs: Citizen and Socialist* (Champaign: University of Illinois Press, 1982).

66. Samuel Johnson (1709–1784), one of Great Britain's most celebrated writers.

67. *Eugene V. Deb's Canton Speech* (Chicago: Socialist Party of the United States, 1921).

CHAPTER 7

1. "Text of the President's Address Asking a Great Defense Fund," *New York Times*, May 17, 1940.

2. Doris Kearns Goodwin, *No Ordinary Time: Franklin & Eleanor Roosevelt: The Home Front in World War II* (New York: Touchstone, 1994), 48.

3. Charles A. Lindbergh, "The Air Defense of America," in *The Radio Addresses of Col. Charles A. Lindbergh, 1939–1940* (New York: Charles Scribner's Sons, 1940), 9–11; speech transcript available at http://www.charleslindbergh.com/americanfirst/index.asp; "Text of the Speech," *New York Times*, May 20, 1940.

4. Goodwin, *No Ordinary Time*, 47.

5. "Lindbergh Decries Fears of Invasion," *New York Times*, May 20, 1940.

6. *Congressional Record*, 76th Cong., 2nd sess., October 2, 1939, 66.

7. Charles A. Lindbergh, "Neutrality and War," in *The Radio Addresses of Col. Charles A. Lindbergh, 1939–1940*, ed. Edward R. Fields (New York: Charles Scribner's Sons, 1940), 5–8; speech transcript available at http://www.charleslindbergh.com/pdf/NeutralityandWar.pdf.

8. Goodwin, *No Ordinary Time*, 48.

9. Lindbergh, "America and European Wars," in *The Radio Addresses of Col. Charles A. Lindbergh, 1939–1940*, ed. Edward R. Fields (New York: Charles Scribner's Sons, 1940), 2–4.

10. Transcript of press conference, April 25, 1941, in *The Public Papers and Addresses of Franklin D. Roosevelt* (New York: Harper & Brothers, 1950), 1941:136–38.

11. Hadley Cantril, "Opinion Trends in World War II: Some Guides to Interpretation," *Public Opinion Quarterly* 12, no. 1 (spring 1948): 30–44.

12. Goodwin, *No Ordinary Time*, 194.

13. Transcript of press conference, "Fireside Chat," December 29, 1940, in *The Public Papers and Addresses of Franklin D. Roosevelt* (New York: Harper & Brothers, 1950), 1940:638.

14. "Radio address of Senator Burton Wheeler, December 31, 1940," *Vital Speeches of the Day* VII (1940): 203–5.

15. Geoffrey R. Stone, *Perilous Times: Free Speech in Wartime* (New York: W. W. Norton, 2004), 236.

16. Stone, *Perilous Times*, 237.

17. Henry Steele Commager, "To Secure the Blessings of Liberty," *New York Times Magazine*, April 9, 1939.

18. Richard W. Steele, *Free Speech in the Good War* (New York: St. Martin's, 1999), 30.

19. Charles Lindbergh, "Election Promises Should be Kept: We Lack Leadership That Places America First," speech delivered at Madison Square Garden America First Committee rally, May 23, 1941, http://www.charleslindbergh.com/pdf/speech7.pdf.

20. John Woolley and Gerhard Peters, "Franklin D. Roosevelt, Radio Address Announcing an Unlimited National Emergency, May 27, 1941," American Presidency Project, http://www.presidency.ucsb.edu/ws/?pid=16120.

21. "Alien Registration Act," in Henry Steele Commager, ed., *Documents of American History*, vol. 2, *Since 1898*, 7th ed. (New York: Appleton-Century-Crofts, 1963), 433.

22. Geoffrey Perrett, *Days of Sadness, Years of Triumph: The American People 1939–1945* (Madison: University of Wisconsin Press, 1985), 99–100; Stone, *Perilous Times*, 245.

23. Stone, *Perilous Times*, 247–50.

24. Goodwin, *No Ordinary Time*, 295.

25. Steele, *Free Speech in the Good War*, 58–61, 80.

26. Ibid., 75, 81.

27. Francis Biddle, *In Brief Authority* (Garden City, NY: Doubleday, 1962), 211.

28. Stone, *Perilous Times*, 255–56.

29. Ibid., 258–60.

30. Leo P. Ribuffo, "United States v. McWilliams," in *American Political Trials*, ed. Michal R. Belknap (Westport, CT: Greenwood Press, 1981), 205.

31. Stone, *Perilous Times*, 257–58, 262–63.

32. Scott Beekman, *William Dudley Pelley: A Life in Right-Wing Extremism and the Occult* (Syracuse, NY: Syracuse University Press, 2005), 137–39.

33. Alan Brinkley, *Voices of Protest: Huey Long, Father Coughlin, and the Great Depression* (New York: Alfred A. Knopf, 1982), 82–83, 266–67.

34. "Voices of Defeat," *Life*, April 13, 1942.

35. Lewis Wood, "28 Are Indicted on Sedition Charge," *New York Times*, July 24, 1942.

36. "Indictments and New Spy Hunt Point to Subversion Crackdown," *Newsweek*, August 3, 1942; "How We Descended to Propaganda Trials?" *Christian Century*, August 5, 1942.

37. Steele, *Free Speech in the Good War*, 206, 211–21; Stone, *Perilous Times*, 272–75.

38. "Nye Defends Sedition Suspects," *New York Times*, January 15, 1943.

39. Steele, *Free Speech in the Good War*, 217.

40. Stone, *Perilous Times*, 274.

41. *Taylor v. Mississippi*, 319 U.S. 583 (1943), U.S. Supreme Court Center, http://supreme.justia.com/us/319/583/case.html.

42. *Hartzel v. United States*, 322 U.S. 680 (1944), U.S. Supreme Court Center, http://supreme.justia.com/us/322/680/case.html.

43. *West Virginia State Board of Education v. Barnette*, 319 U.S. 624 (1943), U.S. Supreme Court Center, http://supreme.justia.com/us/319/624/case.html.

44. Steele, *Free Speech in the Good War*, 232.

45. "William Edgar Borah," *Dictionary of American Biography*, http://galenet.galegroup.com/servlet/BioRC.

46. *Congressional Record*, 76th Cong., 1st sess., October 2, 1939, 66–68.

47. A. Scott Berg, *Lindbergh* (New York: G. P. Putnam's Sons, 1998).

48. *Hearings before the Committee on Foreign Affairs, House of Representatives, 77th Cong., 1st sess., on H.R. 1779, A Bill to Further Promote the Defense of the United States and for Other Purposes*, January 15–18, 21–25, 29, 1941 (Washington, DC: U.S. Government Printing Office), 371–80.

49. "Robert Maynard Hutchins," *Dictionary of American Biography*, http://galenet.galegroup.com/servlet/BioRC.

50. Robert M. Hutchins, "America and the War," *Journal of Negro Education* 10, no. 3 (July 1941): 435–41.

51. Matt Bai, "He Said No to Internment," *New York Times Magazine*, December 25, 2005; Greg Robinson, *By Order of the President: FDR and the Internment of Japanese Americans* (Cambridge, MA: Harvard University Press, 2001), 3–5, 209; Justice Frank Murphy, dissenting opinion, *Korematsu v. United States*, December 18, 1944, available at Cornell Law School Legal Information Institute, http://www.law.cornell.edu/supct/html/historics/USSC_CR_0323_0214_ZD1.html.

52. Justice Frank Murphy, dissenting opinion, *Korematsu v. United States*, December 18, 1944, available at Cornell Law School Legal Information Institute, http://www.law.cornell.edu/supct/html/historics/USSC_CR_0323_0214_ZD1.html.

CHAPTER 8

1. Walter LaFeber, *America, Russia and the Cold War, 1945–2006* (New York: McGraw Hill, 2008), 18.

2. James T. Patterson, *Grand Expectations: The United States, 1945–1974* (New York: Oxford, 1996), 113.

3. LaFeber, *America, Russia and the Cold War*, 17.

4. Ibid., 35.

5. Patterson, *Grand Expectations*, 113.

6. X [George F. Kennan], "The Sources of Soviet Conduct," *Foreign Affairs* 25 (July 1947): 566–82.

7. Winston Churchill, "The Sinews of Peace," March 5, 1946, Westminster College, Fulton, MO, http://www.winstonchurchill.org/learn/speeches/speeches-of-winston-churchill/120-the-sinews-of-peace.

8. Patterson, *Grand Expectations*, 116.

9. Joseph C. Goulden, *The Best Years, 1945–1950* (New York: Atheneum, 1976), 257.

10. Patterson, *Grand Expectations*, 116.

11. Henry L. Stimson and McGeorge Bundy, *On Active Service in Peace and War* (New York: Harper, 1948), 642–46; William H. Chafe, *The Unfinished Journey: America Since World War II* (New York: Oxford University Press, 1986), 63.

12. David Mayers, *Dissenting Voices in America's Rise to Power* (New York: Cambridge University Press, 2007), 295.

13. Henry A. Wallace, "I Shall Run in 1948," *Vital Speeches of the Day* 12 (October 1, 1946): 738–41.

14. Hugh Ross, *The Cold War: Containment and Its Critics* (Chicago: Rand McNally, 1963), 12–13.

15. *Congressional Record*, 79th Cong., 2nd sess., March 20, 1946, 2463–69; William S. White, "Pepper Urges Big 3 Unite Beyond UNO," *New York Times*, March 21, 1946.

16. Thomas G. Paterson, ed., *Cold War Critics: Alternatives to American Foreign Policy in the Truman Years* (Chicago: Quadrangle, 1971), 27–28.

17. Paterson, *Cold War Critics*, 167–77.

18. "Warning to Russia," *New York Times*, March 13, 1947.

19. George F. Kennan, *Memoirs: 1925–1950* (Boston: Little, Brown, 1967), 319–21.

20. Paterson, *Cold War Critics*, 129–30, 179.

21. C. P. Trussell, "Congress is Solemn," *New York Times*, March 13, 1947.

22. Robert J. Donovan, *Conflict and Crisis: The Presidency of Harry S Truman, 1945–1948* (New York: W. W. Norton), 286, 179.

23. Ibid., 155–56, 180–81.
24. Henry Wallace, "I Shall Run in 1948," *Vital Speeches* 14 (January 1, 1948): 172–74.
25. Walter L. Hixson, *George F. Kennan: Cold War Iconoclast* (New York: Columbia, 1989), 74–75.
26. *Congressional Record*, 81st Cong., 1st sess., July 11, 1949, 9208–9.
27. Patterson, *Cold War Critics*, 176.
28. Hixson, *George F. Kennan*, 74–96.
29. "Claude Denson Pepper," *Encyclopedia of World Biography*, http://galenet.galegroup.com/servlet/BioRC.
30. *Congressional Record*, 79th Cong., 2nd sess., March 20, 1946, 2463–69.
31. "Henry A. Wallace," *Biography Resource Center*, http://galenet.galegroup.com/servelet/BioRC.
32. Wallace to Truman, July 23, 1946, Papers of Harry S. Truman, President's Secretary's Files, Harry S. Truman Library, Independence, Missouri.
33. Robert Mann, *A Grand Delusion: America's Descent Into Vietnam* (New York: Basic Books, 2001), 16, 38–49; Paterson, *Cold War Critics*, 167–95.
34. *Congressional Record*, 81st Cong., 1st sess., July 11, 1949, 9205–9.

CHAPTER 9

1. Harold F. Gosnell, *Truman's Crises: A Political Biography of Harry S. Truman* (Westport, CT: Greenwood Press, 1980), 465–66.
2. Ibid., 466–67.
3. Alonzo L. Hamby, *Man of the People: A Life of Harry S. Truman* (New York: Oxford University Press, 1995), 538.
4. James L. Stokesbury, *A Short History of the Korean War* (New York: Morrow, 1988), 35; Hamby, *Man of the People*, 521; "M'Arthur Pledges Defense of Japan," *New York Times*, March 2, 1949.
5. William S. White, "Congress Adheres Swiftly to Action," *New York Times*, July 1, 1950; "Republicans: Critical, but in Line," *Newsweek*, July 10, 1950
6. Ronald J. Caridi, *The Korean War and American Politics: The Republican Party as a Case Study* (Philadelphia: University of Pennsylvania Press, 1968), 40.
7. Robert Mann, *A Grand Delusion: America's Descent Into Vietnam* (New York: Basic Books, 2001), 40.
8. Stokesbury, *A Short History of the Korean War*, 65–78.
9. *Congressional Record*, 81st Cong., 2nd sess., June 27, 1950, 9268–69.
10. Margaret A. Blanchard, *Revolutionary Sparks: Freedom of Expression in Modern America* (New York: Oxford University Press, 1992), 254.
11. Matthew Edwin Mantell, "Opposition to the Korean War: A Study in American Dissent" (PhD dissertation, New York University, 1973), 31–35.
12. Ibid., 37.
13. "U.S. Move to Imprison Bridges as Menace to National Security," *New York Times*, August 1, 1950; "Harry Bridges Put in Jail as Menace to Security of U.S." *New York Times*, August 6, 1950; Mantell, "Opposition to the Korean War," 86–88.
14. Lawrence E. Davies, "U.S. Court Orders Bridges Set Free," *New York Times*, August 25, 1950.
15. "Four Men and Women Sentenced to Prison for Painting 'Peace' Signs in Prospect Park," *New York Times*, August 2, 1950.
16. Russell Porter, "Red 'Peace' Rally Defies Court," *New York Times*, August 3, 1950.

17. Stokesbury, *A Short History of the Korean War*, 51–65.

18. "The Concert," *Time*, August 21, 1950; "GOP Hammers at Far Eastern Policy" and "Blood on Whose Hands," *Time*, August 28, 1950; "Confusion? There's an Election Coming," *Newsweek*, August 21, 1950.

19. "5 of 'Peace' Group Here Indicted," *New York Times*, February 10, 1951.

20. David Levering Lewis, *W. E. B. Du Bois: The Fight for Equality and the American Century, 1919–1963* (New York: Henry Holt, 2000), 545–52.

21. John E. Mueller, *War, Presidents and Public Opinion* (New York: John Wiley & Sons, 1973), 42–52.

22. Stokesbury, *A Short History of the Korean War*, 65–78.

23. "Internal Security Act," Henry Steele Commager, ed., *Documents of American History*, vol. 2, *Since 1898*, 7th ed. (New York: Appleton-Century-Crofts, 1963), 561–64.

24. Robert Griffith, *The Politics of Fear: Joseph R. McCarthy and the Senate* (Amherst: University of Massachusetts Press, 1970), 117.

25. Commager, *Documents of American History*, 564–68.

26. Hamby, *Man of the People*, 428–29, 548.

27. Stokesbury, *A Short History of the Korean War*, 79–111.

28. Gosnell, *Truman's Crises*, 471–73.

29. James T. Patterson, *Grand Expectations: The United States, 1945–1974* (New York: Oxford University Press, 1996), 226–27.

30. Harry S. Truman, *Memoirs by Harry S. Truman, vol. 2, Years of Trial and Hope* (Garden City, NY: Doubleday, 1956), 384.

31. Truman, *Memoirs*, 416.

32. Dennis D. Wainstock, *Truman, MacArthur and the Korean War* (Westport, CT: Greenwood Press, 1999), 101–2, 121–23.

33. Dean Acheson, *Present at the Creation: My Years in the State Department* (New York: W. W. Norton, 1969), 518.

34. Wainstock, *Truman, MacArthur and the Korean War*, 121–22; Hamby, *Man of the People*, 554–55; Gosnell, *Truman's Crises*, 474–75.

35. Hamby, *Man of the People*, 475.

36. Acheson, *Present at the Creation*, 520.

37. Wainstock, *Truman, MacArthur and the Korean War*, 125–26; David Halberstam, *The Coldest Winter: America and the Korean War* (New York: Hyperion, 2007), 591–606.

38. Robert Ferrell, *Harry S. Truman: A Life* (Columbia: University of Missouri Press, 1994), 334.

39. *Congressional Record*, 82nd Cong., 1st sess., April 11, 1951, 3618–19.

40. Ibid., 3655.

41. John W. Spanier, *The Truman-MacArthur Controversy and the Korean War* (Cambridge, MA: Belknap, 1959), 215–16.

42. "Cheers & Second Looks," *Time*, April 30, 1951; "Shifts & Middle Ground," *Time*, May 7, 1951; "MacArthur Approved," *Time*, April 30, 1951; Dennis D. Wainstock, *Truman, MacArthur and the Korean War* (Westport, CT: Greenwood, 1999), 133–35.

43. Steven Casey, *Selling the Korean War: Propaganda, Politics, and Public Opinion in the United States, 1950–1953* (New York: Oxford University Press, 2008), 335.

44. Stokesbury, *A Short History of the Korean War*, 254–55.

45. *I Vote My Conscience: Debates, Speeches and Writings of Vito Marcantonio, 1935–1950*, ed. Annette T. Rubinstein and Assoc. (New York: Vito Marcantonio Memorial, 1956), 1–8, 352.

46. *Congressional Record*, 81st Cong., 2nd sess., June 27, 1950, 9268–69.

47. "Kenneth Spicer Wherry," *Dictionary of American Biography*, http://galenet.galegroup .com/servlet/BioRC.

48. *Congressional Record*, 82nd Cong., 1st sess., 1951, appendix, A2027–29.

CHAPTER 10

1. "War Critic Burns Himself To Death Outside Pentagon," *New York Times*, November 3, 1965; John Corry, "Death of a Quaker," *New York Times*, November 7, 1965; Paul Hendrickson, *The Living and the Dead: Robert McNamara and Five Lives of a Lost War* (New York: Alfred A. Knopf, 1996), 187–95; Nancy Zaroulis and Gerald Sullivan, *Who Spoke Up? American Protest Against the War in Vietnam, 1963–1975* (New York: Doubleday, 1984), 1–3; Sallie B. King, "They Who Burned Themselves for Peace: Quaker and Buddhist Self-Immolators During the Vietnam War," *Buddhist-Christian Studies* 20 (January 1, 2000): 127–50.

2. Robert Mann, *A Grand Delusion: America's Descent Into Vietnam* (New York: Basic Books, 2001), 374–75.

3. Zaroulis and Sullivan, *Who Spoke Up?* 16, 22–23; Mann, *A Grand Delusion*, 342–70.

4. Geoffrey R. Stone, *Perilous Times: Free Speech in Wartime* (New York: W. W. Norton, 2004), 439; Charles DeBenedetti, *An American Ordeal: The Antiwar Movement of the Vietnam Era* (Syracuse, NY: Syracuse University Press, 1990), 114–15.

5. "15,000 White House Pickets Denounce Vietnam War," *New York Times*, April 18, 1965; Zaroulis and Sullivan, *Who Spoke Up?* 38–41; DeBenedetti, *An American Ordeal*, 111–12.

6. Stone, *Perilous Times*, 440–41; DeBenedetti, *An American Ordeal*, 118.

7. Lady Bird Johnson, *A White House Diary* (New York: Holt, Rinehart and Winston, 1970), 262.

8. Stone, *Perilous Times*, 440.

9. "15,000 White House Pickets Denounce Vietnam War," *New York Times*, April 18, 1965.

10. DeBenedetti, *An American Ordeal*, 129.

11. Zaroulis and Sullivan, *Who Spoke Up?* 56–58; Stone, *Perilous Times*, 442.

12. Stone, *Perilous Times*, 471–77; Edith Evans Asbury, "David Miller and the Catholic Workers: A Study in Pacifism," *New York Times*, October 24, 1965; Victor Jew and Adam Land, "Conscientious Objectors," *Encyclopedia of the Vietnam War, ed.* Stanley I. Kutler (New York: Charles Scribner's Sons, 1996), 148.

13. Douglas Robinson, "Policy in Vietnam Scored in Rallies Throughout U.S." *New York Times,* October 16, 1965.

14. William L. Lunch and Peter W. Sperlich, "American Public Opinion and the War in Vietnam," *Western Political Quarterly* 32, no. 1 (March 1979): 21–44.

15. "Red Infiltration Alleged," *New York Times*, October 15, 1965.

16. Robert B. Semple Jr., "Johnson Decries Draft Protests," *New York Times*, October 19, 1965.

17. Max Frankel, "Demonstrators Decorous," *New York Times*, November 28, 1965.

18. Mann, *A Grand Delusion*, 492–93.

19. Ibid., 496–97.

20. Stone, *Perilous Times*, 443.

21. Roy Reed, "Rights Unit Quits Parley in Capital," *New York Times*, May 24, 1966.

22. David J. Garrow, *Bearing the Cross: Martin Luther King, Jr., and the Southern Christian Leadership Conference* (New York: Vintage Books, 1988), 543–45.

23. Ibid., 553.
24. Stone, *Perilous Times*, 445.
25. "Dr. King's Error," *New York Times, April 7*, 1967; Gene Roberts, "Dr. King and the War," *New York Times*, April 14, 1967.
26. Douglas Robinson, "100,000 Rally at U.N. Against Vietnam War," *New York Times*, April 16, 1967.
27. Zaroulis and Sullivan, *Who Spoke Up?* 113–14.
28. Stone, *Perilous Times*, 447; Randall B. Woods, *LBJ: Architect of American Ambition* (New York: Free Press, 2006), 805.
29. Woods, *LBJ*, 808; DeBenedetti, *An American Ordeal*, 204–5.
30. Mann, *A Grand Delusion*, 556.
31. Stone, *Perilous Times*, 449.
32. Mann, *A Grand Delusion*, 570.
33. Ibid., 572–75.
34. Ibid., 609–14; DeBenedetti, *An American Ordeal*, 226–28.
35. Mann, *A Grand Delusion*, 615.
36. Maureen Harrison and Steve Gilbert, ed., *Landmark American Speeches, vol. 3, The Twentieth Century* (Carlsbad, CA: Excellent Books, 2001), 184–87.
37. Stone, *Perilous Times*, 478.
38. John H. Fenton, "Dr. Spock Guilty With 3 Other Men In Antidraft Plot," *New York Times*, June 15, 1968; John H. Fenton, "Spock and 3 Others Given 2-Year Terms in Draft Conspiracy," *New York Times*, July 11, 1968; John H. Fenton, "U.S. Court Upsets Spock Conviction In Fight On Draft," *New York Times*, July 12, 1969.
39. Stone, *Perilous Times*, 487.
40. DeBenedetti, *An American Ordeal*, 257.
41. James M. Naughton, "Nixon Vows Again Not To Be Swayed By War Protests," *New York Times*, October 14, 1969.
42. Mann, *A Grand Delusion*, 644–45.
43. Ibid., 648; DeBenedetti, *An American Ordeal*, 261–63.
44. Mann, *A Grand Delusion*, 658–61; George C. Herring, *America's Longest War: The United States and Vietnam, 1950–1975* (New York: John Wiley & Sons, 1979), 231–32.
45. Charles W. Colson, *Born Again* (Old Tappan, NJ: G. K. Hall, 1976), 41.
46. Stone, *Perilous Times*, 487–94.
47. Mann, *A Grand Delusion*, 672.
48. DeBenedetti, *An American Ordeal*, 264.
49. Mann, *A Grand Delusion*, 680–81.
50. DeBenedetti, *An American Ordeal*, 267.
51. Keith Beattie, *The Scar that Binds: American Culture and the Vietnam War* (New York: New York University Press, 1998), 21.
52. "Pentagon Aide Says Clinton Helps Enemy," *New York Times*, July 20, 2007.
53. DeBenedetti, *An American Ordeal*, 408.
54. Mason Drukman, *Wayne Morse: A Political Biography* (Portland: Oregon Historical Society, 1997).
55. The Geneva Accords were signed in 1954 by representatives of North and South Vietnam, Cambodia, Laos, France, China, the Soviet Union, and the United Kingdom. The United States did not sign the document—which divided the nation into north and south—but agreed to abide by its terms and called for unifying elections. Almost immediately after the agreement, both sides began violating its provisions.
56. *Congressional Record*, 88th Cong., 2nd sess., *August* 5, 1964, 18132–39.
57. *United States v. Spock*, 416 F.2d, 192–93 (1st Cir. 1969).

58. Mann, *A Grand Delusion*, 293, 659–70.

59. *Congressional Record, 91st Cong., 2nd sess., September 1, 1970*, 30682.

60. "Legislative Proposals Relating to the War in Southeast Asia," April 22, 1971, United States Senate, Committee on Foreign Relations; transcript available at http://www.c -span.org/2004vote/jkerrytestimony.asp.

CHAPTER 11

1. Andrew A. Wiest, *The Vietnam War: 1956–1975* (Oxford: Osprey Publishing, 2002), 89.

2. Tom Matthews, "The Path to War," *Newsweek* 117, no. 9 (Spring–Summer 1991): 32. *Academic Search Complete*, EBSCOhost.

3. "Persian Gulf War," *The Oxford Companion to American Military History*, ed. John White-clay Chambers II (New York: Oxford University Press, 2000), 544–46.

4. Herbert S. Parment, *George Bush: The Life of a Lone Star Yankee* (New York: Scribner, 1997), 449–50; George Bush and Brent Scowcroft, *A World Transformed* (New York: Alfred A. Knopf, 1998), 315.

5. Matthews, "The Path to War."

6. Bush and Scowcroft, *A World Transformed*, 332–33.

7. Dilip Hiro, *Desert Shield to Desert Storm: The Second Gulf War* (New York: Routledge, 1992), 169–74.

8. Fred Kaplan, "Poll: Most in US Oppose All-Out War With Iraq," *Boston Globe*, September 30, 1990.

9. Mary Curtius, "This Week, A Stern Test for US Bid for UN Resolution," *Boston Globe*, November 26, 1990.

10. Matthews, "The Path to War."

11. Lawrence Freedman and Efraim Karsh, *The Gulf Conflict, 1990–1991: Diplomacy and War in the New World Order* (Princeton, NJ: Princeton University Press, 1993), 211.

12. Zhongdang Pan and Gerald M. Kosicki, "Voters' Reasoning Processes and Media Influences During the Persian Gulf War," *Political Behavior* 16, no. 1 (March 1994): 117–56.

13. P. Fessler, "Bush Quiets His Critics on Hill by Sending Baker to Iraq," *Congressional Quarterly Weekly Report* 48, no. 48 (December 1, 1990): 4006; Michael R. Gordon, "2 Ex-Military Chiefs Urge Bush to Delay Gulf War," *New York Times*, November 29, 1990; Michael Gordon, "Democrats Press Bush to Put Off Military Action," *New York Times*, November 28, 1990.

14. Andrew Rosenthal, "Senators Asking President to Call Session over Gulf," *New York Times, November* 14, 1990.

15. R. W. Apple Jr., "Bush Says Iraqi Aggression Threatens 'Our Way of Life,'" *New York Times*, August 16, 1990.

16. Thomas L. Friedman, "No Compromise on Kuwait, Bush Says," *New York Times*, October 24, 1990.

17. Maureen Dowd, "President Seeks to Clarify Stand," *New York Times*, November 2, 1990; Freedman and Karsh, *The Gulf Conflict*, 224.

18. Freedman and Karsh, *The Gulf Conflict*, 218.

19. Max Elbaum, "The Storm at Home," in *Beyond the Storm: A Gulf Crisis Reader*, ed. Phyllis Bennis and Michel Moushabeck (New York: Olive Branch Press, 1991), 142–49.

20. Ibid.; Ari L. Goldman, "Council of Churches Condemns U.S. Policy in Gulf," *New York Times, November* 16, 1990.

21. Micael DeCourcy Hinds, "Antiwar Effort Buds Quickly, Nurtured by Activism of 60's," *New York Times*, January 11, 1991.
22. Freedman and Karsh, *The Gulf Conflict*, 290.
23. Ibid., 291.
24. Matthews, "The Path to War."
25. Freedman and Karsh, *The Gulf Conflict*, 291.
26. Patrick E. Tyler, "Baghdad Accepts U.S. Offer to Meet Baker in Geneva," *New York Times*, January 5, 1991; Andrew Rosenthal, "Bush, Noting a Hussein 'Stiff-Arm,' Finds Hopes for Peace Waning," *New York Times*, January 10, 1991.
27. Adam Clymer, "Senate Prepares for a Gulf Debate Soon after Baker Meets With Aziz," *New York Times*, January 5, 1991; Freedman and Karsh, *The Gulf Conflict*, 291–92.
28. C. J. Doherty, "Bush Is Given Authorization to Use Force against Iraq," *Congressional Quarterly Weekly Report* 49, no. 2 (January 12, 1991): 65.
29. Adam Clymer, "Congress Acts to Authorize War in Gulf," *New York Times*, January 13, 1991.
30. "Ground Rules and Guidelines for Desert Shield, Memorandum from Pete Williams," in *The Media and the Gulf War*, ed. Hedrick Smith (Washington, DC: Seven Locks Press, 1992), 4–12.
31. Robert Lichter, "The Instant Replay War," *The Media and the Gulf War*, ed. Hedrick Smith (Washington, DC: Seven Locks Press, 1992), 224–30.
32. Max Elbaum, "The Storm at Home," 142–49; Heather Rhoads, "Activism Revives on Campus," *Progressive* 55, no. 3 (1991): 15–17.
33. Maureen Dowd, "War Introduces a Tougher Bush To Nation," *New York Times*, March 2, 1991.
34. Patrick Buchanan, "Is Stopping Saddam's Bomb a U.S. Problem?" *The* (Portland) *Oregonian*, November 28, 1990.
35. Patricia Sullivan, "William Crowe Jr.; Joint Chiefs Leader Had Diplomat's Touch," *Washington Post*, October 19, 2007.
36. *Crisis in the Persian Gulf Region: U.S. Policy Options and Implications*, Hearings Before the Armed Services Committee, 101st Cong., 2nd sess., November 28, 1990.
37. *Congressional Record*, 102nd Cong., 1st sess., January 10, 1991, S106.

CHAPTER 12

1. Peter Carlson, "The Solitary Vote of Barbara Lee," *Washington Post*, September 19, 2001.
2. Matthew Cella and Gerald Mizejewski, "Patriotism Blooms at Area Campuses," *Washington Times*, September 19, 2001.
3. Lou Cannon and Carl M. Cannon. *Reagan's Disciple: George W. Bush's Troubled Quest for a Presidential Legacy* (New York: Public Affairs Press, 2008), 184.
4. Bill Carter, "ABC to End 'Politically Incorrect,'" *New York Times, May* 12, 2002.
5. Richard Huff, "White House Sees Red over Maher's Remarks," *Daily News* (New York), September 27, 2001.
6. "Washington Post Poll: Attack on Afghanistan," *Washington Post*, October 8, 2001.
7. Barton Gellman and Thomas E. Ricks, "U.S. Concludes Bin Laden Escaped at Tora Bora Fight," *Washington Post*, April 17, 2002; Philip Smucker, "How Bin Laden Got Away," *Christian Science Monitor*, March 4, 2002.
8. Audrey Hudson, "Daschle Scolds Bush for War's Lack of Focus," *Washington Times*, March 1, 2002.
9. Helen Dewar, "Lott Calls Daschle Divisive," *Washington Post*, March 1, 2002.

10. Hudson, "Daschle Scolds Bush for War's Lack of Focus."

11. "The USA Patriot Act: A Sketch," CRS Report for Congress, April 18, 2002, *Congressional Research Service*, Order Code: RS21203.

12. Neil A. Lewis, "Ashcroft Defends Antiterror Plan," *New York Times*, December 7, 2001.

13. John Ibbitson, "The War on Terrorism: In Ashcroft We Trust," *The Globe and Mail* (Toronto, ON, Canada), December 10, 2001.

14. "Ashcroft's Contempt," *St. Petersburg Times*, December 10, 2001.

15. Marcus Raskin and Robert Spero, *The Four Freedoms Under Siege: The Clear and Present Danger for Our National Security State* (Westport, CT: Praeger, 2007), 18; David Cole and James Dempsey, *Terrorism and the Constitution: Sacrificing Civil Liberties in the Name of National Security* (New York: New Press, 2006), 178.

16. Cole and Dempsey, *Terrorism and the Constitution*, 183.

17. Geoffrey R. Stone, *Perilous Times: Free Speech in Wartime* (New York: W. W. Norton, 2004), 553.

18. "MSRG Special Report: Restrictions on Civil Liberties, Views of Islam, & Muslim Americans," December 2004, Media & Society Research Group, Cornell University, http://www.comm.cornell.edu/msrg/msrg.html.

19. Susan Page, "Iraq Course Set from Tight White House Circle," *USA Today*, September 11, 2002.

20. Steven R. Wiseman, "A New Doctrine," *New York Times,* March 23, 2003.

21. Bob Woodward, *Plan of Attack* (New York: Simon & Schuster, 2004), 1–3, 26.

22. Nicholas Lemann, "The Next World Order: The Bush Administration may have a brand-new doctrine of power," *The New Yorker,* April 1, 2002.

23. Douglas C. Foyle, "Leading the Public to War? The Influence of American Public Opinion on the Bush Administration's Decision to Go to War in Iraq," *International Journal of Public Opinion Research* 16, no. 3 (2004): 278.

24. Page, "Iraq Course Set from Tight White House Circle."

25. Elisabeth Bumiller, "President Notes Dissent on Iraq, Vowing to Listen," *New York Times*, August 17, 2002.

26. Remarks by the Vice President Dick Cheney to the Veterans of Foreign Wars 103rd National Convention, August 26, 2002, http://georgewbush-whitehouse.archives.gov/news/releases/2002/08/20020826.html.

27. Woodward, *Plan of Attack*, 202.

28. Alison Mitchell, "Bush's Address Draws Praise in Congress, but Doubts Linger," *New York Times,* September 13, 2002.

29. Ibid.

30. "Meet the Press," NBC News Transcripts, October 6, 2002.

31. Jonathan Riehl, "Broad Resolution Allows Bush to Set Terms of War Without Review," *Congressional Quarterly Weekly*, October 12, 2002.

32. Lynette Clemetson, "Thousands in D.C. Protest Iraq War Plans," *New York Times, January* 19, 2003; Brian Knowlton, "People Rally across the Globe to Protest a Possible War on Iraq," *New York Times*, January 20, 2003; Thom Shanker, "Rumsfeld Says Iraq Diplomacy Is Nearing the End of Its Road, *New York Times*, January 21, 2003.

33. Condoleezza Rice, "Why We Know Iraq Is Lying," *New York Times,* January 23, 2003; Frank Rich, *The Greatest Story Ever Sold: The Decline and Fall of Truth from 9/11 to Katrina* (New York: Penguin, 2006), 258–60.

34. *The Gallup Poll: Public Opinion 2003* (Lanham, MD: SR Books, 2004), 97; Rich, *The Greatest Story Ever Sold*, 68.

35. Transcript of White House press conference, "New SEC Chairman Sworn-In," *February* 19, 2003, http://georgewbush-whitehouse.archives.gov/news/releases/2003/02/20030218-1.html.

36. John Mueller, "The Iraq Syndrome," *Foreign Affairs* 84, no. 6 (November–December 2005): 44–54.

37. "Trends in Public Opinion about the War in Iraq, 2003–2007," Pew Research Center, March 15, 2007, http://pewresearch.org/pubs/431/trends-in-public-opinion-about-the-war-in-iraq-2003-2007.

38. Jonathan Darman, "The Sleepers," *Newsweek*, November 6, 2006; *New York Times/CBS News* poll, October 27–31, http://graphics8.nytimes.com/packages/pdf/politics/20061031_poll.pdf; Real Clear Politics, "President Bush Job Approval" poll, http://www.realclearpolitics.com/polls/archive/index.php?poll_id=19&page=2.

39. Pollingreport.com, "President Bush Job Ratings" poll, http://www.pollingreport.com/BushJob1.htm.

40. Pew Research Center, "Petraeus' Proposals Draw Public Approval, But Fail to Lift War Support," September 18, 2007, http://pewresearch.org/pubs/596/petraeus-proposals-draw-public-approval-but-fail-to-lift-war-support.

41. CNN/Opinion Research Corporation poll, February 1–3, 2008; CBS News poll, January 30–February 2, 2008; NBC News/*Wall Street Journal* poll, January 20–22, 2008.

42. Editorial, "The Good War, Still to Be Won," *New York Times*, August 20, 2007.

43. Buddhika Jayamaha, et al., "The War as We Saw It," *New York Times*, August 19, 2007.

44. Robert Kuttner, *Obama's Challenge: America's Economic Crisis and the Power of a Transformative Presidency* (White River Junction, VT: Chelsea Green Publishing, 2008), 71.

45. Andrew J. Bacevich, "Should Obama Go 'All In' on Afghanistan?" *Los Angeles Times*, September 7, 2009.

46. George F. Will, "Time to Get Out of Afghanistan," *Washington Post*, September 1, 2009.

47. Katrina vanden Heuvel, "Needed: New National Security Thinking," *The Nation*, November 30, 2009, http://www.thenation.com/blogs/edcut/501905/print.

48. *Congressional Record*, 107th Cong., 1st sess., September 14, 2001, H5642–43.

49. Scott Ritter, "Is Iraq a True Threat to the US?" *Boston Globe*, July 2, 2002.

50. *Congressional Record*, 108th Cong., 1st sess., March 19, 2003, S3954–55.

51. *Congressional Record*, 109th Cong., 2nd sess., September 28, 2006, S10388–89.

52. *Congressional Record*, 111th Cong., 1st sess., February 12, 2009, H1277–78.

53. Karen DeYoung, "U.S. Official Resigns Over Afghan War," *Washington Post*, October 27, 2009, http://www.washingtonpost.com/wp-dyn/content/article/2009/10/26/AR2009102603394.html.

54. Resignation letter from Matthew Hoh to Ambassador Nancy J. Powell, September 10, 2009, http://www.washingtonpost.com/wp-srv/hp/ssi/wpc/ResignationLetter.pdf?sid=ST2009102603447.

CONCLUSION

1. A. J. P. Taylor, *The Trouble Makers: Dissent over Foreign Policy, 1792–1939* (London: Hamish Hamilton, 1957), 23.

2. Oliver Wendell Holmes, *The Common Law* (Boston: Little, Brown, 1881), 1.

3. Taylor, *The Trouble Makers*, 17.

4. Fareed Zakaria, *The Post-Americans World and the Rise of the Rest* (New York: W. W. Norton, 2008), 250.

5. Brien Hallett, *The Lost Art of Declaring War* (Urbana: University of Illinois Press, 1998), 25, 45.
6. Henry Cabot Lodge, ed. *The Federalist* (New York: G. P. Putnam, 1892), 51–60.
7. Charles G. Herbermann and Georg Grupp, ed. *The Catholic Encyclopedia* (New York: Knowledge Foundation, 1907), 1:168.
8. Theodore T. Herbert and Ralph W. Estes, "Improving Executive Decisions by Formalizing Dissent: The Corporate Devil's Advocate," *Academy of Management Review* 2, no. 4 (October 1977): 662–67.
9. Samuel Butler, *The Note-Books of Samuel Butler* (New York: E. P. Dutton, 1917), 217; Samuel Butler, *The Way of All Flesh* (New York: E. P. Dutton, 1916), vii.

INDEX